Psychotherapy

The Art of Wooing Nature

About the Author

Sheldon Roth received his M.D. from the New York University School of Medicine. He was Resident in Psychiatry and Chief Resident at Massachusetts Mental Health Center, and he graduated from the Boston Psychoanalytic Institute. Currently an assistant clinical professor of psychiatry at Harvard Medical School and a training and supervising analyst at the Psychoanalytic Institute of New England East (PINE), Dr. Roth is in the private practice of psychiatry and psychoanalysis. He also teaches at the Harvard Longwood Training Program in Psychiatry.

Psychotherapy

The Art of Wooing Nature

Sheldon Roth, M.D.

Jason Aronson Inc.
Northvale, New Jersey
London

For Cora,
Adam, Eli, and Gabriel

First softcover printing 2000

10 9 8 7 6 5 4

The author gratefully acknowledges permission to reprint the following:

From "Burnt Norton" in *Four Quarters* by T. S. Eliot, copyright 1943 by T. S. Eliot; renewed 1971 by Esme Valerie Eliot. Reprinted with permission of Harcourt Brace Jovanovich, Inc.

From "The Schizophrenic Wallet" in *Psychiatric Opinion*. Reprinted by permission of Opinion Publications.

Library of Congress Cataloging-in-Publication Data

Roth, Sheldon, 1938-
    Psychotherapy : the art of wooing nature.

    Bibliography: p. 281
    Includes index.
    1. Psychotherapy. 2. Psychotherapist and patient.
    3. Psychotherapists. I. Title. [DNLM: 1. Psychotherapy–
methods. WM 420 R845p]
    RC480.R666   1986   616.89'14   86-28763
    ISBN 0-87668-945-4 (hardcover)
    ISBN 0-7657-0252-5 (softcover)

Printed in the United States of America on acid-free paper. For information and catalog write to Jason Aronson Inc., 230 Livingston Street, Northvale, NJ 07647-1726, or visit our website: www.aronson.com

Contents

Preface

While gratified by the excellent reception of this book, I was especially intrigued by a recurring comment of reviewers: "This book will appeal to the neophyte as well as the experienced psychotherapist." How could this be so?

I was reminded of special moments in my formal education when the early lectures on a profound subject were given by a preeminent authority. Such lectures were characterized by starkly simple enunciations of principles, just enough information to allow me far-reaching discussions with advanced researchers of the topic. Further study of the matter, however, usually plunged me out of the light of understanding into a dark tunnel of educational confusion. If I persisted in tracing the labyrinthine details of doubt and fact, eventually I emerged from the tunnel's far end into the light of greater understanding. Yet, when later I could hold more sophisticated discussion of the subject, I still found myself utilizing the same elemental principles I had grasped at the beginning. Naturally, this manifest understanding had latently become permeated by both the known and unknown.

Thus I am moved by the realization that readers have understood my intent. At the beginning of my psychotherapeutic work, as well as along the route up to the present moment, the issues with which I have wrestled intellectually and emotionally have always been the same basic issues. I am constantly observing that my later, hard-won understandings are incredibly similar to precepts I learned many years ago. And because this book reflects my experience with psychotherapy, it is embedded with this history of my comprehension.

Some readers will find a parallel with this educational process and the work of psychotherapy itself, endless integration of the straightforward patterns of the past into a workable, but recognizable, blend in the present. I have no doubt that this is the case. Psychotherapy is cut from the same cloth as good education.

In writing this preface to a new printing of this book, I was also tempted to repeat, and not redo, my original acknowledgments. The sentiments expressed there remain the same, only they have become stronger.

Acknowledgments

An acknowledgments page for a book on psychotherapy is sadly limited, since I cannot list the patients whose lives I have been privileged to share. For those of you who may glance at this page, be assured of my lasting appreciation for your trust and my gratitude for the opportunity to work together.

An additional and powerful source of learning has come from the numerous trainees in psychiatry, psychology, and the varied mental health professions, who have always brought me to understand by having to explain. Indeed, much of this book is a compilation of commentary that seemed useful to students and struggling colleagues.

A number of teachers and colleagues have been invaluable to me in the ongoing process of being a psychotherapist. Listing all of them would be difficult, and I fear I would leave out a valued mentor. Many are mentioned in this book, but many others who have not published have been equally important. By singling out the late Elvin Semrad for special mention, I am noting perhaps not just a person but, rather, a tradition of which he was the quintessence. If you asked me to describe this tradition, my answer would probably be, "It's simple, but complex; perhaps my book will explain."

A special mention must go to Mrs. Elisabeth Gleason Humez, whose assiduous and tactful editing revealed the self-analytic function of trying to write a book from the heart and the head. Further editorial clarity and refining were expertly provided by

Ms. Judy Gelman and Mrs. Lori Williams of Jason Aronson Inc. I am forever grateful to Dr. Jason Aronson for his stimulating encouragement to tackle this project and for his helpful practical advice in executing it.

To my wife, Cora, and my sons Adam, Eli, and Gabriel, I express special thanks for years of love, learning, and unending opportunity for maturation.

1

The Personality of the Therapist: Why Practice an Impossible Profession?

The therapist seasoned in the art and science of psychotherapy knows that this skill has been garnered not only through intensive study of patients but through profound intensive self-study as well. Our early training fashions for us objective, scientific glasses through which we view the patient. We are taught to recognize signs, symptoms, patterns, and clinical syndromes, all of which take place in an external reality—another person—quite separate from ourselves. By assuming the role of therapist, we are unexpectedly thrust into a novel, organic relationship with this tidy objective compilation of clinical labels, the patient. Suddenly, or gradually, there comes an awareness that our own signs, symptoms, patterns, and characteristic ways of being have a realistic impact on the therapeutic process. Subjective intuition and empathy, which depend on our personal self-awareness and self-mastery, are indispensable adjuncts to objective knowledge, if we are to be clinically attuned to the patient, whose unpredictable emotional waters demand that we sink or swim in surprising new ways.

Hostility

The neophyte therapist, as well as the experienced one, is often stunned by the extent of the hostility with which good intentions are met. If any one element is underestimated in approaching a career as a psychotherapist, it is the amount of hostility and rejection that will be one's lot in the pursuit of therapeutic helpfulness. A great threat to personal integrity and self-worth will come about through open rejection of one's most heartfelt efforts to be of use, the sharing of intuitions with the patient, and the provision of great patience and forbearance; the patient may still, in spite of all these, declare the therapist inadequate, short of the mark, and uncaring. The more regressed or disturbed a patient is, the more destructive the hostility will be. All but the most farsighted of therapists never consider, when choosing therapy as a career, the major share of daily experience this open hostility will consume.

An immense sense of personal security about one's value and motives is needed to weather patients' emotional storms and these assaults against one's self-esteem. Unfortunately, this sense of personal value will not be in great supply at the onset of the therapist's training or even during the initial years of clinical practice.

The good therapist is also a realist. Professional self-worth exists only when clinical experience has proven that one possesses skill. During the early years of practice, it is of the highest importance that one has good training and continues to work with supervisors and seek the sustaining wisdom of their own successes and failures. Indeed, even therapists with many years of experience will find ways to continue sharing this onus of self-doubt and confusion through study groups, attentive work at professional meetings, and the reading of professional journals for confirmations, comparisons, and learning.

Isolation

Although the role of psychotherapist tends to attract those who feel deep fascination with the lives and experiences of others, psychotherapy is a profession that paradoxically engenders loneliness. Only a scant portion of one's daily work can be communicated to others, due partly to ethical considerations, limitations of time in sharing case material, and fears of acting out some unbidden countertransference. Equally significant is the regressive dreamlike quality of the intense psychotherapeutic experience, which, like the nocturnal dream, defies full verbal description. In addition, the listening therapist is suffused with such a barrage of instinctual stimulation from the patient's material that a subtle, sanity-saving suppression and repression is put into effect almost as the material unfolds.

Listening

As I begin to hint at the tidal onrush of difficulty for the therapist, it may be helpful to look at those qualities that must already exist in the personality of the therapist who enters this uncertain domain. Frieda Fromm-Reichmann, a therapeutic talent greatly admired for her work with severely disturbed and regressed patients, was asked what was most important in psychotherapy. She stated: "If I were asked to answer this question in one sentence, I would reply, the psychotherapist must be able to listen" (1950, p. 7). Her simple comment reflects on a personal quality that is quite complex, a condensation and surface manifestation of many elements of personality.

One therapist who understood some of the roots of his pleasure in listening explained:

> My mother had no patience with teaching. . . . When I was young, for example, she tried to teach me to play golf. Each time I'd make a mistake she'd fly into a rage, and often couldn't contain herself. She'd hit me on the arm or the head! . . . Finally, she got totally disgusted, gave up on me, and said, "Let your father do it!"
>
> I have infinite patience with my patients. . . . I can listen, listen, listen! They can have all the time they want. . . . I know what it feels like to have someone exasperated, full of rage, and impulsive. . . . I will do anything not to be like that with someone.

Another therapist presented out of her past this element that had shaped her capacity to listen:

> In my family it was like pulling teeth to get people to talk, to open up. I never knew what was on their minds and it

was impossibly frustrating . . . that's why it's wonderful to be a therapist. People never shut up! They don't want to leave, and I can just sit and listen . . . hear stories . . . it's very soothing. . . . From age 12 on, I was on the phone with my friends, and I've just transferred that into the office.

Listening must also result from an insatiable curiosity about others; in addition, it must be informed by empathic appreciation for another's experience. There is a constant back-and-forth trial identification, in which we move in and out of the patient's psychic shoes. Often enough they fit and we wear them for a while. Because of the repetition compulsion, people repeat again and again what they have done and said before, at times for masochistic self-defeating purposes, at times in repeated attempts at self-mastery. The therapist must be in the position of a lover of good music, eager to hear the themes and variations over and over. The good therapist is the ultimate nostalgia buff; he or she never tires of hearing about the good old days. The past—good, bad, but never indifferent—is a storehouse of mood, melancholy, pleasure, and pain—heroes and villains, loves and hates. Contrasting how things were for me with how they are for the patient brings me satisfaction, restoration of self, and a furthering self-understanding and appreciation while fostering exactly those processes in another.

Repetition is daily fare in the mental life of most of us. There are archetypal experiences that we chant to ourselves almost daily, like those ritualistic prayers of most organized religions, which recount the major historical events of their own history. For some individuals, the experience is a fleeting feeling, an old defeat or success, a lost love, a fragmentary picture. For the more obsessional, repetition can be an elaborate and carefully rendered psychic drama. In any event, this intrapsychic phenomenon is cast into the dramatic interpersonal space of the therapist's office every day, and lack of interest in this wonder will eviscerate the therapy of whole areas of mental life. This is a condensed micro-drama of the larger enactments of the repetition compulsion.

Sometimes when patients despair of my bearing their endless recounting, I note for them how many years I have lived in the same neighborhood, and yet delight in walking exactly the same path I have trod endless times before. Indeed, familiarity is even part of the walk's attraction. As avid as one is for novelty, just as avidly will one seek familiarity. We have inexhaustible capacities to creatively spin out the functions of childhood's comforting blankets and teddy bears into the comfortable everyday happenings of later life.

I would say that, like the voyeur, the good therapist is an "entendeur" par excellence. Great pleasure is obtained through hearing. In theoretical formulations of the therapist's psychosexual roots, emphasis is usually placed on voyeurism stemming from exhibitionistic impulses of early life and from the satisfactions of seeing tabooed scenes from which one was excluded. Similarly, there is a great deal of early conversation to which one is denied access, sounds of closed rooms filled with secret happenings within the early family life. Perhaps psychologists have written little of the role of the therapist–entendeur in psychotherapy because it is acted out daily, and in general what is acted out remains to a great extent outside the field of self-observing consciousness.

Eavesdropping, listening to the intimate lives of others, from the days of the aural tradition of Homeric tales to the present, remains a steadfast need for most of us. Within our own culture, despite the advent of movies and then television, the voice of radio has not lost its imaginative appeal. Notwithstanding our highly visual, "medium is the message" cultural atmosphere, there has been an astounding increase in the number of "talk" shows on radio, many stations carrying them around the clock. There is no end of people willing to call in and be listened to. Across the full range of diagnoses, from the beginning of one's practice to the very end, some of the most moving comments from patients will stem from their deep gratitude for the therapist's ability, willingness, and interest in listening.

Therapy for the Therapist

For this psychological traveler, insatiable curiosity purged of the superego (no condemnation as one learns another's mental

mores) is invaluable. The therapist, with the avidity and respect
of a good anthropologist, archeologist, or explorer, brings natural tact and care to delving into the unknown life unfolding before him or her. The patient is usually filled with intense guilt
and conscious shame, and the less the therapist fills the room
with more of the same, the less complicated is the task of the
patient.

As we begin to talk of these issues, we enter the realm of personal therapy for conflicts and traits that hinder and perplex the
therapist. There is no question that personal therapy is essential
for the therapist. All through this discussion it has been evident
that although one must come to our profession with certain
given psychological abilities, these can be enhanced and released through personal treatment. Even more essential is the
therapist's need to find help through the very treatment he or
she provides for others. Conviction that the treatment works
provides the therapist with a deep well of faith and hope in an
endeavor characterized by ongoing uncertainty, doubt, and self-
questioning. The therapist's sense of hope for the patient is
mightily refreshed by drafts from this well of experiential conviction.

One cannot analyze into a therapist the capacity for psychological insight, however, or the inclination to intuit the arcane
maneuvers of the unconscious. Such talents must be there initially in some quantity. Personal therapy or analysis may enhance these aptitudes, as well as enhance the important ability
to bear anxiety without rapid flight into behaviors designed to
blunt awareness. Conversely, one must increase the capacity to
experience affect to the extent that excessive intellectualizing
and theoretical understanding do not play havoc with more
valid empathic affectual resonance with one's self and the
patient.

Suffering

As Freud stated:

> Here let us pause for a moment to assure the analyst that
> he has our sincere sympathy in the very exacting demands

he has to fulfill in carrying out his activities. It almost looks as if analysis were the third of those "impossible" professions in which one can be sure beforehand of achieving unsatisfying results. The other two which we have known much longer are education and government. Obviously we cannot demand that the prospective analyst should be a perfect being before he takes up analysis, in other words that only persons of such high and rare perfection should enter the profession. But where and how is the poor wretch to acquire the ideal qualifications which he will need in his profession? The answer is, in an analysis of himself, with which his preparation for his future activity begins. For practical reasons this analysis can only be short and incomplete [1937a, p. 248].

This recommendation for treatment ("physician, heal thyself") brings us to a source of great tension for the therapist. There is no doubt that those attracted to the healing profession come with a variety of ailments and psychic pains themselves. Indeed, this is the wellspring of our capacity for empathy with the patient's suffering. Lewis Thomas, in his autobiography, stated that in the future, with control of infectious diseases, including the common cold and flu, it may be extremely difficult for physicians to empathize with and intuit the clinical needs of their patients, since these physicians may have grown up virtually disease-free. It might be necessary for medical education to include subjecting young medical students to the cold virus or the flu so they may know what it means to be ill and a patient, and thus provide an experiential groundwork for the growth of clinical empathy. Within the realm of psychoanalytic psychotherapy, I doubt that this will ever be a problem!

Consider the following interchange between Elvin Semrad (the model of the devoted empathic therapist for a generation of Boston-trained therapists) and a resident in psychiatric training:

Resident: What do you think helped build your capacity to help people bear intense feelings of loneliness and loss?

Semrad: A life of sorrow, and the opportunity that some people gave me to overcome it and deal with it [1980, p. 206].

It seems to be part of the therapist's sensibility that he or she has suffered, uncovers further suffering in the course of personal therapy, and suffers further in greater or lesser degree as the transference exacts its inevitable toll. The therapist is permitted to have neurotic problems of character — they may actually be desirable — but they must be of a nature that does not limit the therapist's further growth and development. Excessive sadism, inability to profit from life despite earlier neurotic difficulties, and rigidity of defenses based on anxiety arising from challenges to narcissistic issues (such as infantile omnipotence) are some of the foremost barriers to becoming an effective therapist. Persons with substantial components of these factors should consider another profession.

Sadism, in particular, creates havoc in the therapeutic relationship. Patients suffer from the tendency of aggressive impulses to splinter personality into primitive self-destructive elements. When similar affects are felt to be coming from the therapist it becomes a losing battle for the patient. A certain amount of sadistic straw may be spun into therapeutic gold. According to Sharpe (1930), the urge to cure rests in part on the desire to nullify infantile, sadistic impulses to maim, destroy, or kill. Enduring anxieties over these issues lead to the wish to heal, cure, and make well.

How Perfect Must the Therapist Be?

It is clear that personal therapy is necessary to help us, as therapists, try to resolve what is resolvable, make as clear as possible what our psychological blind spots are and which personal scars are intractable, and familiarize ourselves with the slipperiness of the unconscious. It is important to shift the balance between the guilt-ridden superego's regulation of perception of reality, both internal and external, and that of the ego. We must strive to see life as it is, not as it should be. Increasing the ego's capacity to bear anxiety (Zetzel 1949), allows us keener appreciation of facts that we might be eager to disavow, deny, suppress, and repress. Quite linked to this capability is the need to aid the ego's capacity to bear sadness and to recognize the defense of depression against this primary affect.

But to what degree is this to be done? To be sure, an analysis is incomplete, but when is it sufficient? To what degree are our clinical failures based on our own so-called unanalyzed problems? Personal fantasy is easily introduced into such areas of mental vagueness. The Myth of the Perfectly Analyzed Therapist is one such fantasy. As Glover (1955) has suggested, this is a latter-day version of the Myth of the Hero. It is a childish idealization rekindled out of disappointment, a sense of inferiority, and a need for a restitutive, narcissistic perfection.

Since guilt stimulated by aggressive and sexual impulses toward patients is narcissistically unbearable, the therapist may present a stilted picture of a religious-seeming, masochistic surrender of the id to a purified, rational ego, a virtue achieved through an act of psychological auto-castration. It is as though an offending complex or character trait could be totally (qualitatively, not just quantitatively) "analyzed out," as was mistakenly thought possible in the earliest days of psychoanalysis, when the symptom was viewed as completely separate from the whole personality.

This mythical therapeutic resolution leaves a therapist bound to fantasy professional transference figures, and blocks fresh learning. One of the sources of this problem may be the strange nature of our professional training analyses and therapies, where getting off the couch or chair, for example, never means "good-bye" as it does for all our patients. Instead, the analysand/therapist says "hello" professionally, often then joining the same society, institution, or training center to which the analyst or therapist belongs. Doing this leads to lack of a sharp differential between the new therapist and the old therapist. What follows is many years of the young therapist's struggling loose from the style and points of view of his or her former therapist, to emerge as a more spontaneous student in the process of learning from the newly acquired patients. One of our most esteemed analysts, American-born, stated that when he first began to do analysis he was startled to hear himself speaking with a German accent.

Training Transferences

In a similar fashion, "training transferences" linger on and inhibit the new therapist's learning. The weight, opinion, and protective wisdom of esteemed teachers and supervisors receive an
idealization that protects these magical figures. Idealization lasts
as long as we need it in order to feel secure and adequate in a
psychological field where obscurity and inscrutability of daily
happenings are the rule. Burdened by the need to be responsible, good therapists, we carry mental images of these Dr. Spocks
of theory and technique, and often those, rather than the patient, are what we see.

Flowing from the myth of the perfectly analyzed therapist often comes a similar subtle, but steady, demand for a perfection-
ism in our patients, and an edge to technique that becomes
superego in quality. This fuels the need for a fantasied "completed" therapy, or "full resolution of the transference." For ourselves, and our patients, it is useful to bear in mind the comment
of Hans Sachs that the best of analyses is like a scratch on the
surface of a continent.

Throughout this discussion, it is clear that I do not under-
estimate the need for a thorough, personal therapeutic experience for a practitioner. I am merely pointing to some of its
iatrogenic effects that taint technique and sensible purpose. Indeed, I reiterate that a positive therapeutic experience for the
therapist is essential in instilling a sense of hope for our patients.
It is essential to the inner conviction of the therapist to know that
the technique being practiced actually works. Only a personal
therapeutic experience can provide this confidence. It is never
obtained from textbook or article, no matter how brilliantly con-
ceived or presented.

The Projective Receptacle

I have often observed a special family constellation in the back-
grounds of therapists with talent for their work, marked especially by empathic comprehension and patience for the foibles
and pains of their patients. These people often served in their

families as the bearers of painful awareness of the unhappiness and sadness, rages and tensions between family members: unhappy marriages, intense sibling rivalries, the tensions of being an only child, and so on. Within these families, the only member who took note of the underlying emotional tensions was the future therapist. Often the personality of mother or father was characterized by avoidance, denial, or repression of painful psychological realities. Although the therapist may have found places or persons outside the family to share burdens, within the family life there was little affirmation of his or her perceptiveness and awareness.

Borrowing from Bion's group dynamics, we may say that the future therapist served as the projective receptacle for the unacceptable and painful facts of family life and thereby decreased the conscious psychic burden for the other members. Out of this isolation stems one source of empathy for the emotional estrangement of one's patients, particularly the psychotic ones. One has an eagerness to do for the patient what one wishes had been done for oneself, a natural variant of the Golden Rule (do onto others as you would have others do unto you). This current runs so deep in the character of the therapist that it is rarely stated, but is rather felt like an urge toward the person of the patient: Listening is enhanced as one listens to oneself through the life of the other. Listening becomes the therapeutic expression of Harry Stack Sullivan's observation that "we are all more human than otherwise."

At the same time, this receptivity is not inconsistent with respecting, even admiring, the inherent differences in the life and values of another person. There seems to be a balance of pleasure in finding universalities in people's experience and the marvel of true differences, the wonderment of the psychological traveler to the unknown realms of another's mind and experience. In part, this wonderment stems from the childhood capacity for play which must linger in the exploratory impulses of the therapist. Sustained playfulness of personality is often the hallmark of the child therapist. Linked to playfulness is humor, which is the redeeming salve of painful experience, differing from wit in its parental warmth and observant, sharing nature.

Empathy and the Therapist as Parentified Child

Empathy, the psychological capacity to "taste" the experience of another, is a trait most often linked to the early mother–child contact (and, with the changes in contemporary childrearing, should also include the ministrations of fathers), in which early bodily and emotional needs of the infant are sensed by the parent. Empathy becomes a form of reestablishing contact with the mother (Greenson 1967), a nonverbal reunion; it bridges a separation between people. Consequently, it can be enhanced by depressive experiences in the early life of an individual. Empathy becomes an attempt to feel for and into the mother who is not completely present for the child, and particularly so with the mother who is depressed.

Many therapists are motivated by unconscious desires to cure the mother of depression, to rescue her through depth of compassion and understanding manifested in empathy. The journey into depression and mastery of this difficult experience, through either life experiences or personal therapy, provides one of the greatest foundations for the understanding therapist. It lends a natural backdrop to listening to the mourning issues inherent in the psychotherapeutic experience.

The prototherapist who is given the family role as rescuer is an example of what family therapists call the parentified child. There may be many members of the family, other than the mother, who need rescuing. This special role is a two-edged sword. It not only precociously heightens personal responsibility and bolsters self-esteem, it also fosters excessive guilt for shouldering burdens in excess of one's capacities. In the therapist, this lingering dynamic can lead to masochism in relation to the patient, as, for example, with patients whose abusiveness requires limit-setting.

An important talent, ancillary to empathic intuition, is the capacity to communicate. Contemplating it, one can only marvel at its innumerable manifestations: The line runs all along the gutsy, folksy, down-home, earthy catchwords and idiomatic style to that of the elegant, careful, sophisticated, and intellectualized rendition of the same dynamics. The essential qualities of being understood remain outside the style, falling more under the rubrics of tact, respect, timing, dosage, and care for the self-esteem and self-respect of the patient. In addition, the therapeutic pair build a mutual style of communication, special to themselves only, and not immediately present at the beginning of treatment.

Facing the Facts

Kohut (1977) painted a powerful picture of Freud's personality as being significantly motivated and sustained by a love for the truth. Certainly a passion for the facts and a refusal to allow anxiety to blunt understanding are valuable assets in a therapist, and many have attempted to understand the beginnings of such intellectual attitudes. Some have placed it early in development, particularly in oral receptivity (Greenson 1967). Outside this strict psychosexual formulation one might imagine the infant and young child as having been encouraged to take pleasure in foods, new activities, toys, transitional objects, and, perhaps most important, aspects of the mother's bodily warmth, presence, and unknown mysteries. Mastery of the unknown is a new, pleasurable experience, and gives a sense of competence.

Dialectically, at the same time that the developing therapist needs confidence to plumb the isolating darkness, he or she needs the opposite pleasurable desire, the wish to experience sameness. The early mother–child merging, symbiotic fusion in body and psychology leads to tendencies to collect and integrate similarities under one roof. This function is most clear in great art that amalgamates, integrates, fuses large realms of experience in color, form, content, language, or performing communication. Art, even when it depicts aloneness, has a tendency to bridge physical and emotional gaps and bring people together and enhance mutual appreciation.

These two tendencies of opposite nature—fusion and difference—resonate with the basic psychological issues of integrating one's past with the present and one's needs for separation and individuation. The therapist's natural attitude toward these tendencies will influence his or her capacity for facing seemingly conflicting truths.

Special Traits

Many people speak of the necessity and value for the therapist of having broad cultural education and experience, familiarity with great literature, art, music, and other esthetic expressions, a knowledge of history, politics, sociology, and the realms of science, both natural and physical, as well as medicine. I have no doubt that immersion in these endeavors, explored out of genuine pleasure in learning, will enhance and broaden the empathic and cognitive capacities of the prospective therapist. It has been just as clear to me, however, that persons with few of these sophisticated interests may display an extraordinary talent, and on one or two occasions even genius, for engaging patients and pursuing profoundly meaningful psychological therapies.

How else do we recognize some of the qualities of such talented people? For one thing, they take spontaneous and genuine pleasure in making intimate acquaintance with the significant (and not so significant) details of the personal psychological existence of others, and, moreover, they take continued pleasure in the further development of others as well as being fascinated by past development.

Certain of the successful therapists have the feel and function of a large teddy bear, available for mental hugging, sustenance, abuse, and cherishing, usable for the while and discardable when no longer necessary. This reassuring quality is not immediately apparent in many therapists, and only over time does the unconscious truth emerge as the patient feels safe to depend and lean on this former stranger. The greater the therapist's teddy-bear quality, the more natural is the therapist's facility with hungry, object-deprived patients such as borderline personalities and psychotics. The more this transitional object availability retires into the background of the therapist's personality, the more likely the therapist is to work with patients at the neurotic end of the spectrum (who have sufficient internal teddy bears of their own, and come for different troubles). Some unusual persons work with the entire spectrum of patients. Others find that at various periods of their development one kind of patient or the other holds a special interest and attraction.

Some have conjured up as basic for a therapist's appeal the image of the physician as a figure permitted to view instinctual secrets of the patient, just as the physician is the one accorded the knowledge of all the products and areas of the body kept out of everyday view. Even prior to experiencing the physician in this way, however, is the image of the mother, a rather more constant and dramatically available person, who cares for the infant in toto. If the physician imago plays a role in the mind of the patient, it is strongly based for the most part on the power of early experiences with the mother and partakes of this transference. The history of psychotherapy is replete with great therapeutic talents who came from professional fields distant from medicine.

Maternal Identifications

Let us briefly note that these basic personality traits and sources of empathy, which are predominantly derived from the provenance of the mother, lead to strong female identifications on the part of the therapist, regardless of sex. Discomfort with this psychological reality will greatly inhibit a therapist from being empathic, openly caring, and capable of symbiosis in the deepening of the therapeutic relationship. The parental image and identifications are most important in long-term psychoanalytic psychotherapy, which, like childrearing, depends on the capacity to wait patiently for the unfolding of development, a great deal of which occurs independent of the actions of the parents. Passivity in this instance becomes a receptivity to the developmental process within the psychotherapeutic process. Failure to wait patiently and receptively amounts to a failure in empathy.

Gratifications

Empathic immersion in the psychological past and present of the patient, when linked with resonating experiences in the therapist, suggests the heady and fascinating material that is the daily bread of the working therapist. Although the frustrations and heartaches are many for the thoughtful therapist, the rewards in human enrichment are inexhaustible: the special pleasure and joy of accomplishment, the integrating sense of mastery when the method works, when ethereal principles produce concrete results. Not the least of one's gratifications is the privileged opportunity to gather into oneself so many diverse, rich, and passionate lives. In his autobiography, Jung puts it well:

> From my encounters with patients I have learned an enormous amount, not just knowledge, but above all insight into my own nature . . . my patients brought me so close to the reality of human life that I could not help learning essential things from them. Encounters with people of so many different kinds and on so many different psychological levels have been for me incomparably more important than fragmentary conversations with celebrities. The finest and most significant conversations of my life were anonymous [1961, p. 145].

In addition, humans are so prone to destruction that it speaks to the deepest social urges of man and woman to provide a setting whereby two people can sit together for an unspecified time with a basic assumption that eventually, given the proper opportunity, out of chaos and misery a healing process will emerge. This twosome creates a structure for decreasing the destructive consequences of wanton aggression and for enhancing the creative capacity for affection and love, to the mutual benefit of both parties. In our current civilization this is no mean feat. For many of us, it is clearly a central factor in what makes our "impossible profession" possible.

2

Transference: Ariadne's Thread

Psychotherapy and Transference

Psychotherapy is the study and understanding of the vicissitudes of love. It entails finding the point at which development was frustrated and the adaptive patterns that were used to cope with this frustration. Aggression as it occurs either as anger and guilt, or sadism and masochism, is most often secondary to the frustration of love, and the insecurity and aggressive disharmony emanating from such failure.

For this tangled human state of affairs, deep reliance has to be placed upon the personality's form of summarized history, the transference—an event wrought out of skill and time—that provides an Ariadne's thread through the dark reaches of the labyrinthine unconscious. The transference thread leads therapist and patient back to the scene of the crime, as it were (usually many scenes and many crimes), to a drama of the reenactment of both wish and reality, with curious comminglings of the two. The complexity of life, both external and intrapsychic, creates a Rashomon of these scenes as they are viewed through the adult eyes of the patient, the reflected view of the therapist, the remembered eyes of the child, or mother, father, siblings, et cetera, or the retrospective understandings at various past stages of the life cycle. Reconstruction of the past, in order to make sense of the present, turns into an ongoing process: one, in fact, that proceeds through one's entire life beyond the termination of treatment.

Transference

Transference is the unconscious tendency to shift our emotional interest and investment toward new persons or inanimate objects in the hopes of reexperiencing old persons or objects, or in the hopes of succeeding where formerly we failed. It is maladaptive to the extent that we are left a perpetual victim to the repetition compulsion. It is potentially adaptive to the extent that it reflects the urge to master the past and provides repeated opportunity to do so. It is integrative when it draws the richness of the no-longer-visible past into the present.

When a young man begins college and first meets his professors, he bears toward them a basic emotional valence that is a compilation of past experiences with parents and other important educators. Perhaps he idealizes his professors quickly, and as time goes on and he sorts out reality from fantasy (transference), he may change his opinion accordingly. To the degree that reality does not alter his basic emotional valence, he is caught up in an unconscious transference. Here I am pointing out that transferences exist outside the clinical situation of psychotherapy. Psychotherapy is merely a technique that capitalizes on those factors that exquisitely cull out and maintain transference tendencies.

Transference as Adaptation

That transferences occur is an observable fact, but what actually motivates such behavior is less clearly understood. It seems obvious that if a capacity for transference did not exist, the original family sources of love would be irreplaceable. During a critical period of development an imprinting would occur that was unalterable, and we would be like the experimental duckling that follows only the wooden duck–mother with which it was presented in the first few days of life. Adaptation has provided humans with a certain degree of flexibility to combat the reality of the family's inability to satisfy all of a family member's needs. As these needs mount in pressure (particularly with the development of sexual drives in adolescence), suitable replacements are sought with great intensity.

Transference as it occurs in everyday life is a complex mixture of many things. An adolescent boy may seek the early idealized mother in his girlfriend (a replay of fantasy), while he attempts to have this young lady be all the things his mother couldn't be for him in the past (a wish). He may have urges to mastery, to redo unresolved conflicts of the past. Certain inhibitions and shyness in emotional and sexual matters may be overcome in his new love relationship.

At the same time, the transference becomes an integrative attempt on the part of the maturing ego, a synthetic function. Through the new relationship, the young adolescent will bring into creative harmony past cultural patterns and socializations, and will come to focus many disparate sexual urges (oral, anal, genital) onto one person. Some of these feelings will be experienced directly and others sublimated.

However, depending upon his adaptability, as contrasted with his psychological rigidity, a certain number of conflicts will remain unresolved in his new love relationship. When the compromise between conflicting impulses is too psychically costly, there will be signs, symptoms, or dysphoric affects, reflecting untenable psychological compromise (Brenner 1982). Excessive idealization, for example, can play havoc with growing sexuality if it inhibits sexual expression by invoking the superego incest taboo. It is these untenable psychological compromises (clinical conflicts) that block continued growth and development. Inhibiting compromises, as they are manifested in transference, are the major sources of resistance and the focus of crucial interpretive work within psychoanalytic psychotherapy.

Wishes, Dreams, Action, and Transference

Freud developed the science of psychoanalysis out of his study of dreams, both his own and those of his patients. It was first in reference to dreams that the notion of transference was observed. He described the transference of affect from one dream image to another (displacement) as a means of achieving a hidden, and forbidden, gratification in an unconscious manner. A man focuses, in a dream, great manifest attention on a dachshund (symbolization), whereas the latent affect—a lovely woman—is wishfully attached to the other end of the leash.

Later in his clinical work, Freud recognized that powerful feelings developed toward the person of the analyst as he pursued the uncovering of traumatic memory. These distracting feelings, usually erotic ones, were first dealt with as resistances to uncovering memory, but soon were recognized as the memories themselves being unconsciously, affectively acted-out in a contemporary version of the past (real or wished for). He designated this acting-out as transference. What was formerly viewed as a resistance to the treatment now became the focus of treatment itself. For example:

> A young man arrives for psychotherapy under the influence of marijuana. He is vaguely aware that he wishes me to be irritated with him, angry enough to set limits on his behavior and control him. This is soon revealed to be a repetition of his delinquent childhood behavior, which was designed to mobilize his remote and distracted mother into being a responsible parent. Rather than the patient's remembering, he presents by transference the memory in action. This is transference as repetition.

Freud's first full awareness of transference as resistance, and the necessary focus of treatment, came belatedly in the case of Dora, after she had abruptly broken off treatment. She had left Freud as she had been left by Herr K., who rejected her love. This was transference as a wishful reenactment of the past.

As Greenson (1967) has noted, wish and fantasy about past experience are more often represented in the transference than is simple repetition. Ontogeny recapitulates phylogeny—the development of the individual recapitulates the development of the species. Each therapist will find in the transference experience many areas of wishful fantasy that, on long-term examination, prove not to have occurred outside the bounds of imagination. Tales of aggression or sexual expression between parental figures and the patient, for example, reflected in transference, may prove, when analyzed, to be nothing more than fantasy and wish. This experience will repeat Freud's path of discovery, as he originally thought all neurotics to have actually been seduced in childhood, only to discover the high degree of fantasy in such memory. It is particularly this wishful fantasy element of transference—the turning from painful reality—that makes transference the major resistance and consequent focus of psychotherapy.

Clinical Transference

In understanding transference resistance, it is important to distinguish between transferences in general and the special form and blend of transference that, following Freud's usage, are commonly referred to as the transference neurosis. Suppose I am driving along a highway, seemingly doing nothing illegal, and I am pulled over to the side of the road by a state trooper. Like most people, I become somewhat anxious, fearful I've done something wrong, and suspect punishment in the form of a ticket. My autonomic nervous system is working overtime. I have an immediate superego transference to the image of a uniformed officer of the law. Now, when the trooper informs me that he is lost and asks me for directions, I have an immediate cessation of the anxiety and a complete dispelling of the superego image. This is a floating transference, easily removed with simple reality testing.

Transference neurosis is different. There comes a point in regular therapy, even when it takes place only once a week, at approximately eight to ten months in the treatment, when a set of feelings tends to gravitate toward the person of the therapist and simple reality testing no longer dissipates the anxious notion. Despite reassurances or interpretations, a patient may, for example, begin to feel unwanted by the therapist, less favored than other patients, and boring. This situation may repeat the experiences that brought the patient into therapy in the first place, and also may be similar to events of the past, particularly of the infantile past.

This weaving of the transference thread into the cloth of the patient's mental fabric takes the person of the therapist deep into the unconscious frame of the patient's emotional sense of self. As the transference to the therapist is clarified, so, too, the inner mental fabric of the patient undergoes a certain amount of alteration. For example:

A reasonable and rather rational young woman begins therapy with a fair degree of optimism, energy, and enthusiasm despite the presenting complaint of social inhibition and occasional depression. I am at first seen as warm, straightforward, and receptive, as well as understanding and empathic. By six months into treatment the patient becomes depressed, increasingly experiencing me as cold, unavailable, and not understanding. When I am verbally active I remind her of her dictating, authoritarian, and often violent father; when I become quieter to combat this reaction, I then seem like her schizoid, distant, and apathetic mother.

There seems to be no stance I can take and win, and it is exactly this that I communicate to the woman, suggesting that this was the plight she experienced in her home environment. She is struck by this empathic suggestion and can see herself more clearly as she sees the position she puts me into.

This helps her to understand, provides a road map to help structure her transference experience. But we must be perfectly clear that many whys and wherefores, for many years, will be necessary before there is a significant diminution of this isolating and depression-producing transference.

Note also how this dual emotional thread—the violent and the emotionally distant—that was woven about me keeps us in constant contact with two hidden museum wings of the past—father and mother—and in a deft manner keeps us in touch with great historical complexities.

Transformation in Transference

When Freud's psychotherapeutic encounters with patients were of a briefer duration, particularly in his early work with hysterics in the 1880s and 1890s, he focused primarily on the neurotic symptom: massive phobias, hysterical paralyses, tics, and all the observable kinds of symptoms to which a patient might easily point and consult a physician for. The early formulation of transference neurosis thus looked for the reproduction of the neurotic symptom in relation to the physician therapist. As psychotherapeutic exploration lengthened in time, a more sophisticated awareness of transference neurosis developed. Freud stated:

> When, however, the treatment has obtained mastery over the patient, what happens is that the whole of his illness's new production is concentrated on a single point — his relation to the doctor. . . . When the transference has risen to this significance, work upon the patient's memories retreats far into the background. Thereafter, it is not incorrect to say that we are no longer concerned with the patient's earlier illness but with a newly created and *transformed* neurosis which has taken the former's place. . . . All the patient's symptoms have abandoned their original meaning and have taken on a new sense which lies in a relation to the transference; or only such symptoms have persisted as are capable of undergoing such a *transformation* [1917, p. 444].

As Weinshel (1971) has also stressed, this transformation takes into account that the transference neurosis is not just a static replay of the past, but also an integrative accounting of the present. The elements present in the transference neurosis reveal multiple levels of development and their interaction with the present. Thus a phobic man or woman will not necessarily become primarily phobic of the therapist. The phobia may be displaced to certain elements of mental content (oedipal victories, for example), or the phobia may not come into the office, but may be enacted instead outside of the therapeutic setting.

When we speak of the transference neurosis, we are speaking not only of presenting symptoms, but a totality of conflictual personality that enters the office. This includes general attitudes of character, ego defenses, affects that may be used for defense, discharge, communicative signals, as well as fantasy, wish, and past reality. Contemporary psychoanalytic psychotherapy is really a therapy of character problems. The sources of current untenable compromises are traced through the transference thread into the reaches of past experience. Transference reveals the integration of these experiences in the current fabric of the personality. Transference as a vehicle for character analysis is important across the full range of diagnoses, from neuroses through borderline to psychoses.

Ego Attitudes in Transference

The transference pulls into view the ego-vulnerable elements of character that lead to nonadaptive behavior. A paranoid woman, for example, may not feel that I am one of those responsible for sending radio waves into her bedroom each night, but she will relate to me with great distance, suspicion, and aloofness, perhaps rarely mentioning my importance in her life. We are both able to agree, however, that she is terrified of depending on me, fearing separation and loss, and is entrenched in transference aloofness. A superficially similar transference distance may be developed by an obsessional neurotic man. He too may rarely discuss my importance in his life, but is aware of homosexual anxieties in feeling too close to me and conscious discomfort in competitive feelings with me. Separation anxiety may play a role in his feelings, but on a smaller and less-feared scale than in those of the paranoid woman. In both patients, however, regardless of original or persisting symptomatic distress, the transformation of these symptoms into the transference neuroses primarily reflects characteristic ego attitudes for distancing important, loved persons in their lives.

Let me reemphasize that the term *transference neurosis* is historically dated by Freud's original conceptualizations, which grew out of the study of what were then considered neurotic symptoms. Many of these symptoms occurred in patients who would be referred to today as borderline or even psychotic. Rather than coin some new phrase such as "sustained transference reaction" or "permanent transferential displacement," I believe it is important to emphasize the enduring nature of the pattern of transference, and retain the historical phrase *transference neurosis*.

The libidinous energies (the degree of psychological interest, or importance), when transferred to the image of the therapist, have a "stickiness," or "adhesive" quality, as Freud noted. The patient may then see the world somewhat through transference-colored glasses:

> A colleague revealed to me that when deep in the transference neurosis of his analysis he went to a wedding and was amazed to see his analyst there, dancing, dining, socializing, but mostly ignoring the patient, who felt quite hurt. When he confronted his analyst with this abhorrent behavior at the next analytic hour, he was educatively chagrined when the analyst informed him that he absolutely was not at the wedding.

This mistaken identification in a preoccupied hunt for the loved person is not a neurotic symptom per se, but would conceptually be an example of transference neurosis.

Migration of Symptoms to the Transference

In general, the longer the psychotherapy lasts, and the greater in frequency the visits are, the more likely it is that original symptoms take on a more sophisticated character in the transference neurosis. In contrast, the psychotic symptoms of chronically psychotic patients will often devolve upon the therapist: he or she may become the devil, the source of radio-waved sexual impulses, or even the stimulus for hallucinations.

There are also other occasions in clinical work where the symptom comes to rest on the therapist, remains there, and the patient, free of his or her burden, leaves treatment.

> A tortured man in his mid-twenties came to see me with a concatenation of textbook symptoms: handwashing, obsessive thoughts that "God blows," fears of contracting syphilis from his girlfriend of long standing, and, most debilitating of all, a chronic fear he had killed a pedestrian

while driving. This latter fear caused him to phone police stations endlessly, trying to counteract fantasy with fact. Connected to his fear of acted-out aggressions were work inhibitions. He was a brilliant physicist, whose findings were being used for military goals, and he feared vague retaliations from God for this temerity.

After a year of dedicated work, all symptoms were gone, a degree of alteration had eased his overworked superego, and he felt better than he could remember. His only remaining anxiety, he felt, was seeing me in the hospital setting in which I then practiced: He was sure to contract an incurable disease by seeing me in this fashion. He terminated quite satisfied with his progress.

As a source of disease, I was clearly a potentially destructive transference for this man, and the relationship ended with little resolution of this negative element.

The unresolved negative transference is a common source of premature rupture of an analytic psychotherapy, and the source of most stalemated treatments (Bird 1972).

This leads us to an important clinical point regarding the negative transference neurosis. The young man just discussed contacted me several years later, subsequent to his marriage. His symptoms were not as severe as before, but he was quite anxious (a baby was coming) and feeling vague guilt and depression. Since I practiced so far from his current home, and still worked in a disease-ridden hospital, he suggested that I refer him to someone closer, which I did.

It would be the job of the next therapist to explore not only his past and the transference that would develop between them, but also the unresolved transference to me. It is quite common in clinical practice to see patients whose psychological stress and strain have been woven about the mental figure of their last therapist, have never been resolved, and, like the issues of earlier life, still haunt them. Cardinal to working through this unresolved transference are the issues of mourning, giving up the attachment to the transference ghost of the therapeutic past.

It is a commonplace observation of the contemporary therapist that most people seen in consultation have seen one or more therapists already, and often suffer from insufficiently worked-through transference experiences. We might say these are iatrogenic illnesses, although not extraneous to the presenting problem, yet illnesses as a result of partial treatment.

Rapid Development of Transference

When starting therapy with a patient who is still enmeshed in deep unresolved transference issues to a former therapist, we may observe rapid development of a transference neurosis. The mantle of the patient's former therapist may be cast over us, as "new" therapists, or ours may be cast over the patient's last therapist. Whereas the previous therapist may have been seen as bungling, incompetent, or unempathic, the current therapist, as the harbinger of new hope, is idealized with all the opposite attributes. This idealization may be necessary to get a new therapy underway, but the debt to the negative transference will eventually have to be paid if meaningful work is to be done. Startling idealization masks unconscious devaluation.

While discussing this form of rapid appearance of the transference neurosis, let us mention some other instances in which this special phenomenon holds true. Grossly psychotic patients, particularly patients in the throes of acute psychoses, often immediately suffuse the therapist with their unconscious imagos. Deep attachments are formed with great rapidity, especially if the therapeutic situation is correctly structured and the therapist continues with the patient in the compensating stages of the patient's clinical course.

> An acutely psychotic, megalomanic, and paranoid man was in a catatonic stupor for several weeks, during which, he later told me, he believed I was a sorcerer with the keys to a pink Cadillac. I was waiting for his "good" behavior in order to present him with the keys. "Good behavior" meant relinquishing his world destruction fantasies (letting go of his psychosis).
>
> As he compensated I moved into the figure of a pastor of God (like his father) observing his balance between good

and evil living. When he was fully compensated, I was the wise and astute "shrink" who could pass judgment on his wild and scandalous life and lead him to more thoughtful (virtuous) living.

This intense focus of cascading transference images flowed out in a matter of three months. In nonpsychotic egos, only the most faint and derivative thoughts and feelings akin to these could ever be observed, given such brief acquaintance, and they would certainly lack the felt passion of the psychotic.

Borderline Personalities and Immediate Transference

Certain borderline personalities will commence therapy with a rapid development of a transference neurosis, usually one of a deeply dependent, idealized, maternalized variety, with the patient making great demands on and having expectations of the therapist such as only a young child might expect from a mother. This regressive ability of borderline personalities splits the psychotherapeutic community into two camps.

Zetzel (1966, 1971) suggested seeing such patients only once a week and keeping the material of the hours directed primarily to nonexploratory topics. She recommended being supportive, directive, and reassuring. She also recommended relinquishing the neutrality of the therapeutic stance to ensure not misleading the unconscious transference hunger of such patients into transferences that would be unmanageable by their fragile egos. This attitude assumes that within such patients the original sense of early deprivation (primarily maternal) is so enormous that a permanent defect is left within the ego of the patient. No one can make up for past hurts and lost love, and it would be senseless to suggest that the patient can retrieve that love through the transference. Certainly the patient could never tolerate the frustrations inherent to a neutral therapeutic stance.

In this view, the power of the unconscious is such that the patient would almost want the therapist to be a mother in reality, rather than using the transference as a springboard toward understanding present problems in loving (primarily outside the therapeutic hour). To be sure, all patients who allow themselves deep immersion in the transference neurosis feel at some point or points that the therapist can, must, or will be the longed-for transference figure. The difference between these persons and the borderline personality, in the view of those who recommend limited and structured treatment, is that the borderline does not easily pass through this wishful transference phase into a period of realistic consideration (interpretation and working-through of the transference).

Kernberg (1972, 1976), like many others at the opposite end of the continuum of treatment recommendations, asserts that only a full-blown development of the transference in such patients will allow any meaningful structural change in personality. Structural change is change that develops in a permanent fashion, independent of the link to the therapist: for example, increased capacity to bear anxiety and depression, sadness and separation, which would be reflected in increased tolerance for frustration, and decreased regressive and acting-out tendencies as a means of discharging dysphoric and painful affect. Persons with such changes presumably would feel good about themselves without needing a therapist's reassurance.

Kernberg's view is that "supportive" therapies tend to perpetuate the signs, symptoms, and difficulties of borderline personalities rather than offer the opportunity for continued maturation and growth observed in psychoanalytic, exploratory psychotherapy. It must be stressed that the exploratory pathway often leads to hospitalization to bolster the patient's capacity to tolerate intense, primitive transferences and to find the means to work them through. Perhaps this takes us back to Chapter 1 and the role of the therapist's personality in determining patient preference and technique.

Hospitalization as Consultation for a Transference Impasse

The therapist who practices in an inpatient hospital setting is well acquainted with transference as the immediate stimulus for decompensation and hospitalization. Ironically, although more overtly dysfunctional than the young physicist mentioned earlier who terminated treatment with me, these patients have decompensations that are often an attempt to hold onto the therapist, to master an unbearable transference, but who are now resorting to last-ditch means. When the ego of the patient is felt to be inadequate to work out problems of frustration and love with resulting primitive rage and aggression, the hospital is sought as an auxiliary ego.

In these cases, the hospital-based therapist often functions in the consultative role as a quasimarital therapist. The transference impasse between the patient and the therapist becomes the focus of the hospitalization. The consultant therapist and the milieu work on mastering the current impasse. The most obvious of these impasses are the psychoses resulting from therapist vacations, but more subtle, and just as frequent, are the impasses in the working-through of the negative elements of the transference. All psychotic and many borderline patients fear the upsurge of their resentment and anger toward a therapist just as they feared it with the original important persons of the past. Rather than risk murdering the therapist, committing suicide, or, on a less intense level, risk the loss of a loved therapist, the patient will decompensate.

It often happens that the therapist with such difficult patients is having problems (countertransference) with a transference impasse similar to the patient's. There is something unbearable or unmanageable about the clinical situation. It may even be that the therapist is unaware of this difficulty and views the crisis as stemming primarily from the patient. The inpatient service, with its multiple sources of information, is well-geared to bringing such a problem to conscious focus and providing a clinical forum within which to seek a solution. The hospital becomes a safer environment for both patient and therapist to broach seemingly unspeakable issues.

Transference Psychosis

Special features of early development may enhance the risk of the patient's becoming psychotic as the transference deepens. If the early important people in the patient's life were psychotic and the patient is closely identified in personality with such persons, he or she may relive the psychotic features as these identifications are fully reawakened in regressive, analytic psychotherapy. Additionally, if the patient has a history of childhood or adolescent psychosis, there is a high risk of psychosis as the past is reawakened.

Just as transference neurosis theoretically recreates infantile patterns of neurotic experience, these two instances, in the strictest sense of the concept, might be referred to as transference psychosis (Reider 1957), since by definition they rely on the core infantile past for reenactment in the present.

> A woman who had functioned for most of her life on a borderline level had both a schizophrenic mother and father, as well as a chronically schizophrenic brother. Intense panic states brought her into treatment. Her levels of anxiety were usually discharged in frenetic sexual behavior. As her transference to me deepened and the reawakening of longings for her "good" mother came to the surface, along with her desire for closeness with her mother came the necessity to merge with her psychotic features. This rekindling of early psychotic identifications with her mother resulted in a psychosis that required hospitalization.

For such patients, love of mother is mingled with the greatest and seemingly inhuman torture. It is as if the mother were fire; to be warmed by her is to be burned by her.

Psychosis that occurs during the treatment of borderline personalities, or even of patients with adult-onset psychoses, is more accurately described as a process of becoming psychotic in the transference, rather than transference psychosis. These patients have fragile egos prone to the use of denial, distortion, and projection. When the ego is threatened with extensive anxiety, sadness, and murderous rage, the result is often unconscious domination of reality sense and reality testing. Although the patient may in the past have had psychotic potential, and prior close clinical examination may have revealed ominous trends in affect and thinking, there usually has not been a history of grossly open psychotic experience. What in effect has been transferred to the present has been some mood, perception, or thought process that may have been somewhat appropriate for a distant developmental stage, such as early childhood, but the use of which in an adult is clearly psychotic.

Allow me to confound understanding, however, and recall Sullivan's assertion (1962) that close examination of adult schizophrenics will reveal a brief or fragmentary psychotic experience during adolescence. This will be in connection with some adolescent heterosexual impasse or failure, unbearable sadness around loss of or attainment of love, from which a mini-psychosis results. The strain of cyclonic adolescent experience will reveal the frayed edges of the ego in the future schizophrenic.

My own clinical experience has often borne out this clinical maxim. However, the episode was not understood as such by the patient at the time, and rarely was seen as psychotic by those around him or her. Indeed, it is usually the adult transference experience that elaborates and clarifies what was a terrifying and mystifying past experience for the patient. It is important to note that this obscure episode occurs during adolescence, a time when those persons at even the more neurotic-to-normal end of the functioning spectrum have moods and periods of thinking that from later perspective are seen to have been significantly irrational. The moods of adolescents, we might note in passing, have the tidal-wave quality of the feared moods in psychotically prone individuals. In general, we remember the facts of adolescence better than its affective storms, while we remember the mood of early childhood better than the facts of it.

Transference as Adaptation

In early research in nutritional biochemistry, experimental animals were deprived of certain selective vitamins. It was observed that these vitamin-starved animals, when offered an array of foods, gravitated toward those that alleviated their deficiency. In an analogous sense, what the patient primarily seeks in the transference relationship will be those frustrated elements of past life that have continued unfulfilled into the present. This is an important point, for otherwise the unraveling of the transference experience would have little rhyme or reason, no unconscious structure (Ariadne's thread) to guide us. This is the ego-adaptive function of the transference that pulls the patient close to the unresolved failures of the complicated development of the capacity to love. Ironically, although the pain attendant to this process stimulates repressive tendencies, the transference is *antirepressive* (Bird 1972) as it thrusts the forgotten past center stage in dramatic form.

Setting the Stage for Transference

The therapist sets the stage for the appearance of the transference, but need do little in the way of manipulation in order to foster its appearance. There are, however, quiet elements of technique and setting that will encourage the hibernating bear to appear from its lair. Perhaps first and foremost is suggestion.

Freud was repeatedly frank on the role of suggestion in psychotherapy. We suggest to patients that if they allow themselves to reveal themselves in full, tell all (content as well as what prevents the telling of content), the possibility of meaningful understanding will help them master unresolved conflict (the legacy of childhood helplessness). Just as the dream attempts to tell all, pulling together as much experience as the primary process will allow, the therapist points the patient in the same direction. In therapy, as in dreaming sleep, we exclude the outside world; we keep things quiet, the door closed, and try not to interrupt the patient needlessly. We keep our pattern regular, so that the office environment may recede into the background. Our own behavior borders on what we call "neutral." We try not to let our own opinions override the experience of the patient, and we maintain a backdrop on which the patient may project his or her own drama. To some extent, we must be a willing participant without constantly informing the patient that we are not what is being described.

Allowing Transference to Develop

It is important, especially in early stages of treatment, to allow the spontaneous transference to come forth and develop. In many ways, this is how the patient becomes comfortable with us, since initially we seem strange and different. Excessive early interpretation destroys the "as if" quality. For example:

> I recall one therapist working with a young Catholic woman, who early on experienced the therapist as one of her beloved and idealized priests. In a mistaken attempt to assure the negative transference, the therapist kept informing her how mistaken she was. The patient was confused, irritated (as a result of mistaken empathy), and blocked in deepening her transference relationship.
>
> I suggested to the therapist that he allow this woman to make his office "homelike" first, before jarring her sense of security, and allow her to find the idealized love she was looking for. How else was she then to understand all the vicissitudes of failure and unhappiness that might be attached to that sought-after love?

As Freud noted quite early in regard to transference, "For when all is said and done, it is impossible to destroy anyone *in absentia* or *in effigie*" (1912a, p. 108). The transference must be allowed to form with intense, living vividness. Fleeting transference reactions are harder to clarify, point out, explore, and, most important, to believe — for both therapist and patient.

Tact

Great tact and appreciative empathy are gifts from the psychological gods in a therapist's handling of the resistance elements of the formed transference neurosis. For one thing, as Freud illuminated in "Remembering, Repeating, and Working-Through," the transference is an instance of the repetition compulsion. It is a form of acting-out this memory in lieu of affectively linked, verbal recall. In a brilliant description Freud stated,

> For instance, the patient does not say that he remembers that he used to be defiant and critical towards his parents' authority; instead, he behaves in that way to the doctor. He does not remember how he came to a helpless and hopeless deadlock in his infantile sexual researches; but he produces

a mass of confused dreams and associations, complains that he cannot succeed in anything and asserts that he is fated never to carry through what he undertakes. He does not remember having been intensely ashamed of certain sexual activities and afraid of their being found out; but he makes it clear that he is ashamed of the treatment on which he is now embarked and tries to keep it secret from everybody [1914, p. 150].

In these instances the impulse life of the past is kept at bay through transference attitudes, and also kept at bay are the fears that motivate and necessitate repression. In removing this cloak, one lays the patient open to great vulnerable anxiety, exquisite sadness over failed ventures in loving, and the enormously difficult position of admitting that one's best psychological intentions are misadventures.

Transference love, especially in mixed-gender therapies, is often painfully difficult to analyze in its aspects of resistance (the "nonresistance" aspects will be discussed in another chapter). The passion experienced is real, the affects genuine. Besides, there is a period when analysis of this affect is totally futile. It is much like telling an adolescent girl or boy that their current "crush" is a mistake, and outlining a more proper choice. Similarly, premature interpretation is met by the patient with unbelieving dismay and a sense of being deceived and misunderstood.

Therapeutic experience and wisdom recommend sensitive, passive receptivity and waiting through the initial passionate upheaval. At some point, when the patient begins to feel the pain of frustration and an inkling of maladaptation to this passion, one begins to tell the patient what one knows. In those instances where adequate working-through of this transference occurs, the therapist may later be viewed quite differently. One woman who for three years had found me the answer to her dreams, gently and tactfully informed me during termination that she was mistaken. With extraordinary perceptiveness she briefly enumerated a list, which was rather on target, of key personality traits of mine (which I shall forgo listing here), all of which she didn't much care for.

Eroticized transferences that develop rapidly in initial stages of treatment and reveal a smoky aura of sexuality and seductiveness are usually a sign of the degree to which early maternal issues will be cardinal in the future development of the transference neurosis. Patients who display such transferences despair of forming adequate and safe trusting relationships except with sexuality as the bonding force. The history is usually marked by experiences of early deprivations in the sphere of adequate mothering and nurturant relationships. Such women, for example, wish men to be primarily mother figures for them, and only when these features become evident in the transference do the underlying unmet desires and needs come to the conscious fore.

The Power of Positive Transference

Sometimes a patient breaks off treatment in order to maintain the positive transference and to hold onto the gains obtained under its sway.

A young professor of medicine came to me in dire, depressive crisis as his marriage dissolved. He had lost 25 pounds, was insomniac, could neither work nor think, and paced back and forth most of the day in an anxious frenzy. He felt paranoid and on the verge of suicide. In frequent and intense sessions he developed a rapid positive transference to me. I could say, or do, no wrong. Concomitantly he compensated totally, and returned to productive work.

After four months he informed me that we would have to stop treatment, which he felt had been highly beneficial. He stated that the original referring psychiatrist had informed his wife's lawyer that he was "emotionally disturbed" and my patient felt this statement a great betrayal. He feared it would be used in court against him. He became paranoid and full of rage at this other psychiatrist, while feeling nothing of the kind toward me. He explained that it might not look good in court if he continued seeing me, considering the poor behavior of the other psychiatrist, and it would be best to terminate since he felt so good.

Gentle questioning of this stance produced great resistance, and it was considered best judgment to allow the man to regulate his own internal psychic traffic and to assume he was more in touch with what it could bear than I was.

Let us pause for a moment, however, and pay due respect to the power of a sustaining, positive, and unanalyzed transference. Long ago, Dr. Karl Abraham told of a neurotic psychopath he had had to examine during his military duty in World War I. This man had committed any number of criminal acts devoid of empathy or superego. Yet he was careful enough to have transgressed just so far that his punishment was only dishonorable discharge. Years later, Dr. Abraham came upon this man in a small German town. He wore the robes of an honored citizen, had the medals of a burgomeister, and was clearly the darling of the local gentry. Dr. Abraham reacquainted himself with his former patient, and asked about the source of his success in life. Shortly after the war, the man had come upon a widowed woman of means, with children, had married her, and had moved into her life. His entire existence had changed since then. "And what," Dr. Abraham inquired, "would ever happen if you lost your wife?" "Ah," said the man, "if I ever lost my little mother, I'd be right back where I started from!"

Transference Layers

Transference has no end of mysterious expression. At times a civil, positive transference that remains tenaciously static wards off tumultuous negative transference and in turn leads to more sexually passionate positive transferences.

A bright young man had dealt with a devastating sense of personal defectiveness by entering a seminary, hoping to raise his self-esteem by a pure life and deeds of charity. Despite outstanding performance, which was mostly an activity defense against depression and a way of gaining approval, this course came to grief. It culminated in a brief psychotic episode during which he harangued the fathers with delusionally inspired evangelical suggestions. Leaving the seminary, he began psychotherapy.

For a few years his transference attitude consisted of civility, rationality, kindness, and gentle self-mocking humor. When tiny bits of negative transference emerged, such as his feeling I favored other patients, or noticing a few minutes' lateness on my part, I elaborated these few morsels of discontent. I suggested he was shy about revealing his unhappinesses and frustrations with me lest I ignore him or, worse, find some civil manner of getting rid of him. He became overwhelmed with images of biting off men's penises, thoughts of raping his mother with a "razor penis" (his father was a knife salesman), and intermittent images of subjecting me to various of these and other perverse, destructively sexual acts.

My allowing him to elaborate these images and thoughts over several weeks, without much interpretation, eventuated in new fantasies. He began to view himself as he had in adolescence, fat, flabby, and with pendulous breasts. His father had pulled his "little penis" as a child and often ridiculed him when the patient felt vigorous and competitive. He became terrified that I would do the same (at times literally) in our hours.

He feared for my capacity to listen to this material and was flooded with wishes for me to beat him as his mother had done when she was irritable, tense, and depressed. He felt that doing this gave her some relief from her unhappiness with the father (a complicated masochism since it wins him mother over father, and also cures the mother of depression). He assumed that by beating him, I would get similar relief.

As these feelings were elaborated and clarified over the next year, a new, strong positive transference emerged. This became a central focus of the therapy, and from it the patient took great strength. It led to marked compensation in his ego state and personal life. I became the strong, longed-for father, the father who could not only make the mother happy and thus make her available for him as well, but also who could lend strength to the patient, did not fear his competition, and even looked forward to it.

This newer positive transference reworked the flabby feminine experience of adolescence into a homosexually tinged, positive transference. Through this, he elaborated all the longed-for love he missed from his schizoid father, and had sought fruitlessly from the priests of the seminary. The earlier frozen rationality was a partially schizoid, positive-transference resistance against violent negative feelings, and even more threatening homosexual needs. These latter paternal needs, expressed in an enduring positive transference, became the major locus for his remaining therapeutic work.

Summary

We have made a first pass at defining transference and showing some of its clinical manifestations. Transference unconsciously displaces the experience of the past to a symbolic representation in the present. This may be a reflection of fact, lived fantasy, or the way we may have wished things to be. As an aspect of the repetition compulsion, such transference activity may be adaptive or maladaptive; it provides an opportunity to increase conscious memory by returning to it repressed material; and it can at times be used in new mastery of past failure. Creatively, transference also integrates past stages and epochs of life with ongoing newer experiences.

The keen clinician has respect for transference as the compendium of summarized history of the patient, and trusts the transference to emerge in such a form as to lead both patient and therapist to the clinically relevant events and conflicts of psychic life. Recognition and empathic tact in the handling of the resistance element of transference are cardinal.

The process of transference and transference neurosis is so complex that its weave is found in virtually all the warps and woofs of the psychotherapeutic relationship. It is only through a continued explication of this process, that a more realistic and meaningful conception of transference will emerge.

3

Countertransference:
A Rose by Any Other Name

A Mental Sorbet:
Transference and Countertransference before Freud

In his discussion of dreams, Freud was fond of pointing out that before psychoanalysis was developed, people dreamed. Similarly, transference to a curative figure had been observed by the psychologically astute prior to Freud's research. The regressive need to reproduce the past, to state one's history in action and affect, in order to master it in the present through the helping presence of another is evoked in the following example of intuitive psychology, drawn from the homiletic tales of Rabbi Nachman of Bratzlav (Bratislava), a teacher and mystic who lived from 1771 to 1810 (Matt). Rabbi Nachman was one of those turbulent Chassidic "souls on fire," whose endless energies focused on earthly mysteries as well as heavenly ones.

A Story about a Man Who Became a Turkey

Once a prince went crazy and convinced himself that he was a turkey. He took off all his clothes and sat naked under the table, and refused to eat any real food. He put into his mouth only some oats and tiny bits of bone.

His father, the King, brought all the doctors to cure him, but they could do nothing. Finally, one wise man came to the King and said, "I take it upon myself to cure your son."

Right away the wise man took off all his clothes, sat under the table next to the prince and began collecting oats and bits of bone, and putting them into his mouth.

The prince asked him, "Who are you? What are you doing here?" The wise man responded, "Who are you? What are you doing here?" The prince answered, "I am a turkey." The wise man said, "I also am a turkey."

The two turkeys sat together until they got used to each other. Once the wise man saw this, he hinted to the King to bring him a shirt. The wise man put it on, and he said to the prince, "Do you think that a turkey isn't allowed to wear a shirt? He is allowed, and if he wears one, he is not any less a turkey." These words the prince took to heart and he agreed to wear a shirt, too.

A few days later, the wise man hinted to the King to bring him a pair of pants. He put them on, and said to the prince, "Do you think that a turkey is forbidden to wear pants? Even if he wears pants, he is still a full-fledged turkey." The prince admitted that this was true, and he too started wearing pants.

This went on, step by step, until finally, having followed the wise man's instructions, the prince was wearing a full set of clothes. Later, the wise man asked that human food be served on top of the table. He took some and ate it, and he said to the prince, "Do you think that a turkey is forbidden to eat some good food? One can eat the best food in the world and still be a true-blooded turkey." The prince accepted this, too, and began eating like a human being.

Once the wise man saw this, he said to the prince, "Do you really think that a turkey must sit under the table? No, not necessarily so! A turkey can walk around wherever he likes and no one holds it against him." The prince pondered this and accepted the wise man's view. And once he stood up and walked like a human being, he began acting like a real human being and forgot that he was a turkey.

The prince in the tale has regressed to some earlier infantile, naked state of life. He rules a childish realm beneath the protective roof of a maternal symbol, the table, upon which the parental nourishment of food is set. In this state he is stubborn and negativistic and exhibits his distress before all. What has caused the regression is unclear from the tale. Exactly why the regression moved to this level is also unclear. What is clear is that the prince has left himself in a dependent position relative to those around him, while apparently rejecting help. This is a classic position for many psychotic patients.

From our modern point of view, the actions of the wise man are uncanny. It is as if he had read Freud and Searles (1965), possibly even the Existentialists, since knowing and judging are put aside in the interests of being and sharing. He works slowly, with little confrontation, takes the empathic position, and allows the prince to move from a neutral observing position to a slow symbiosis and fusion, whereby he and the prince both experience themselves as turkeys. Only when this turkey-transference symbiosis has been achieved does the sage behave in ways that are basically action-interpretations aimed at separation and individuation. This illustration is similar to Searles' description of the phases of interaction between patient and therapist in schizophrenia (1961b).

The flexibility of the wise man's "work ego" is in the spirit of H. S. Sullivan's participant-observer. While accepting the transference, he also allows for an ego-split that sits outside the psychosis, and offers a nonpsychotic ego for identification by the prince. The prince develops two transferences: the infantile turkey fantasy and a second that stems from a mature ego still residing within him. We might call this the nonpsychotic part of the ego. Using this more mature transference, the sage attempts to modify the punitive turkey superego, allowing tabooed impulses and expanding the ego's relation to reality accordingly.

The daring flexibility of the wise man in adapting to the transference needs of the prince lends a bridge to our next topic, countertransference. The empathic role-responsiveness of the wise man was a regression in his "work ego" put in service of the therapeutic process. In more recent times John Rosen created a stir when he used similar techniques for engaging the out-of-contact, acutely psychotic patient ("direct analysis"). Rosen, for example, might play the role of "God the Father" and enter the religious delusions of a psychotic patient, shouting, exhorting, and commanding the patient's attention. Such action may not be an essential curative factor, but role-responsiveness in the therapist is an important ingredient of empathic resonance with the regressive needs of the patient.

There is a great temptation to start with the assumption that transference is a one-sided process. The patient transfers to the therapist, and the therapist, inert as a door kicked in displaced anger, mirrors the process to the patient, following some variant of Freud's recommendations. He said that therapists should

> . . . model themselves during psychoanalytic treatment on the surgeon, who puts aside his feelings, even his human sympathy, and concentrates his mental forces on the single aim of performing the operation as skillfully as possible. . . . The emotional coldness in the analyst creates the most advantageous conditions for both parties. . . . [1912b, p. 115].

The doctor should be opaque to his patients and, like a mirror, should show them nothing but what is shown to him [1912b, p. 118].

Recognizing the lack of surgical precision among analysts, Freud first used the term *countertransference* in 1910 as he outlined avenues for broadening psychoanalytic understanding.

> Other innovations in technique relate to the physician himself. We have become aware of the "countertransference," which arises in him as a result of the patient's influence on his unconscious feelings, and we are almost inclined to insist that he recognize this countertransference in himself and overcome it. . . . No psychoanalyst goes further than his own complexes and internal resistances permit; and we consequently require that he shall begin his activity with a self-analysis and continually carry it deeper while he is making his observations on his patients [1910a, pp. 144-145].

We can parenthetically note here, however, the familiar remark that "the major barrier to self-analysis is the countertransference."

It was only later (1918) that personal analysis with another analyst was set up as a major training goal. Clearly, though, Freud recognized that the unconscious of the analyst was affected in the process of experiencing and recording the patient's transference. The history of countertransference at this point was similar to that of transference—at first it was not expected, then it was noted but viewed primarily as resistance. Its becoming a vehicle of treatment, similar to transference, was a development that came after Freud. Indeed, the pursuit and clarification of the meaning and use of countertransference are perhaps among the greatest creative innovations of psychoanalysis and psychotherapy since Freud. The concept of countertransference led the way out of a narrow one-body, intrapsychic psychology to an extraordinarily complex two-body psychology, which explores the effects of two psyches in mutual interaction.

A Two-Body Psychology

Even before Freud's death, attention was turning toward a two-body psychology. W. Reich wrote:

> Finally, it is a mistake to interpret the general analytic rule that one has to approach the patient as a blank screen onto which he projects his transference in such a manner that one assumes always and in every case, an unalive, mummy-like attitude. Under such circumstances, few patients can "thaw out," and this leads to artificial, unanalytic measures. It should be clear that one approaches an aggressive patient unlike a masochistic one, a hyperactive hysteric unlike a depressive one, that one changes one's attitude in one and the same patient according to the situation, that in brief, one does not behave neurotically oneself, even though one may have to deal with some neurotic difficulties in oneself [1933, p. 139].

Heimann (1950) moved toward using countertransference as a major instrument for understanding the patient, not merely a form of resistance to understanding. Once this stance was taken, countertransference had retrod the path of transference. Sandler and coauthors (1970) summarized Heimann's contribution:

> The analyst's unconscious understands that of his patient. This rapport on the deep level comes to the surface in the form of feelings which the analyst notices in response to his patient, in his countertransference. . . . [The analyst must] sustain the feelings which are stirred up in him, as opposed to discharging them [as does the patient], in order to subordinate them to the analytic task in which he functions as the patient's mirror reflection. . . . an analyst may become aware of rising emotionally-tinged reactions to a patient which cannot immediately be linked with the surface content of the patient's associations, but which nevertheless indicate the existence of a role which is being unconsciously forced on the analyst by the patient. The analyst's awareness of his own responses can thus provide an additional avenue of insight into the patient's unconscious [p. 85].

At about the same time, Little, who worked with patients capable of deep regression, discussed transference and countertransference as inseparable phenomena: "Countertransference is no more to be feared or avoided than is transference; in fact it cannot be avoided, it can only be looked out for, controlled to some extent, and perhaps used" [1951, p. 40].

Definition and Forms of Countertransference

With this brief historical perspective, let us attempt some preliminary definitions and clarifications of the meaning of countertransference. In the strictest sense, it is the therapist's counterpart to the transference of the patient. Countertransference is the unconscious tendency of the therapist to shift his or her emotional interest and investment from persons and experiences of the past onto the person and image of the patient. The therapist's unconscious transference to the patient is most deleterious when it is primarily an enduring transference neurosis. As a transference neurosis, it implies (as it would for the patient) a *resistance* to conscious awareness, and by definition an acting-out on the part of the therapist. Since the patient has a less neutral image of the therapist than the therapist has of the patient, the neutral backdrop as a stabilizing aid to reality testing and interpretation is somewhat lost to the therapist. In addition, different types of countertransference may arise from several different factors. Let us briefly mention these forms of countertransference and then explore each one in more depth.

1. *Empathic Countertransference.* The therapist unconsciously shapes and amplifies actual and/or potential facets of his or her personality in response to transference demands of the patient. For example, the therapist is uncritically credulous toward a paranoid's complaints about the world's injustices, or provides increasing availability to a needy borderline personality's wish for an endless source of love and understanding. More subtly, the therapist may respond with anger and irritation to a patient who unconsciously seeks rejection and abandonment.

2. *Unique Countertransference.* The therapist and patient have an unfortunate, ready-made fit between their personalities, which provides marked built-in resistance to working through major transference conflicts of the patient. A therapist's unresolved homosexual issues may make working with homosexual patients difficult and frightening. A therapist who has unresolved adolescent rebellion issues may have difficulty in setting limits for impulse-disorder patients or rebellious acting-out. A markedly masochistic therapist may receive unconscious guilty gratification from a keenly sadistic patient.

3. *Situational Countertransference.* Two elements are represented in situational countertransference: the therapist's own special circumstances and special circumstances of the therapist's milieu and surrounding culture. The effects within the therapist of drastic developmental and personal changes must be considered. These are more or less enduring or more or less

transient (e.g., illness, deaths, marriage, births, shifts in professional goals). The milieu may have impact on the therapist
through hospital views of psychotherapy, regression, long or
short stays of treatment, and through the larger cultural attitudes toward psychoanalytic forms of treatment.

  4. *Characterological Countertransference*. Characterological factors are the therapist's built-in attitudes toward the world in
general, attitudes not related to the individual patient. They are
significantly based on transference residues, as well as on the
therapist's biological amalgam. In this bailiwick lie the characteristic level of tolerance to stress and frustration, amounts of optimism versus pessimism, and the degree of dedication and
concern.

Transference, Countertransference, and Reality

Winnicott uses the term *objective countertransference*: "Objective
countertransference [is] the analyst's love and hate in reaction to
the actual personality and behavior of the patient based on objective observation" (1947, p. 195). Although part of this phenomenon falls under the category of "empathic countertransference," Winnicott is also referring to an aspect of the
therapist's response that is realistic and appropriate—one most
people would have to the patient in question. It is confusing to
call such responses countertransference, to the degree that the
above is the case, since nothing is being transferred to the patient. In taking the stance that it is possible for a therapist to react
"realistically," one is also stating that not everything that takes
place between patient and therapist is, strictly, transference.
This looser use of the term *countertransference* occurs in many
discussions of the topic and leads to a good deal of confusion as
well as dilution of the concept, particularly in terms of viewing
countertransference as both a barrier and a route to understanding the specific dynamics of the patient's transference. Transference implies an overriding, coloring influence of the past on the
perception of present reality. Realistic responses imply the influence of current reality on one's ability to form reasonable judgments and perceptions. A similar distinction might be drawn

between a person's transference-driven "acting-out," and "living." There is a distinction between the two, or else there can be little meaning to concepts of growth, development, and reality.

Empathic Countertransference

Empathic countertransference touches the heart of anyone fascinated by the process of psychoanalytic psychotherapy, a process that tempts the transference to come from its lair with palpable vividness. Psychotherapy comes close to tempting the Fates by virtue of living so close to a passionate emotional edge. Unconsciously, we taste and live the multitude of roles and partial roles assigned to us by our patients, and more often than we know, we act-in these assigned roles before we are aware of them. There must be some pleasure obtained by therapists when, like clay, they are molded to the transference needs of the patient.

Offering a patient the opportunity to project requires a certain give in the therapist's personality. One rather astute woman remarked to me that she could never function in my profession; "Your job is my symptom!" she said, referring to her lamentable malleability in the face of others' desires. This is the participant in the observer (Sullivan 1954) and reflects the role-responsiveness (Sandler 1976) inherent in the countertransference reaction. The therapist displays a certain degree of this malleability at any moment until he or she is aware of it; certain levels may run long courses prior to this awareness. Since it is not only the patient, but the therapist as well, who continues to integrate the treatment after termination, it may be only after separation that certain roles we have unconsciously played, and perhaps intuitively interpreted without full understanding, come to the front of our consciousness.

Using Empathic Countertransference

It is often difficult to know which transference reactions will move into the realm of words and understanding and which will not. The therapist will often experience great upsurges of countertransference (of which he or she might despair), until, with some relief, verbal understanding ensues. For example:

After several months of therapy, a woman mounted an intense campaign of dispute and demands. She questioned with prosecuting acuity my every comment and interpretation, became insistent that I explain my motives, techniques, goals, and intentions. Finding our time in sessions not up to such scrutiny, she barraged me with long, articulate, and detailed letters, insisting I outline and structure the treatment and become more active and open. She began making frequent telephone calls with similar content. It was as if I were the patient and she some active, intervening therapist. The roles were reversed, or, as some like to put it, the object and the self-representations were reversed in the patient.

Although I tried to maintain what I hoped was a sympathetic, tactful, but neutral approach in exploring her behavior, I increasingly realized I couldn't stand to be with the patient. I dreaded her assaults, her overwhelming visual scrutiny (I could hardly blink without her noticing and commenting), and felt as if she were occupying my body as well as my mind. "Disgust" would not be too strong a word for the discovery I made in the brief moments when I could escape my guilt as a therapist and be honest with myself.

What burst forth, when least expected, was a moving saga of her mother's horrible illness, which had begun in the patient's adolescence. Their roles had been reversed. The mother had insisted that the daughter be her personal nurse, and attend to many of her intimate bodily functions. This included not only attending to her urinary and bowel needs, but included placing vaginal suppositories in the mother, and frequent cleaning of the genitals. The patient re-experienced her disgust, helplessness, and intolerable sense of being overwhelmed and controlled. I then sensed that in her behavior to me she had for several weeks been the dreaded, ill mother's body, and seemed in her current rendition of the past to be suggesting that I perform the functions and experience the feelings that she had had with her mother.

As therapists, we don't consciously offer ourselves up for such explicit roles; we find ourselves taking them, and then, if we are fortunate, understanding them. Of great value to the comprehension of the transference is the fact that our understanding is consequently experiential, and not merely an abstract intellectual conception.

Countertransference Hate

Winnicott (1947) emphasized the role of countertransference hate, especially in the treatment of psychotic patients. Since projection is a major defensive style of the psychotic patient, the intense preoccupation with destructive fantasies and impulses leads to seeing these qualities in the therapist. Hence, the therapist is constantly prodded in the direction of behavior that the patient interprets as intense dislike or hate. The patient embarks upon a provocative testing that increasingly fatigues the therapist's capacity to meet the patient's mounting fantastical demands, ultimately producing in the therapist real dislike and suppressed feelings of hatred.

A paranoid woman with a penchant for exacting descriptive detail found few things I said to her to be on the mark, and often accused me of outright misunderstanding. Her frequent condemnation of my psychological clumsiness was so common in our discourse that for long periods I marveled at how she could remain in treatment with me. She often laughed at my personal habits, form of dress, or office arrangements. She made disparaging comments about people in my social circle, which clearly were meant to include me and my family. She was often in a rage about a list of past misdemeanors of mine which she "gunnysacked" and had ever ready to refresh my dim memory of these derelictions of psychotherapeutic duty. The slightest attempt on my part to analyze her behavior was met with regressive paranoid states, replete with biting diatribes about my lack of empathic concern for her well-being and vulnerability to stress.

Apart from these well-aimed forays into destroying my sense of competence, she ignored me; I rarely came into her thoughts. After years of treatment she had not a shred of romantic concern for me, and, going her own intellectual way, continued to "analyze" herself. Despite my efforts to understand the dynamics of such behavior, which are not difficult, since her background is replete with traumatic events and persons (her father was borderline at best, and her mother recurrently psychotic), despite conjuring up my own ghosts of the past (all the infinitely patient mentors who had skill with disturbed patients), and despite my wish to be kind to a suffering person, after a long while I began to resent this woman.

Years of such treatment led to frequent realizations that at times I actually hated her and was quite pleased and relieved when she missed an hour. I continued with the patient primarily because she continued to show up for her appointments (which never ceased to amaze me), and because her outside life showed significant change and improvement.

Hostility is wearing, however, and at some point my narcissism experienced its final straw. I unleashed some of my hate in accurate interpretations of her iciness, feeling that she could take it or leave it. I had my own right to existence as much as she did. Basically, I effected a separation in myself from the patient. If I couldn't rescue her with "empathic" cure, it didn't mean I was judged guilty. This separation was one that the patient, as yet, could not attain in her own relation to a psychotic mother.

Perhaps because of the lack of guilt in my altered attitude toward her, I was surprised to find that the patient could listen to me. Indeed, she outlined my importance to her survival, and, citing her woeful and terrorized childhood, also explained why she needed disparagement to distance me and keep herself protected from attachment. Her need to bear the slings and arrows of outrageous misfortune in

the hopes of healing her psychotic parents was in part relived by me in the countertransference. I had become her
helpless childhood self, and she played out the aloof, psychotic mother, a haughty humiliating woman who defended in this fashion against massive unhappiness.
Unlike the patient, however, I had cured myself and found
a route to relatively guiltless separation.

My painful psychological odyssey is related to a deep wish in
many disturbed patients: If they cure the despairing transference figure of the therapist – an amalgam of the disturbed parents and their own disturbed childhood selves – then hope for
their current selves is possible. Following the period of psychotherapy with the woman described above, I found my hate had
markedly diminished. A deeper fondness developed, along
with greater empathic tolerance. A more intense version of the
same process was then repeated in the patient and led to important changes. She found for her parents the love she had desperately concealed in childhood as a means of bearing the chilling
emotional atmosphere of a psychotic household. She had
identified with the aggressor.

In such cases, once the emotional watershed of hate is trav-
ersed, it is easy to put the unpleasant feelings to rest. As a therapist, one cannot tolerate the notion of hating a patient – in such
states of mind it makes sense to say, "If I feel this way, why continue with the patient? Or, better yet, why don't I find another
line of work!" Once the negative transference and countertransference are within control, however, this level of hatred is repressed in its vividness for both patient and therapist.

In any thorough analytic psychotherapy, the revival of the
earliest and most infantile forms of aggressive defensiveness
will be awakened. The therapist is not an objective computer-
ized machine. The ability to feel is one of the therapist's keenest
assets and must always be available to him. Recall the remarkable statement of Winnicott that "the mother hates the baby before the baby hates the mother, and before the baby can know
his mother hates him" (1947, p. 200). Winnicott suggested that a
therapy is incomplete if a patient never comes to an understand-

ing of what the therapist had to put up with in maintaining the treatment. Without this comprehension, Winnicott stated, the patient "is kept to some extent in the position of an infant—one who cannot understand what he owes his mother" (1947, p. 202). Clearly, then, in this form of psychotherapy the therapist pays a price for understanding. The neutral reflecting mirror of Freud's famous simile becomes, in the treatment of disturbed patients, the looking glass of Lewis Carroll's Alice: The patient jumps through and lands in our emotional landscape, causing surprise, amazement, consternation, and, perhaps, pleasure.

Unique Countertransference

Unique countertransference capitalizes on a readily available interlocking match between the transference needs of both patient and therapist. It is one of the sources of stalemated or deteriorating treatments, for its resolution is a potential threat to the mental economy of the therapist, who either cannot be aware of the countertransference resistance or is reluctant to face the painful consequences of personal therapy.

This transference–countertransference complication often attracts attention when it involves acted-upon sexual feelings as a means of resisting transference interpretation and resolution. These are usually sagas of great sadness on the parts of the participants.

A rather beautiful and elegantly mannered young designer of women's clothes found herself increasingly anxious, unable to concentrate, and addicted to drugs. In addition, she was disturbed by her compulsive promiscuity. In therapy with a male therapist, over several months, she found that all of these symptoms diminished. The intensity of her thrice-weekly visits to her idealized therapist preoccupied her mind and energies more and more. The therapist, a man fresh from a miserably failed marriage (and with a long history of failed relationships with women), found himself equally preoccupied with this idealizing feminine presence.

As the patient began to express overwhelming longings to be held and comforted by her therapist, recounting all her past failures in receiving this unconditional love, the therapist slowly began to comply. At first there was just a gentle and passing embrace at the end of the hour, but before long this moved to actual sexual relations during the hour. In this case the therapeutic pair moved the relationship beyond the office and conducted a passionate love affair. At the same time, the therapist continued to see the patient in treatment (and, in a striking twist for such cases, did not charge her).

Before long the patient began to find the previously idealized therapist weak, dependent, and incapable of making her happy. Her unhappiness, even more intense, returned with all her old symptoms.

In this case, driven eroticization was being used to cover deeper issues concerning maternal failure, issues that would involve fragmenting depression in a therapeutic working-through. Both therapist and patient used eroticism to fend off unmanageable and frightening sadness derived both from current events and the past. An additional determinant in the woman's history was a sometimes depressively psychotic mother who had made bizarre, lesbian advances to the the patient as a child. Driven heterosexuality protected against these early terrors as well as the depression accompanying them.

Consulting on this case, I referred the patient to a therapist who was quite skilled in handling this form of resistance to depression and who understood the role of mourning, which was necessary for an adequate coming to terms with the past. The first therapist refused to take part in the consultation, but did return to his own analyst for consultation. It is important to note that the second therapist was not immune to sexual feelings aroused by this patient as she transferentially relived her past and her ways of dealing with its anxieties. The major difference is that he did not act on them but drew on these feelings within himself to appreciate the patient's experience.

The patient's transference in this new therapeutic setting was an exquisitely painful one. If she seduced her therapist she would ultimately have to face losing him, as she would come to see him as vulnerable and untrustworthy (like her seductive father); she feared the terror of object-loss and abandonment if she failed to seduce him, as she felt confidence only in sexuality as a human bond.

This is the affliction of the compulsively eroticized transference for which the therapist must have great self-understanding in order to master the submerged issues of mourning.

Quite the reverse match may also occur.

A woman was kept in treatment for many years as her therapist worked on the issues of early maternal failures, her narcissism and lingering infantile omnipotence, and many others deriving from the early years of life. These issues were there, and working on them was indeed helpful to the patient, but after termination of this successful treatment she seemed still to run into her typical difficulties with men. She entered therapy with a different therapist, who did not focus as much on nurturant issues as on sexual feelings toward men and rivalries with women. She recalled that many of these issues had come up in her earlier treatment, but had not had the adult sexual focus of her current treatment. (This patient was not alone in her experience with the first therapist.)

Avoiding Negative Transference

A common countertransference problem is the inability to bear the direct experience of the negative transference. Therapists with such a problem slowly accumulate a caseload of primarily grateful patients. These therapists will be excessively supportive, unusually available by phone or extra appointments. They rarely point out the patient's inherent aggressiveness, and may even engage in actions that make it difficult for the patient to experience anger. Fees may be unusually low or large indebtedness may be allowed to accumulate, incurring in the patient guilt and reluctance to irritate such an obliging therapist. At times, when the patient is also a mental health professional, the therapist may make patient referrals to the patient, thus linking the patient's livelihood to the good will of the therapist. The therapist may engage in an indulgent, idealizing transference in the mistaken conception that a nurturant, empathic holding environment is providing a "corrective emotional experience." Such events are usually clear to onlookers, friends of the patient, or colleagues of the therapist who accumulate consistent anecdotes over many years. When such onlookers comment, in however tactful a manner, to this kind of therapeutic pair, the unworked-on negative transference usually finds its resting place with ease and vigor.

The possibilities for forms of mismatch are legion, but the actual number of occurrences is unknown. Apart from nonreporting, there is the added issue of nonawareness, which makes the relative frequency of these therapeutic mismatches unknowable. What can signal a therapist to a situation in which he or she is avoiding negative transference, however, is a deteriorating or stalemated therapeutic process (while the therapist bears in mind that other factors may also produce such a picture).

Situational Countertransference

This category of countertransference contains some special circumstance or situation within which the therapeutic process takes place and by which it is highly conditioned. In part, these situations include developmental factors in the therapist's life such as illness, deaths of important figures, love and marriage, births of children, and key professional stages of development. Apart from the therapist proper, there is also the attitude of the milieu in which the therapist practices.

Treatment Failures, Rescue Fantasies, and Masochism

Certain key periods of development leave the neophyte therapist prone to intense reactions that, as time and experience accumulate, may not recur at the same intense level. A number of years ago I asked that each member of a seminar group of advanced psychiatric residents select a case in which the resident had invested a lot of energy, that he or she had treated intensively for at least one year, and that had failed. The choices of cases were notable for their similar characteristics and the course of the transference–countertransference interaction.

The patients were all severe borderline personalities or outright psychotic. In several cases it was the first or earliest patient of the therapist's experience. These patients had histories or conflicts not too dissimilar to the residents', and they were close in age. The early identification of the therapist with the patient was absorbingly intense. For example, one patient was approximately the same age as his therapist, of the same sex, was an outstanding ballplayer of the same type, and, like the therapist, had gone to an outstanding school on an athletic scholarship. Similar issues existed in regard to women, and the therapist in his characteristically candid way even commented on how alike their basic defensive styles were. Other remarkable comparisons existed between their respective families. The other cases revealed analogous dramatic identifications between therapist and patient.

Each therapist had, in the early fervor of an analytically oriented training program, felt committed to "rescue" the patient. This rescue fantasy tended to place the therapist in an indulgent, ever-empathic position in bearing the transferences of these patients. The patients sensed the intense care and concern of these devoted therapists. The first stage of treatment revealed outstanding positive changes in the patients' mental status, which served to imbue each therapist with greater interest and fervor.

As the "honeymoon" period of the transference waned, however, the transference became increasingly negative. Therapeutic sympathetic acceptance blurred into masochism as all of these therapists found themselves increasingly blamed (by their patients) for their patients' faltering lives. The therapists were unable to interpret unbridled narcissism, fearing the shattering of what they experienced as the "fragile ego" of these patients.

A vicious cycle developed whereby the more the patients' paranoid sadism was expressed, the deeper was the masochistic position in which the therapists found themselves. One of the therapists, for example, found his suicidal patient turning assaultive, threatening him with a knife attack and claiming to have access to guns. The therapists all came to despairing and depressive positions in relation to their patients. It was they, rather than their patients, who experienced sadness and depression as they felt the loss of their fantasy, and they felt isolated from the possibility of effective work with their patients. The patients maintained a paranoid position of blame and entitlement, unable to master this attitude in order to work through the depressive issues in their lives.

What finally crystallized in much too abrupt a fashion, with little advance working through, was a sharp turn in the therapists' stance. In a strikingly similar way, the therapists all reported a period of "laying down the law," a setting of limits, which in two cases amounted to a take-it-or-leave-it attitude. Several of the patients broke treatment, never to return, while the level of interaction of the other patients with their therapists moved toward a "maintenance" position.

This sequence, so forthrightly presented by this group of rather insightful psychiatrists, is not unique to them. One sees in the early years of a therapist's training similar sequences, which, as time goes on, never quite reappear in such a guileless fashion.

Countertransference Cures

Special care for a patient, early in a therapist's training, may also have a positive outcome.

> A schizophrenic woman in her late twenties was transferred from one hospital to another, where she was assigned to a first-year resident in psychiatry. She had suffered almost total disability for several years, had had multiple fruitless hospitalizations, and had been treated by one of the leading therapists of disturbed patients in the city. This therapist had told the resident, "Don't waste your

time; she is a lost cause," and told the resident of his many
years of futile effort.

The resident was impressed by this advice, but confessed to his supervisor that he liked the patient and she
seemed to speak rather openly to him. (However, she had
done the same with the exasperated former therapist.) The
resident was encouraged to follow his natural inclination,
become as involved as he could be, and deal with issues as
they came up.

The woman's life was turned around over a period of
several years and she did not need further hospitalization.
Her life has continued to improve, and some fourteen years
later she is still in treatment with the same therapist.

This process has been noticed in many training programs
(Barchilon 1958). Seemingly chronic treatment failures, often
with experienced therapists, yield in new and surprising ways
to the nurturing warmth of the intense positive countertransference of a neophyte therapist. Although older therapists sigh
with relief at the safe distance from their early, excessively intense countertransference-ridden therapies, many will admit to
missing the wonderful enthusiasm of their earliest experiences,
which often led to special forms of success not repeated in later
years.

Crises of Development and Fate

Cardinal developmental moments in the lives of therapists are
unpredictable in their exact impact. Naturally, this impact depends greatly on the personality in which these moments occur.
What is predictable, however, is the fact that they do have an impact. When a therapist falls in love, for example, it may make
him or her more appreciative of similar processes in a patient,
but it is also not uncommon that one becomes distracted, and
finds a transient decrease of interest in one's patients. This is
also true when a therapist gets married, has children, or falls ill,
particularly if the illness is terminal.

Every therapeutic community has its share of horror stories

concerning therapists suffering either from deteriorating mental capacity or terminal illness. Countertransference here often spreads to the community, and few will dare even to consider informing some respected and aged therapist that his or her powers are failing and it is time to close the office. It is remarkable how much a patient will tolerate in this situation and either deny, repress, or rationalize away the failing abilities of a valued and trusted therapist. Terminal illnesses may provoke very unusual reactions in therapists; some deny the extent of the illness, refusing to recognize that energies are limited concerning patients.

I have seen therapists refuse to tell their patients the truth, and the few patients who suspect that something is wrong may have their doubts interpreted as a form of transference. Great guilt and anxiety is induced in such situations. The patient is not given the chance to mourn the loss with the person they are losing, nor is the patient given an appropriate referral while the therapist is still alive. It is not uncommon for a patient to be notified by phone of the therapist's death (by another therapist taking over the caseload, or by a friend), without ever having known that the therapist was dying.

On the other hand, there are many instances of therapists' presenting the facts to patients and patient and therapist together evaluating the best course of therapeutic action. In these cases a deeper and more meaningful termination is found than in those where the therapist holds a seemingly "neutral" stance until the very end.

Milieu and Culture

Leaping to a different framework of situational countertransference, let us consider some of the ramifications of the therapeutic milieu. Wards and hospital settings that are geared to economically determined needs for short-term stays will provide a distinctly antiregressive atmosphere for the structure of psychotherapy. Patients with psychoses and other personality decompensations resort to regressive expressions of conflict and defense as last-resort measures for self-stabilization. Such a complex and painful process, when hurriedly truncated, forecloses all communicative value these states have, communication for which the patient has desperately thrown in his or her last mental chips.

In such milieus, the therapist will be told regression is "bad"; one will be accused of harmful acting-out when suggesting the patient might need a certain level of regression or a long hospitalization. Pushing the therapist has its impact on the patient as the therapist hurries the patient and may seem to shortchange the "talking cure" through aggressive somatic approaches to states of decompensation. The patient might think that the therapist does not wish to listen, while the therapist is responding to the great crush of persuasion from the milieu. Under other circumstances he or she might be quite willing to listen. For example,

> A young psychiatrist in practice, in supervision with me, excitedly reported a most unusual experience. An elderly man he was treating for severe depression could not be given antidepressant medications because of poor health, and the psychiatrist had "merely" talked with him a few times a week. Much to the psychiatrist's amazement, the old gentleman got better. At first I thought the therapist was pulling my leg, since he knows my analytic orientation. But he was serious. This young man, despite reading widely in Freud and other analytic writers and seeing me for supervision, had been so heavily influenced by an excellent and sound somatic psychiatric training that it was necessary for him to rediscover on his own the "talking cure."

It is worth reminding the reader that Semrad used to remark on the learning pattern of the serious psychotherapist: Ontogeny recapitulates phylogeny. The development of the individual goes through the developmental steps of the species. Similarly, therapists who undergo psychoanaltyic training often find that the constraints of classical analysis, which are appropriate for the situations for which they are designed, begin to be used with nonpsychoanalytic patients. The neutral-mirror simile mentioned earlier takes over their technique. Like many analysts of earlier generations, they may take years to retrace their intuitive steps toward the creative use of spontaneous and empathic countertransferences.

Countertransference in the hospital milieu is a whole topic unto itself. Disturbed patients who are hospitalized often have difficulty in integrating disparate and contradictory portions of their personality. They have trouble hating the person they love, so they look for someone to hate and another someone to love. This dilemma can be further split into someone to have sexual feelings toward, and someone else for dependency. The process can split further along many emotional lines.

Each of the ward recipients (various nurses, attendants, and so on) of these emotions will think he or she is the sole comprehender of the patient's "true" emotional state. Stubborn, bitter struggles between therapist and various staff members may result, for the various ego states of the patient have been dealt out to a large number of staff members like a deck of cards, each recipient thinking him- or herself the one with the winning hand. This is because each individual ego state is authentic but not actually conclusive. It falls to the lot of the chief of the ward to reshuffle the deck and lay the complete set of cards out for the whole ward on one psychological table. This clarification is best done through daily ward discussion, as well as strategic case conferences with everyone present (including the therapist).

In short, the ward functions here as the integrative, synthetic function of the patient's fragmented ego. An important role for the milieu is drawing these countertransference threads into one completed tapestry. This can be quite enlightening for the therapist and staff members, each of whom may have been working in isolation with only certain portions of the patient's experience.

Characterological Countertransference

Characterological countertransference takes in the therapist's inherent attitudes toward the world and people in general: the countertransference is not based on how the therapist responds to the patient as an individual. Therapists differ in their basic interests in and attitudes toward varieties of patients and forms of psychotherapy. Some therapists do not like to work with children or adolescents; others find these raw levels of development exhilarating and look forward to the challenges and flexibility that children require. I recall seeing a film of a family interviewed first by N. Ackerman and later by M. Bowen. The children in Ackerman's interview were allowed free rein and roamed all about the room like embodiments of the family id. With the same family, M. Bowen suggested that the children leave the room, since it was questionable whether adultlike serious talk could take place between the parents with the children present.

This calls to mind a 12-year-old boy who came to my office in an irritable frame of mind. We had been working together for several months. He had brought his baseball cards to share with me, and in the process began to demonstrate his prowess at "flipping," designed to reveal his accurate aim and speed. In little time there were approximately two hundred cards variously distributed about my office and person. I allowed this behavior because I judged that he needed to feel I could tolerate his impulsiveness and aggressiveness without feeling either terrorized or paralyzed.

With five minutes left in the hour, I informed him that although his prowess was most educational and enlightening, I had another patient due in the office in several minutes and requested that he please clean up with alacrity. He cheerfully acquiesced. I mentioned this clinical vignette to a colleague, who blanched several shades of obsessionally ordered dismay and noted, "That's why I would never work with adolescents!"

Each of us has a general attitude and temperamental tolerance toward activity within the office which serves as a basis of countertransference toward all patients. Within this framework much can happen, but it does happen within a characterological framework. For example, Fromm-Reichmann (1950) pointed out that being bound to convention and cultural norms greatly inhibits the therapist's chance for success with schizophrenic and schizoid patients. The personal adjustments of such patients may lie in mores that stand apart from or outside the usual manner of life for most people of our culture. A therapist's inability to respect this difference will lead these patients to sense rejection, and therapeutic results with them will be poor.

On the other hand, with some patients the therapist may have to stand fast by standards of culture that the patient reviles, shuns, and phobically avoids. (Examples may be rebellious adolescents, whose antisocal behavior prematurely forecloses possibilities for continued emotional growth and maturation.) Consequently, a general characteristic countertransference that may be unworkable for one group of patients may prove to be exactly what the doctor ordered for another.

Among certain characteristic attitudes desirable in all therapists is one mentioned earlier: the capacity to listen. Another important and powerful one is dedication. Berman (1949) eloquently described the complex elements of a therapist's "dedication" (p. 161), which contains the staying power and presence of the therapist through all manner and mode of emotional baptismal fire. He likened it to the stability, patience, and experienced overview of parents in relation to the multiple strains of raising children. He felt that the therapeutic situation "represents a unique way of arranging for the commonplace – the commonplace of experimentation and learning through human intercourse" (p. 162). The mature parent, Berman suggested, was the prototype for the dedicated therapist.

Countertransference and the Internal Gyroscope

With the conviction that countertransference is possible in its various forms (empathic, unique, situational, characterological), one begins to understand the *impact of the personality of the therapist* on the evolution and working-through of the transference. Clearly, transference does not occur in a vacuum. Countertransference becomes an important form of internal information about events occurring within the patient and between the therapeutic pair. With a therapist's experience and

self-understanding, countertransference functions most opti-
mally when it has a *signal* value for the therapist's ego. The
participating ego of the therapist provides the data, and the observing ego collates it for an integrated conclusion. Although patients are always unique, no matter how similar, over time we
develop a sense of our own orienting internal countertransference gyroscope, a general feeling for our usual level of functioning under conditions we have known. When this internal
gyroscope seems to tilt to the left or right in response to some patient, this tilt becomes our first indication that a special process
has been initiated in us by the patient. At such times close acquaintance with ourselves is required. A sage cardiologist, early
in my medical training, advised his young flock of aspirant physicians to study the normal heart, to listen again and again and
never stop this activity, for then, the slightest abnormality
would startle our senses, demanding that we seek its meaning
and origin.

4

The Outer Borders of Transference: Working–Therapeutic Alliance and the Real Relationship

Freud's Natural Working Alliance

Freud brought to psychoanalysis, his scientific creation, a strong European and nineteenth-century medical point of view: The patient was afflicted with a symptom, an illness, a disease. This attitude led him to relate to patients as if he and the patient were faced with an irrational third event—the symptom. Together, as intelligent and motivated civilized adults, they were to join forces and deal with the recurring marauder who intruded into natural homeostasis. In addition, the early excitement of discovery lent an air of coinvestigator status to the patient struggling with the demons of unconscious forces. Patients (for example, the Wolf-Man) were often aware that the material of their hours became the building blocks of Freud's science. Although we can sense that this coinvestigative relationship carried unspoken implications of positive transference, we should also be aware of the enormous motivational push such a setting lent to the conscious and unconscious efforts of Freud's patients. Civility and science induced "rapport," a natural working alliance. In contemporary psychoanalytic psychotherapy, such a natural alliance has been reformulated into actual tech-

nical recommendations, the aim of which is attaining the kind of
working relationship Freud seemed regularly to obtain with his
patients.

Enhancing Cooperation

To enhance cooperation, one can cull out important elements
of the transference, its "unobjectionable" portions (Stein 1981),
into a series of propositions describing a work relationship between therapist and patient. To do this is useful not only
conceptually, but also technically. Patients may be openly in-
structed or told of the general format of treatment, educated
about their role in the therapeutic process. Fantasy should be encouraged, along with open revelation of the patient's experience
(thoughts, imaginings, feelings, bodily sensations) during the
hour, as well as the reporting of dreams and daydeams. Therapists should suggest the importance of discussing feelings, both
pleasant and unpleasant, toward themselves. The structure and
guidance of such methods offer a cognitive route of action toward change, which can augment an essential motivational
force in psychotherapy: hope.

We shall see later that many unconscious and irrational factors play a role in the ostensibly rational, cooperative motives of
those who seek treatment. In the mélange of unconscious transference motives, there are certain ones that cooperate with the
aims of the treatment. Desires for gratification of unconscious
infantile wishes, urges to please, to be favored, to be the favorite, among others, will induce patients to engage in therapy with
great energy. Patients will reveal hidden motives, follow inter-
pretative suggestions, review therapy hours in between sessions, and in many ways follow the work program outlined by
the psychotherapist. This is a program that may have been made
explicit, or may appear implicit in the therapist's manner of
working, or may reflect fantasies of what therapy is or should
be. To the degree that such activity on the patient's part advances understanding and leads toward progress in the treatment, we therapists can feel that we have a good working
alliance, or therapeutic alliance, with our patient.

Depending upon the element emphasized, this process has been called working alliance (Greenson 1967), therapeutic alliance (Zetzel 1958), rational alliance (Fenichel 1941), therapeutic contract (Menninger 1973), mature transference (Stone 1961), and a multitude of other terms such as narcissistic alliance, existential alliance, and irrational alliance (Gutheil and Havens 1979).

The Working Alliance and the Therapeutic Alliance

These conceptualizers all basically fall into one of two camps. One emphasizes the rational elements of the ego, including its cognitive capacities. This view acknowledges Sterba's early (1934) division of the ego into an observing entity as well as elements dominated by the unconscious. Out of this split the patient's observing ego identifies with the tasks of the therapy and the working model (the work ego) of the therapist.

The other view concentrates on and elucidates some element of the positive transference that binds the patient to the unpleasant tasks of self-exploration. The coloring of this form of alliance may depend on the diagnostic type and special transference needs of the patient. Zetzel, for example, emphasizes in her therapeutic alliance the early dyadic, one-to-one relationship with the therapist, which is based on early maternal trust. Such trust enables a patient to engage in the suggested activities of the therapy. This form of alliance remains in many ways unanalyzed; it becomes the cushioning emotional absorber of various unwieldy emotions induced by regressive transference experiences. The patient is encouraged to build up this basic trust early in therapy. Creating and strengthening trust is activated by the therapist, who utilizes explanations, encouragements, and a certain degree of direction and early interpretation of treatment expectations. The degree of this activity varies with the degree of basic trust that needs to be built up.

The concept of the working alliance falls somewhere in between. On the one hand, it reflects inborn qualities of the ego, conflict-free, such as perceptual acuity, memory, inductive and deductive reasoning, learning, and the complex mental characteristics that intelligence comprises. On the other hand, the working alliance is influenced by the past history of the individual and therefore is molded by the state of the transference. The patient's experiences with past educators and mentors, apart from familial influences, will be reflected in how various transference states enhance or detract from the working alliance.

The more borderline or psychotic the patient, the less one can rely early in treatment on a natural working alliance. With such patients the therapist works carefully to obtain a relationship of basic trust (therapeutic alliance) in whatever fashion possible, in order to decrease the patient's anxiety and to foster attachment to the therapist. Over time, when basic trust is developed, more full attention may be paid to elements of a working alliance.

The closer the patient is to the neurotic element of the diagnostic spectrum, the more the therapist can take basic trust for granted, turning attention earlier in the therapy toward the elements of the working alliance. These latter comments are gross generalizations; in some cases, one approach may be called for, in other cases, a different approach may be used. Many psychotic patients, for example, may have deep trust in the omnipotent and motherly qualities of the therapist and, in the depth of psychotic regression, may embrace in total fashion a trust of the therapist. It is not uncommon for such a patient to wish to plunge unexpectedly into a very relevant discussion of the source of his distress. Prior good experience with a therapist will enhance such *psychotic* tendencies to trust, even if the therapist is totally new to the patient. Total transference is made to the new figure.

Effects of Transference on Alliances

The working alliance is a fragile creature when it comes under the sway of the transference.

> A borderline woman informed me after a year of treatment that she was deeply in love with me. If it made me happy, she would do "therapeutic work" in order to maintain her relationship with me. Thus she would bring in

dreams, think of fantasies, attempt to work on the unconscious meaning of her behavior, but while under the sway of her transference love, her doing this had little impact in terms of changing her character structure. Any true analysis of the transference threatened her with its loss, and the maintenance of love was more important than change or reality. In time the frustrating nature of this love made it necessary to reutilize working-alliance attitudes to help her undo what in reality was an inadequate state of chronic frustration with an unobtainable object, myself.

The Alliance Used Defensively

Although the therapist appeals to the reasonable elements of the patient's ego in asking for cooperation in the tasks of therapy, the very reasonableness of the patient frequently becomes used as a defensive resistance against the treatment. This behavior is cooperation in the letter of the law rather than the spirit. For example:

A rather intelligent and obsessional patient whose major complaint in entering psychotherapy was inability to feel and to know his underlying feelings began treatment with educational enthusiasm. He talked to all those he knew who had been in psychotherapy, and read many books on the topic. In the beginning of treatment this allowed him to gloss over his anxiety about entering a dependent relationship with a man. A clear "rationale" carried him along.

Several months later, his feelings, as revealed in dreams and actions outside treatment, indicated increased concern over dependency on a man. He felt anxious about coming to sessions, and rather than experience anything directly toward me, he hypothesized with great prolixity about the various transferential possibilities that might be "unconsciously" behind his difficulties. He felt none of these possibilities as conclusive or real, but as rather fascinating lines of speculation.

Here, the working alliance born of cognitive capacities,

jointly used by the reasonable ego and the defensive ego, had been submerged by the defensive use of obsessional forms of thinking.

Similarly, a therapeutic alliance cemented by strong basic trust, perhaps with little actual thought given to such a stance, may become used for defensive purposes.

A woman who initially viewed me as having many of the qualities she most liked in her mother ("You have an earthy, New York Jewishness") was able to surmount an early paranoia over intimacy. Her former therapist had failed her as her mother had, but warmth toward me, she suggested, would allow her to face the inevitable transference regression of another therapy. This was a therapeutic alliance, where emotional trust was allowing the patient to enter into and engage in the process of treatment.

Later when it was clear that there were brewing within her deep misgivings about her precipitous plunge into treatment with me, it became difficult to get her to focus on this. She continued to speak panegyrically of my many virtues in contrast to her previous therapist and to point out how her trust in me had allowed her to try psychotherapy again. Her early basic trust was so important that it was preventing the patient from including in early therapeutic alliance areas of the transference that would dissolve key portions of the basic trust.

The Effect of Negative Transference on Alliances

In both these examples, when the negative transference was more than the psychic traffic could bear, the working or therapeutic alliance broke down into the everyday bread-and-butter of psychotherapy, transference as resistance. It is essential to keep this possibility in mind rather than getting so caught up in the seemingly humane approach of fostering the working or therapeutic alliance that one forgets that, although such an alliance may aid a bit in the therapeutic process, under the onslaught of a true, regressive transference everything else falters.

The cardinal element of transference and its technical management should be reemphasized as the central elements in an emotionally meaningful psychotherapeutic process.

A Slow Development of Alliance

Although it is a bit artificial to talk of a working alliance apart from the elements of transference, which it represents, it is important to note that it may appear and crystallize after several years of unspoken transference relationship.

A very remote borderline adolescent was hospitalized after almost a year of isolative retreat from school, friends, and his family. Although not psychotically mute, he chose abstinence from direct communication with adults as a modus vivendi, especially if those adults represented a form of authority as I did as his psychiatrist. He was highly intelligent, artistic, creative, and the little he did say made pungent, realistic sense and quite captivated my interest in him. Despite several years of relatively silent sessions we continued our mutual interest in each other.

At some point, when he had concluded I was not out to mold him into some vested image of my own, and I seemed in general to comprehend what he was about, he began to talk with me. He became analytic about his behavior and motives and demonstrated a strong working alliance, which had been all but hidden for years. The basic trust had held us together in the interim with little understanding of the dynamics.

Although the trust had stabilized his regressive trend and brought him out of isolation, little progressive psychological change was possible until the working alliance, with its features of utilizing understanding and mastering frustration and depression through emotional and intellectual comprehension, was present.

The working alliance weaves its way into the concepts surrounding understanding, which will be more fully discussed in a subsequent chapter.

Cautions about the Concept of Alliance

A great danger lurks in an alluring guise for those who become too entranced by the attractive rationality of these concepts that foster collaboration. The danger lies in its ready appeal to intellectualization as a way of coping with uncomfortable instinctual derivatives of sex and aggression. By excessive focus on the "we" looking at the "it," the charge of passion is diminished in the transference experience and excessive verbiage is spent on "contracts," "therapeutic agreements," and supra-emotional interchanges that pass over more unmanageable feelings. Thus, certain feelings are mutually passed off as mere transference, or dreams are quickly funneled into palatable symbols that we all apparently understand. Experienced therapists will also count many occasions when "contracts" and "alliances" dissolved into nothingness as suicidal patients were swallowed in a tidal rush of unmanageable affect, wreaking destructive havoc upon themselves.

In this cautious vein we can take heed from Freud's 1910 comments on "wild analysis."

It is a long superseded idea, and one derived from superficial appearances, that the patient suffers from a sort of ignorance, and that if one removes this ignorance by giving him information (about the causal connection of his illness with his life, about his experiences in childhood, and so on) he is bound to recover. The pathological factor is not his ignorance in itself, but the root of this ignorance in his *inner resistances*; it was they that first called this ignorance into being, and they still maintain it now. The task of the treatment lies in combating these resistances. Informing the patient of what he does not know because he repressed it is only one of the necessary preliminaries to the treatment. If knowledge about the unconscious were as important for the patient as people inexperienced in psychoanalysis imagine, listening to lectures or reading books would be enough to cure him. Such measures, however, have as much influence on the symptoms of nervous illness as a distribution of menu-cards in a time of famine has upon hunger [1910b, p. 225].

He goes on to suggest that the patient not be provided with such information until two conditions are met: (1) through preparation, the patient is in the mental neighborhood of what he has repressed, and (2) the attachment to the therapist ensures that there will be no fresh flight from the resulting psychological pain of uncovering the repressed ideas and affects.

The Real Relationship

In both of the models just cited there is often the suggestion that there is a real (nontransferential) figure that emerges out of this interaction with the patient. In the rational model, the analytic therapist provides realistic mental tools for analysis—tools that presumably are so real that the absorbing patient will carry them away from the therapeutic experience and have them for personal self-analysis beyond the time of actual contact with the therapist. These tools would include some facility with free association, attention to dreams and waking fantasy, slips, recognition of characteristic anxieties and defenses against them, knowledge and tolerance of affects, and ability to use them as signals, and so on.

In the transference model of alliance, the notion is that a real sense of trust is built up: a trust that, for the most part, continues all through the therapeutic experience. Apart from interpretation of various levels of fantasy concerning the therapist, such as omnipotence, the element of trust should be warranted. It is expected that the patient is not seduced, abandoned, nor misused for purposes other than therapeutic ones. Such trust in the process and the provider of the process in an ethically and reasonably conducted treatment must be based on reality. Into these two areas of therapeutic relationship—the working and the therapeutic alliance—appears the notion of the real relationship within the transference relationship.

Action Speaks Louder than Words

The therapist's conduct, over time, will determine what kind of working or therapeutic alliance is communicated to the patient.

Consistency of approach, attention to meaningful detail and affect, attention to dream and fantasy, recall of prior sessions and material, regularity of meeting times with little untoward lateness—in short, without enumerating all the essentials of good technique—a devoted craftsman's approach to a serious human situation will be the best explicator of the working alliance to the patient.

Out of this blend of devotion to therapeutic work and a genuine concern for one's patients emanates the real relationship, an element apart from the transference proper and the hypothetical working alliance. Although the relationship may stem from basic qualities of the therapist's character, it is conceptually separable from these factors by virtue of comparable technical and therapeutic standards of dedicated therapists, despite differences of style and personality.

The dedicated therapist is a nonfantasy flesh-and-blood figure, providing a consistent role and function not readily available in the daily course of human events. This real aspect of the therapist is not to be minimized as a strong factor in helping a patient maintain and endure the pains of sadness and anxiety attendant on a meaningful therapy. That a therapist has shared these experiences with the patient creates a relationship special unto itself, and in that sense is real and a new event in the actual ongoing events of a patient's life.

It is not unusual for patients to be overwhelmed by the fact that no one in their past lives has been privy to the knowledge offered up to the interested therapist. Indeed, it is often the patient him- or herself who has been blind to facts of personal history and behavior and is profoundly moved by the depth of awakening self-understanding. Although, as noted above, there are transference elements that promote and support the collaborative features of psychotherapy, during treatment they are used in ways that are novel and creative as well as repetitive. An emotional and sophisticated appreciation of such an advantageous situation forms a powerful, special, and realistic bond and respect for the therapist, who is the agent providing it.

5

The Initial Interview

Beginning with the End

Let us begin our discussion of the initial interview with its end. The last question I pose at the end of a first meeting is, "Will you be satisfied after you leave that I have grasped and appreciated what you wanted me to know about you, or will you feel that I have missed something essential?"

This question goes to the heart of a meeting designed to provide help and understanding to a distressed individual. The therapist wants to be in empathic concord with the aware portion of the patient's ego, and wants to be sure that the patient feels that he or she has been understood. Farther down the road, this understanding may prove to be misleading, superficial, or even wrong, but for the initial meeting, agreement on this point has a great deal to do with whether or not the patient shows up for a second session. Even if the answer to this query is negative, the interviewer is alerted, and appropriate measures can be taken to regain an alliance with the patient before the door closes, or at the first available opportunity.

Many patients view the therapist with great fantasy and mysticism, reducing themselves to passive bearers of information to a psychological shrine, and then hoping for sibylline results. By asking for a conscious opinion, the therapist immediately conveys the notion that the patient is quite active in the process that is unfolding, and alerts a patient to the fact that commenting on the therapist's impact and technique are an important part of the patient's role. This action brings the transference into the first interview without concerning the therapist with genetic meanings (although they might be apparent) but rather with the spontaneous and meaningful experience of the patient at the very moment of interaction.

Keen empathy will always tune into the transference. It scans the ongoing experience of the patient, which always includes the therapist's shaping of the experience as the patient sees this shaping. Thus, although my mind may range in many realms during an interview (manifest versus latent content, assessment of mental status, psychosis versus neurosis, suicidal concerns, and so on), my heart is always focused on the affectual concern. Am I getting the patient's point? Note that the stress is on the patient's point rather than my own conceptualizations and preoccupations with it. Yet I also do not ignore myself, since getting my own point is also important. Empathy works two ways.

Science and Art

Science approaches art in the initial meeting of therapist and patient. We receive a new patient with a mental wide-eyedness, taking in and recording the human data with freshness and clarity, minimizing prejudicial impressions, remaining open for surprise. This attitude merges with an artistic "willing suspension of disbelief," which allows us to be carried along by the patient's individualistic tale, with its ever-present universal implications. We want to find a way to allow the patient to tell his or her story as the patient understands it. In Semrad's sense, we do not so much want to understand the patient in a purely intellectual vein as we want to *appreciate* the patient's experience. Just as we like to abandon ourselves to a powerful musical or theatrical performance, eager to be swept up by the essence of the art, so too we must find a way of giving ourselves over to the experiential point of the patient. In pursuing this form of empathic comprehension, the patient will respond to the therapist's intent to understand problems through the patient's eyes. If the therapist follows in this fashion, psychopathology will not be the chief focus of therapy. Instead, the therapist will be led to find out what the patient is seeking in life—the health and creativity—and what seems to block this progress and achievement. This attitude builds on the patient's self-esteem, self-respect, and self-trust from the initial moments of the therapeutic relationship.

For the most part, there is little need to focus specifically on objective-descriptive psychopathologic features of an interview. As we pay realistic attention to what a person wants in contrast to what he or she has, all these data are usually blatant. Only certain emergency situations (suicide risk, destructive forms of psychosis, and the like) in which such data do not become obvious will require structured questioning. As we make empathic contact with a patient, we ensure that subsequent meetings are in the offing and that mental roads are appropriately, slowly sketched toward the relevant material.

Some therapists are made anxious by the approach I am outlining here. They fear that important pathology is missed with an approach that seems existential. A patient could leave the office quite suicidal, psychotic, or homicidal; without an organized system for reviewing the patient's mental status, the therapist might miss the key elements of that patient's difficulties. What this concern overlooks, however, is the fact that by paying constant attention to the ongoing experience of the patient as he or she tells and experiences his or her tale, the therapist is constantly assailed by data. We see how affects are handled (or not handled), how thoughts are presented (or not presented), what mood is prevalent, how well or poorly the therapist is related to. One could go on with endless possibilities of data present or absent. In this way, our senses are constantly forming and reforming impressions of the patient as the tale is elaborated and spun out. Toward the end of an initial interview, if the therapist has been alerted to certain emergency clinical situations (dangerous forms of psychosis requiring immediate hospitalization, suicidal or homicidal potential), the therapist can make direct and practical assessments of the patient's mental status.

Early Therapeutic Alliances

By and large, for the purposes of beginning a useful therapeutic relationship right from the initial interview, we are most concerned with gradually engaging the patient on an everyday level of contact: Has the interviewer appeared available, reasonable, and reachable to the patient? It is in this area that concepts of therapeutic alliance and working alliance can be evaluated. When the patient feels he or she has reached the therapist, a sense of trust and therapeutic alliance has been evoked. When the patient is working to inform the therapist of how to understand him- or herself, then an active working alliance is nascent. What I am stressing is that the therapist's endeavor to contact the patient on his or her level of awareness is a goal—an important goal—and from this activity the alliances spring.

The attitude I wish to inculcate in a patient as early as possible is that talking to me should be like talking to him- or herself. Ancillary to achieving this is the observation and discussion of factors that prevent the attainment of this goal (analysis of resistance). Oscillating between expression and analysis of barriers to expression constitutes the vast majority of a patient's work, not only in an initial interview but for the duration of treatment. Bypassing resistances while attempting to ease the patient into the therapeutic encounter is a special feature of the initial interview. A young man may have some homosexual difficulties, the revelation of which would cause great anxiety in an initial meeting. Rather than fully explore the uneasiness, the therapist might, for example, suggest that the patient reveal only as much as comfort dictates. Topics that produce more psychic pain than mental traffic can bear can be returned to at a more opportune moment, a moment designated by the patient in an indefinite future. Support of the patient's delaying tactics is fostered so that the patient feels in control and less vulnerable while negotiating this initial therapeutic meeting. Naturally, this strongly supportive technique will vary with patients: If the patient's sense of ease seems paper-thin, but it appears that brief discussion will dissipate initial anxiety without ripping the sense of ease, then the therapist may forge ahead and inquire what is creating the barrier to expression. This maneuver is early defense analysis.

Timing

It is important to remember that each patient who schedules a first consultation with a therapist usually does so under the propulsion of powerful anxiety. When the patient reaches the office, his or her frenzy has reached the tether end of much fantasy, conscious and unconscious, concerning the prospective interview. Consequently, the therapist needn't jump in too sprightly a manner at each early resistance and defense. It is the rule rather than the exception that an initial interview is no place for bravura psychological interpretations. The therapist's comments must be very close to the material offered and close to the patient's awareness and observed tolerance. At no time do we wish to overwhelm the patient with unexpected proof of his or her raging aggression, unseemly sexual desires, or incipient signs of psychotic potential. A patient must be prepared to accept the unacceptable.

In addition, it is often remarkable how misleading the material of initial interviews may turn out to be for a more complete understanding of what is on a patient's mind. Almost all therapies are a succession of unexpected events that provide a truth that is usually stranger than fiction. A belief in this premise will guard the therapist from impulsive and falsely accurate interpretations. The therapist's conviction will also communicate to the patient that unbiased, ongoing openness will provide the most honest acquaintance with one's self.

Given half a chance, most people after the initial social amenities ("How can I help you?" or "What brings you to consult me?" or simply "What's the matter?") will unravel their tale as they previously sensed they *might*. For the most part, the therapist will initially be viewed as a helpful figure. A neutral and sympathetic attitude will go a long way toward maintaining a working relationship with a patient, not only in an initial interview but well down the road of the first part of treatment. It is wise not to intervene with potentially jarring and painful commentary until patients have accorded you full access to the inner recesses of their pain.

Naturally, there are certain patients who arrive for an initial interview emotionally opened up, virtually begging you to move in rapidly and interpretively. This might be the case, for example, in instances of acute decompensations, psychoses, or suicidal impulses. A patient's sense of fragmentation, sense-lessness, or irrationality can be organized by structuring comments even if the comments are only tentative. For example, an acutely suicidal patient under the influence of a black depressive mood, is convinced there is no other form of mental existence. The therapist's gentle reminder (even in the first interview) that depression is a thief whose booty is the memory of good experiences and rational thinking often suffices to make a temporary bridge of optimism from the first interview to the second.

The Schizophrenic Wallet: Making Contact with Decompensated Patients

The initial interview with deeply decompensated and psychotic patients may manifest as many forms of communicative style for the simple and repetitive ideas that lie behind them as do dreams. For example, with certain mute or highly uncommunicative psychotic patients, I have at times made use of their wallets for beginning meaningful contact (Roth 1968). Laying out the contents of a patient's wallet on the therapist's desk allows an opening for communication. The tangible evidence of a patient's reality sitting there starkly, in the form of pictures, identity and credit cards, address books, scribbled love notes and personal reminders, obituaries clipped from newspapers, lucky coins, prayer cards, calling cards of doctors, dentists, lawyers, paid and unpaid bills, et cetera, allows the patient to say what his or her fragmented thinking is incapable of saying: "You see, doctor? I'm a human being too, with all the family and complications of life that any person has." The full wallet suggests sources of self-esteem.

This technique was taught to me by a 23-year-old acutely schizophrenic woman. When she entered my office for the first time, she was in a fury over a recent comment by her mother: "Poor Mary, she has no friends, nothing to call her own." It was impossible to communicate with this grossly fragmented and agitated woman. She wandered about my office aimlessly loose-associating, while I vainly attempted to gain contact through verbal means. She suddenly flung herself into a chair and began to empty her pocketbook of its contents across the top of my desk while repeating in taunting, sarcastic tones, "Poor Mary, she has no identity, nothing to call her own." I was bombarded with the contents of the pocketbook and then with the inner recesses of a well-stuffed wallet. Each time I picked an item up (with great care considering I was dealing with "life matter") she would quiet and calm down, waiting for my reaction and comment. Increasingly, she began to answer my questions when we focused on her life in this displaced and concrete fashion. We delved into scribbled names on the backs of pictures and cards, and the mysterious items that had found safety in the nooks and crannies of her bag and wallet. I seemed to have contacted the patient by this method; she felt I knew that she was "somebody," and this provided an early basis for trust.

In addition, by this method I collected a wealth of information that would have satisfied even the most determined objective-descriptive psychiatrists in search of an initial anamnesis. Many months later the patient told me that during her acute illness her wallet was one of her greatest reassurances. Its existence told her that she had an identity and hadn't been totally dissolved into the panic and fragmentation of her acute schizophrenic state.

Another young woman of 19 was in a psychotic state of panic at our first interview. She constantly begged, in pressured two- or three-word phrases, for permission to leave the office, and gave the impression of a person being closed in on by a horde of hunting animals. She indicated she was unable to talk, and I asked if she had a wallet. She answered yes, and I asked if we might look at it together. She agreed.

Her wallet was, in many ways, a parallel not only to her conscious feelings, but also to her unconscious. She was carrying around pictures of people she had not seen or thought of for six or seven years, mostly friends from early childhood or elementary school. Indeed, she had to take time to think, smiling with amusement, until the relevance of many of the pictures came to her.

The patient expressed much anger toward people who had ridiculed and laughed at her that day. Her garb was indeed unusual—a large brown corduroy English hunting hat, to show that she was part English, and white moccasins to show that she had Indian blood. She used the wallet to prove her ancestry. Between a picture of her mother and father she had stored a series of obituaries clipped from newspapers, relating to deaths in her family. She proudly traced her genealogy for me, showing where the English ancestors had come from, and where an American Indian had married into the family.

The many pictures and memories we shared in this interview allowed me a place in her world. I had not only heard her speak of her identity; I had had it in my hands, therapeutically revered it, and returned it to her keeping.

For schizophrenic and other psychotic patients who feel a fragmented and lost sense of identity, these nonverbal approaches serve as concrete introductions to the elusive acts of interpretation and questioning. With such patients, one may follow a creative and often intuitive hunch in initial interviews, gearing oneself to the missing and hidden mental links in the patient's illness. I have suggested to other patients that they draw pictures for me and tell a story about the pictures (usually "draw a man, draw a woman, draw yourself or your family, and tell me a story about the picture"). These more directly projective techniques are drawn from the same ones that work in child therapy—the use of action and play activities that allow an acting-out of that which can't be verbalized. I find that these techniques help establish a human and emotional affective link between me and the patient, and, with an adult, rather rapidly lead to verbal exchanges that amplify the material. As I suggest above, with uncommunicative psychotic and severely regressed patients, I allow the development of techniques that bring into play the natural nonverbal means of human communication. It is important to be somewhat adventurous and imaginatively creative in responding to the dreamlike nature of regression.

The Therapist's Style

It should be acknowledged that certain therapists, even good ones, are quite clumsy at initial interviews. They have difficulty relaxing their usual technique to loosen up for the special elements of an initial meeting. Some still reflect the so-called classical psychoanalytic style of maintaining neutrality and standard listening technique right from the start. They feel they are ensuring the patient's capacity to use the therapist as a reflective mirror; they are careful not to be seductive. What the patient sees is exactly what the patient will get. Other therapists are clumsy because their personalities border on shyness and they are ill at ease in the presence of strangers (certain personality traits are analyzable, but not necessarily resolvable). As time goes on and they feel they know the patient better, their underlying warmth and dedication is conveyed to the patient, and their reliability and excellence are apparent.

Many people (therapists included) do not sell themselves well when they feel something productive must be achieved or a conclusion drawn at a first meeting. An initial meeting with a prospective patient contains elements of social pressure that do not exist during most of one's subsequent relationship with that patient. Similarly, certain therapists shine in the limelight of the public-interview situation of a clinical teaching conference, while others absolutely dread such experiences. On the other hand, some therapists, because of their seductiveness, are quite expert at putting a patient at ease in an initial meeting. There is at first a suggestion that they can deliver more than they later produce in treatment. The patient experiences great disappointment and confusion as time goes on. It is in order to avoid such a situation that the neutral-style therapist often errs on the side of drabness. It is an art to put a patient at ease while maintaining the patient's chief complaint as a viable presence, and, simultaneously, to desist from promising any rose gardens.

Money

Patients may avoid many specific issues during a first interview, but money is usually not one of them. The rapidity with
which finance becomes a matter of discussion usually does not
allow for much psychological interpretation of the meaning of
payment. Consequently, everyday tact and civility should be
lent to a patient's questions on this topic. As Freud long ago
noted, there is as elaborate a network of defenses and guilt
around issues of money as there is around the issue of sexuality.
The directness and simplicity that aid in the discussion of sexual
matters are equally useful in the discussion of money.

It behooves the therapist to have a clear and frank understanding of his or her financial policies regarding payment for
treatment and to be prepared to state them in simple terms to the
patient. There are no ironclad rules for specifics, such as
whether to charge for missed sessions with no notice, advance
notice, regardless of notice, and so on. Such matters depend in
part on the individual needs of the therapist, the influence of local practices, and the needs and abilities of the patient. Clarity
about one's own practices and comfort with such clarity are important in setting financial facts before a patient so that the patient can respond to a realistic and open policy.

It is my general impression that many therapists are extremely lenient about missed sessions when they begin their
practice. In part, they are guilty over being paid for a skill that
they are still unsure they possess. They also feel guilt over more
unconscious conflicts, such as being paid for a process they secretly enjoy (that is to say, there are broad libidinal roots in the
pleasures of being a therapist). However, as time goes on, they
resent their early leniency toward not charging for missed sessions. This is especially so with acting-out patients, whose
arcane creativity at missing sessions works so close to the therapist's accepted guidelines that there is no way to confront them.
One's anger, often suppressed, slowly mounts. Anger does not
augur well for a sense of openness and comfort in dealing with
patients.

If one has doubts about handling money, it is wise to discuss these issues early with supervisors, peers, and colleagues as one enters practice. In training, money is less discussed than sex, yet it provides dilemmas often no less subterranean nor central to motivation for both patient and therapist. A good deal of negative transference, a major source of therapeutic stalemate and failure, often comes to focus around undiscussed financial conflicts between patient and therapist.

Initial Impressions and Recommendations

A patient may request a diagnosis at the end of an initial interview. It is wisest in this situation to be most realistic. As best as one can, one formulates the patients' frustrated wishes, goals they have sought and not achieved, and some of the tentatively understood personality barriers that have prevented realistic accommodation to their current state of frustration. Indeed, a therapist may know little of these matters at the end of an initial interview. It is helpful to tell the patient this, perhaps even suggesting why (if you are aware why you are in the dark), and to say that only further exploration could shed light on the darkened matter.

What is needed in such an instance is a tentative *psychotherapeutic diagnosis*, which is different from a psychiatric and nosologic label. The psychotherapeutic diagnosis is a joint effort and results from the work just done by the therapist and the patient. It will be a succinct commentary on the ability of the interviewer to formulate the patient's strivings and the personal strengths and weaknesses that foster or work against those strivings. When a patient does not specifically request such a summary, it is best not to give it if the interview has manifestly produced such an understanding in the patient. In such a case, the therapist should suggest only that the pair continue this manifestly productive exploration in further sessions. The nature of the work just concluded will dictate the nature of the work to come.

If a patient requests some explanation of what is done in treatment, the best answer comes from merely pointing to the productive interchange that has already taken place, and then suggesting that, in general, more of the same is in the offing. It is a bit like the marketplace philosophy of "what you see is what you get." Such an approach is an early natural precursor of a working alliance built on observable work done, and it minimizes expectations of especially mysterious proceedings that will magically dispel unhappiness.

Which potential patients should be allowed to continue beyond the initial interview into a psychotherapeutic relationship? Are there persons who at the initial interview should be told that psychotherapy is not an appropriate vehicle? The answer to this is a pragmatic one; the proof of the pudding is in the eating. It is often quite difficult to predict a priori the ability of a person to benefit from the services of a listening therapist. The initial interview begins with one basic experiment for the patient: Do I feel that it helps to tell someone all this, and does telling it give me hope? Only continued meetings with the patient may answer this question for the therapist—theoretical foreclosures will never give the pair a chance. When the patient is willing, one works with the material at hand, which, when followed empathically, will dictate the necessary forms of technique.

At times one does come across certain patients whose previous psychotherapeutic adventures have, in season and out of season, come to ill ends. Such situations require open discussion and realistic advice about seeking other forms of ameliorative help, such as psychopharmacologic consultation or behavior therapy. For example, a 45-year-old male alcoholic requests evaluation for psychotherapy. The initial interview quickly reveals a history of a seven-year psychoanalysis, preceded and followed by several bouts of lengthy intensive psychotherapy, as well as supportive psychotherapy. All of these efforts have been undertaken with therapists of good reputation, but they have left his substance abuse essentially untouched. With such an unfortunate past history, the most realistic prescription would be referral to a psychiatrist or therapist who specializes in the treatment of alcoholism and an immediate concomitant connection with Alcoholics Anonymous.

Patients who have undergone prior psychotherapy, whether

successful or failed, set the therapist a special task for the first interview or two. This task consists of careful inquiry into the nature and development of the prior therapy, particularly the clinical transference and its successes and difficulties. Careful outlining of this past experience will provide for both patient and therapist the possible snags and deflections that will emerge in the coming psychotherapeutic relationship. Barring the possibility that the past therapist was a figure of monstrous countertransference proportions, it is most likely that past transference trends will reemerge in a new analytic psychotherapy. This mutual exploration of past therapy fosters a working alliance as both participants appreciate the history of the past as outlining the work of the future. With this alliance, they can develop a warning system for possible impasses. For example, a borderline patient who used to phone the past therapist incessantly might well be expected to resort to similar exigencies when the frustrations of dependent longings are awakened in the new treatment. Early discussion and clarification of the current therapist's approach to and view of this behavior will circumscribe the patient's expectations and set an early reference point should limit-setting be necessary.

Many therapists propose that an initial interview should include a general discussion of treatment and ground rules for it. They even present some preliminary formulation of the goals of continued work. For some patients this might be good, but for many, a more open-ended point of view is in order. One can't really be sure so easily just what a person needs and wants. A debilitating anxiety often shrivels into manageable proportions after a meaningful consultation; by the time of the second meeting, a patient might have second thoughts about becoming committed to an open-ended psychotherapy. Allowing the process to clarify a bit of its own accord will give both therapist and patient a clearer notion of what they are getting themselves into. I therefore suggest caution in committing oneself on the basis of one interview with a patient. On the other hand, there are those patients who know their mind, may have a keen sense of the therapist they are facing (particularly if they have past therapeutic experience), and will feel keenly rejected on encountering a modest wait-and-see attitude from the therapist. I have had patients return to a second and third interview of open-ended exploration in which they confessed to anxiety that I did not like them, and wanted to get rid of them (that is, refer them) since I had not agreed at the first interview that I would work with them. My attempt to allow them complete freedom of decision was read as insensitive rejection. Certain other patients have opposite responses, feeling pleased that they are not going to be railroaded (as they might have been in the past) and that they may enjoy the luxury of time and choice. This all indicates how individual a matter these initial impressions are and how unwarranted blanket rules are for this variable and very human situation.

The Central Issue

You may wonder what central issues are investigated in an initial interview. I have emphasized an open view in listening to the patient: a view that does not lean heavily on objective-descriptive psychiatry and a checklist of psychopathology and stigmata by which one can identify problems as psychotic, neurotic, borderline, and so on. Objective signs and symptoms come easily enough as one gauges central problems and the defenses that have been chosen to deal with these problems. Common to all misery that enters the psychotherapist's office is some frustration centered on love. It is love obtained and lost, love sought, or love seemingly never found that disturbs people who seek the attention and care of another person in defining a treatment for their human ailment. Therefore, if I can make any meaningful generalization about what a therapist can specifically look for in an initial interview, it is the line of the libidinal thread. Whom is the person seeking, consciously or unconsciously; whom do they fear losing, or fear not finding? Even in complaints that focus chiefly on professional issues, there are clear links to persons whose love will be lost or found through professional endeavors.

Consider the following succinct summaries of first interviews:

A depressed woman seeks consultation because she has moved to a new area for professional reasons and to seek the roots of her family (looking for the wished-for good father). Her husband wishes to return to another part of the country, to his roots. She is in conflict about whom to love most: the living present or the dead past.

A recently divorced woman, suffering from disorganization both professional and personal, experiencing intense anxiety, reveals material that indicates she will no doubt lose her passionately loved paramour. She is unconsciously aware of this and is seeking treatment and a safe haven before it happens.

A man becomes increasingly schizophrenic and paranoid. Overtly he complains about his boss's persecution of him. It is obvious that he is panicked about his wife's first pregnancy and terrified she won't have enough love for two.

A major emphasis of this book is placed on transference, which leads the therapist to the roots and meaningful preoccupation of the patient's life and conflicts. Transference depends on the frustration of love (libido) and its consequent outgoing and ongoing search for gratification through another person. Although potential for transference rather than a workable clinical transference is evident in initial interviews, there is also present in the material the transference as it is manifested in the patient's current and past life. In these areas of entanglement the threads of love's trial-and-error pattern will always be found. These experiments in life are close to a person's heart and usually close to consciousness. When they are touched in initial meetings, they allow patients to assume with great relief that the therapist recognizes what is important in their lives. Frustration in love as a source of clinical unhappiness may seem obvious everyday material, but it is often remarkably overlooked in clinical practice.

Let us end this chapter with its beginning, reemphasizing the essential task of an initial interview—the question ultimately posed to the patient—"Will you be satisfied after you leave that I have grasped and appreciated what you have wanted me to know about you, or will you feel that I have missed something essential?"

6

Psychotherapeutic Diagnosis versus Psychiatric Diagnosis

It is important that the morbid condition of the patient should not be allowed to blind one in making an estimate of his total personality.
Sigmund Freud, On Psychotherapy

Early in psychiatric training I became aware that in the interview situation I was feeling a mental split. Part of my mind was fulfilling what had been emphasized as a cardinal role and function of a competent psychiatrist—collecting a valid anamnesis and noting objective data for a correct diagnosis. Another part of my mind was begging me to complete this task so that I could relax and enjoy my time with the patient. What I sought was elimination of "scientific" and administrative demands so that the patient and I could get to know each other on more human terms, not in the ordinary sense of friendship, but in the sense of my understanding and appreciating the patient's suffering. In terms of diagnosis, knowing about hallucinations or delusions was undoubtedly fascinating and discerning, but it left me with little sense of the patient as a specific personality. More important, it did not address the issue of whether this person could cross painful interpersonal boundaries to bond with me and pursue psychotherapy.

Accurate diagnosis was supposed to suggest the correct

course of treatment. Indeed, it was helpful in many ways, such as structuring the milieu, indicating somatic treatments, and clarifying what was "wrong" in the minds of the family and the patient. In a very general way, psychotherapeutic technique was suggested: psychoses versus neuroses, depressions versus manias, and so on. Yet, often enough, such diagnostic illumination seemed excessively broad, or excessively narrow, or at times, although accurate, irrelevant for the task of psychotherapy. Unfortunately, psychiatric descriptive diagnoses do not carry in their outlines and prognoses for subsequent therapy the specificities of other medical specialties. In assessing the patient's capacity to benefit from psychotherapy, I began to respond to elements of personality that were more relevant to the use of interpersonal treatment.

Theory suggested that psychotic patients could utilize psychotherapy less well than nonpsychotic patients could. Yet, many schizophrenics made greater strides in treatment than did patients with nonpsychotic character disorders, and often they accomplished even more than neurotics such as severe obsessional personalities did. The elements of psychiatric diagnosis seemed to derive from a level of conceptualization and intellectual concern different from the level that created a useful ambience for psychotherapy. The presence of loose associations, delusions, or hallucinations did not rule out the patient's capacity to become involved with a therapist, maintain motivation to come to sessions, engage in painful mourning processes, or work on clarifications and interpretations. On the other hand, the good reality testing and strong defenses of an obsessional neurotic did not necessarily indicate interest in therapeutic processes, nor did these qualities suggest the necessary psychological mind-set that is important for looking inward in a useful therapy.

For example, an action-disposed lawyer, geared to a reality that consists of external admissible evidence, may have a constitutional reluctance to deal with the gossamer facts of the unconscious. Such persons, when faced with a crisis in their lives, seek a few consultations with a psychiatrist and then find an action-disposed means of putting their minds at rest. All too often, however, they are not able to see that the next solution (wife, mistress, or job), although outwardly different from the last, is actually unconsciously the same. Such persons have no psychotic stigmata, they demonstrate good reality testing of the kinds examined by standard psychiatric criteria, and by and large they have excellent ego strengths, including high-level defense mechanisms such as intellectualization and sublimation. Yet, they are poor candidates for analytic psychotherapy. Why? Quite simply, they are not motivated to look inward, and any prolonged dependence on a therapist goes counter to their self-image of self-reliance and independence.

Ironically, despite marked personality difficulties, a borderline personality in crisis may be more capable of taking advantage of a therapist's skills precisely because the proclivity to dependence (perhaps part of their problem) bends toward the therapist, and the sharpness of their pain increases motivation and the urge to seek understanding. Excessive independence (counterdependence) may be maladaptive, while apparently excessive dependence can have adaptive elements. These nuances are lost in traditional diagnostic approaches, but they do not elude the therapist's often unarticulated, intuitive response to the patient's whole personality.

An Emphasis on Health

A psychotherapeutic diagnosis is geared toward health rather than pathology. The traditional diagnosis aims toward pathologic signs. In looking for what will make a workable psychotherapy, it is important to search out the strengths of the patient. Many of the ingredients of this process are derived from useful knowledge of the elements of normal growth and development. Much of what we expect from the therapeutic process is what, we hope, comes about in ideal parental relations: empathic understanding, tolerance for the ups and downs of the developmental epochs and crises, warmth, a sense of overview and distance with experiential perspective, and value placed on a civilized balance between inhibition and expression of impulses.

The capacity to engage in this interpersonal process, replayed in psychotherapy (Freud referred to psychotherapy as "after education"), reflects the healthy, growth-stimulating aspects of a person. The lexicon of traditional psychiatry has few terms to express health and many terms to particularize psychopathology. In judging psychotherapeutic potential, one finds our professional language so inadequate for the task of denoting health that one often resorts to unspoken intuition instead. This chapter will attempt to provide a few words for this everyday intuition.

The probable successful use of psychotherapy is reflected in factors such as the unique personal psychology of the patient (intrapsychic), plus those that border on the intrapsychic and interpersonal (interactive), and those that flourish primarily in the interpersonal field. I have given the categories indicators that point toward and away, since these factors enhance or diminish the expression of one another.

Motivation

It is unrealistic to single out the one human quality that could be called the most important predisposition for psychotherapy. But, if I had to do this, the factor would be motivation.

Many elements seem to make up the final force called motivation. Certain qualities seem biological in nature, a constitutional thrust of the id, expressing libido in the striving for pleasure

Table 6-1
Factors Encouraging Use of Psychotherapy

Intrapsychic ◄──────►	*Interactive* ◄──────►	*Interpersonal*
Motivation	Honesty	Communicative pressure
Insight	Frustration tolerance	Warmth
Flexibility	Capacity to bear affect	Responsiveness
	Humor	Dyadic resonance

against unpleasure and aggression in forceful self-assertion. Some roots of motivation stem from the complex interaction of an early psychological environment that provided backing for pushing ahead despite obstacles. Other sources are superego dictates of "shoulds"; one should never give up. Elements of nonconflictual ego may play a motivating role through the urge to mastery (Hendrick 1942) or the urge toward competence (White 1963). Embedded in strong motivation is also the psychological experience of hope, a complex emotion that promises safety, security, and ultimate gratification.

Many in-depth studies of psychotherapy have included motivation as a primary factor in a patient's decision to continue therapy or in the therapy's ultimate success (Kernberg and coauthors 1972). Whether all these studies are valid or not, what cannot be denied is the therapist's admiration and respect for a patient with strong motivation. Strong motivation will sustain and support both patient and therapist in a long, often frustrating endeavor. It is a condensed and keen indicator of resources that may be totally concealed in the initial phases of evaluation and interaction, like the intriguing Japanese folded paper flower of old, in which the beauty of the blossom is hidden until it is mixed with the medium of water.

Once a young woman came to see me upon the insistence and recommendation of her mother and her mother's friend, a psychiatrist. My major impression of this worn-looking woman, who seemed old beyond her years, was that of the often described "bag lady." Complete with large shopping bag, she was unkempt, her hair flowing in bedraggled strands around her neck and streaming onto a cloak which all but hid her entire body. Only an averted face was left to reveal her emotions. In a barely audible voice, she spoke two- or three-word sentences. She presented her story mostly in the words and images of her mother and her mother's friend. It was hard to discern whether she had a story of her own. Her passivity was sad and impressive. Thus, I was surprised when she insisted we meet again, and then further surprised when later she insisted we begin in psychotherapy.

For two years little seemed to happen, although my respect for her dogged stick-to-it-iveness (motivation) steadily increased. At this point, it is sufficient to indicate that over the subsequent seven years, slowly but increasingly, she made unexpected and remarkable strides and changes in herself and in her life. It was her motivation alone that carried us through the first two years of the treatment to meet the person who finally emerged.

Insight

The course of insight in psychotherapy is admittedly quite checkered. All too often it is a summer soldier, fluctuating with the level of resistance (psychic pain subsequent to understanding), and the negative and positive transference. It does reflect, however, the degree to which the rational, observing ego of the patient is in alliance with the goals of treatment. In early interviews, the patient's insight may reveal a potential to use the setting of therapy to further self-understanding, one of the major processes of change in psychotherapy. This revelation may occur within a single interview or, more usually, over time, from interview to interview. In addition, insight may be descriptive, a verbal and intellectual comprehension. Or it may be experiential, an affectual window of emotional perception. This is especially true with regard to the transference.

I had a rather difficult first interview with a depressed woman who was picky with my observations; they were always just a bit off the mark. I appeared to her to be clumsy and far from smoothing the path of communication. At the end of the interview I felt I had done a terrible job putting the woman at ease, and wondered if she would show up for our next appointment or call and cancel. She surprised me at the second interview by announcing that no sooner had she left my office after our first meeting than she was struck by her irritating attitude toward me. She deftly suggested that her mother was like that with her father, and in her recent burgeoning depression she was terrified she was increasingly coming to resemble her dreaded mother. In the first interview she unconsciously acted-out a major portion of her chief complaint, rather than stating it. This acting-out certainly gave me a more vivid and immediate picture of her difficulty than a spoken description would have. And, when combined with her subsequent comprehension of the meaning of the acting-out, it undeniably revealed the patient's capacity for self-reflection and insight.

Anxiety may bring a patient to treatment, but after the initial calming effects of consultation, the patient must still feel sufficient anxiety in order to bear the frustration and psychological threat of treatment. Insight, which helps patients link their anxiety to elements of themselves that require continued exploration, helps give patients a structured view of treatment and an intellectual justification for continued exploratory pain. The patient need not be able to pinpoint underlying factors. The acknowledgment that conscious surface anxiety has unconscious roots, particularly when some of them have been demonstrated, is enough to help maintain a rationale for the uncertainties of treatment.

Flexibility

We notice with admiration persons who can describe their foibles and at the same time acknowledge their strengths, present their behavior as childish yet be quite adult in formulating this difficulty, suffer painfully during the hour, shed floods of tears, and yet leave the hour at the required time, ready to face the world. This flexibility may also be understood as the capacity for regression in the service of the ego. It demonstrates the wide range of functioning inherent in the patient's ego, and it implies an adaptability to the needs of the therapeutic setting. The patient is demonstrating ability to be a participant as well as an observer in the therapeutic process. Ultimately, flexibility will be necessary in order to engage in the transference with emotional involvement as well as intellectual understanding. Such a richness of function, when present, invariably impresses a therapist and speaks strongly for a patient's capacity and willingness, through demonstration, to do psychotherapeutic work.

Inflexibility, the initial ego weaknesses of a patient, which may be taken as a poor sign for psychotherapy potential, may alter tremendously with treatment. An initially passive, emotionally monochromatic, inhibited housewife, for example, may later prove to be highly assertive, powerfully passionate, and strongly exhibitionistic. The initial picture may have been part of a psychological guise intended to assuage an easily threatened husband and may have been based on feelings of inadequacy that would yield to psychotherapy. Her seemingly unthoughtful, psychologically limited thinking could have been mostly defensive. At another extreme, when the patient's ego is generally effective in life and the patient feels that this behavior is mostly adaptive, it may appear that the character armor is so syntonic that we cannot imagine it shifting even through interpretation of unconscious conflict. During initial evaluation we must focus more on the potential for change in ego defenses rather than purely upon the current state of the ego. We should gauge how much of the ego is devoted to defensive purposes, and how much room may appear for relaxation and more realistic use of defenses.

The common example of inflexibility is that of the obsessional defenses of intellectualization, reaction formation, and isolation of affect. It is a good sign if these defenses are somewhat painful to the patient (ego-alien) rather than smoothly functioning and unnoticed (syntonic). This discomfort reveals an awareness that suppressed tendencies are being handled by a slightly irrational use of rational processes. Additionally, if these obsessional defenses are used almost solely for warding off emotional experience rather than for purposes of clear thinking and toleration of affect, then the prognosis for treatment, while not totally black on this basis alone, certainly turns a deeper shade of gray. I cannot caution enough, however, against a premature judgment on these matters. A trial of therapy is always preferred to a trial of diagnosis.

Honesty

"We must not forget that the analytic relationship is based on a love of truth—that is, on a recognition of reality" (Freud 1937a, p. 248).

The capacity to deal honestly and realistically with oneself is, of course, quite relative. It is an ongoing developmental process for everyone. Although honesty touches on qualities of insight and the ability to bear painful affects and tolerate frustration, when it is present as a salient feature of personality, it stands out on its own. It is so central to the whole of the psychotherapeutic endeavor that when a patient displays realistic honesty in dealing with the trials and tribulations of life, by definition the patient reveals the capacity to engage in psychotherapy. Often, when I have remarked to a patient that I was impressed by his or her honesty in dealing with disruptively painful material, the patient has commented with some puzzlement: "How can I hope to get out of this mess without dealing with the facts?" When psychotherapy works well, it leave patients with a notion of what they *can* do (in the sense of what they are able to do) rather than what they *want* to do (in the sense of what they wish to do). Without the honest facts, this state of mind cannot be reached. Honesty in psychotherapy also requires the doubly difficult task of being honest not only with oneself, but also with another person.

On its own, however, honesty may not always be entirely adequate:

A charming, successful stockbroker came to see me because he had tired rapidly of his recent marriage, undertaken late in life. His wife no longer had the slightest sexual attraction for him. He was brutally honest in detailing his lack of concern, the family pressures that had caused him to capitulate temporarily and marry, and the affairs he carried on constantly. A woman, for him, he said, meant no more than an "erect penis." He was not caustic or cruel, but merely matter-of-fact; indeed, quite honest about himself. He detailed the amorous adventures of his father, who he

felt had tried to hide similar feelings from his wife, children, and extended family. The patient suggested that he
had less shame and inhibition on this score than did his father. If I could provide some interpretation that would
reestablish his sexual attraction to his current wife perhaps
he would stay married; if not, he would have to divorce. I
was the first psychiatrist the man had seen, and when after
several sessions the magical interpretation did not come
forth, I suspect I had become the last.

Frustration Tolerance

For all patients, but especially for those in need of intense
nurturance, the therapeutic situation holds great frustration.
This wonderful object, the therapist, makes him- or herself
available, but for limited times only, and on a limited basis. This
limit comes in the face of many unmet libidinous and aggressive
needs of the patient. Indeed, the therapy may intensify many of
these needs. The patient must have a capacity to hold back and
limit his or her experience of the therapist to a psychic reality.
"Hands off" is a major rule of the treatment room. When following this rule is a practical impossibility, usually hospitalization is
indicated. Treatment is continued with the borrowed ego
strengths and constraints of a therapeutic milieu.

When patients are acting-out patients, we begin treatment
knowing it will be a long time before they will put into words
and restrained affect the pieces of their impassioned experience.
Ironically, here, the therapist needs a high degree of frustration
tolerance to endure the acting-out. Many therapists are unable
to—and do not—work with such patients. They cannot bear in-
cessant missed appointments, large indebtedness when bills
continue to mount, irrational unending phone calls, recurrent
substance abuse, or self-destructive behavior. Perhaps the most
difficult trial a therapist must bear is being a passive observer to
the patient's destructive behavior toward others. This often
strains the therapist's judgment of where "too much" begins.
With such impulse disorders, the therapy remains for a long

time at Step One. The essential first ingredient of treatment is that the patient be willing to continue the process and hold on to the therapeutic relationship, in which it is hoped that transference will be worked through. This requires special techniques in the treatment of acting-out patients.

Frustration level also indicates a patient's tolerance for allowing experience of their affects as the acting-out ceases and the drama is experienced in the consulting room. The capacity to bear anxiety and the capacity to endure depression, two of the cardinal affects of the work of psychotherapy, are linked to the toleration of frustration. The memories and experiences linked to these affects will provide great pain and recreate earlier, as well as current, trauma; the desire to flee will be enormous. It is at this point that the psychosis-prone ego will develop psychotic symptoms, or the full neurosis will crystallize out a neurotic symptom.

Affect always relates to some real situation of the past as it comes to expression in the present. Transference is the prime example. Dreams, for the most part, utilize visual imagery, displacement, and condensation to disguise intolerable affect. Without bearing the affect, the patient is unable to see what and whom they are fearing and fleeing from in their specific version of inhibitions, symptoms, and anxieties. Much of therapy is strategic development of the capacity to bear affect, particularly the affects of sadness and its defensive version, depression. These relate to object loss and cause exquisite pain in the process of mourning. Early manifestation of frustration tolerance and the capacity to bear affect, or at least the promise of this capacity in the future, will impress a therapist with the potential of the patient to broach the deepest pains of treatment.

Humor

Laughter generated by humor is derived from *empathy* for human foibles and weakness. It is to be differentiated from wit, which expresses more aggression and sadism and often stems from harsh attributes of an overweening superego. Ben Franklin, for example, was one of the great wits of our country: "Three can keep a secret, if two are dead." Severe harshness and rigidity in the superego, as will be discussed later, are two of the great barriers to change and success in psychotherapy. Guilt mandates failure. Humor reflects a different side of the superego as it joins the ego in looking upon itself with the warmth and empathic understanding of the *parent* viewing the inevitable struggles of the developing child. As Freud commented:

> If it is really the super-ego which, in humour, speaks kindly words of comfort to the intimidated ego, this will teach us that we have still a great deal to learn about the nature of the super-ego. Not everyone is capable of the humourous attitude. It is a rare and precious gift . . . the super-ego tries, by means of humour, to console the ego and protect it from suffering[;] this does not contradict its origin in the parental agency [1927, p. 166].

Unlike wit, whose impact is unrelenting, humor has a *forgiving* nature and a recognition of natural forces the control of which is often beyond our reach. Freud was fond of comparing the relation of the ego to the id by relating the tale of Itzhak the Horseman. Itzhak was seen riding wildly one day, and was asked where he was off to in such a rush. Itzhak replied, "Don't ask me, ask the horse!" There is also a *playfulness* that reveals humor's similarity to dream-work. Primary process is allowed expression through the maze of defensive inhibitions. The construction of humor often uses the mechanisms of dream-work—condensation, displacement, and symbolic representation—bringing us close to the unconscious preoccupations of a patient in much the same way a dream might. Once when I commented to a patient that he never brought dreams into our work, he replied: "Dr. Roth, with a life like mine, who needs dreams!"

Humor conveys a sense of dignity and hints at a civilized relationship with the listening therapist, for it implies *mutual* understanding. Once, as a patient lay down on the couch to begin an analysis, he said: "Psychoanalysis is like marriage. It's something you hope you have to do only once!" While this comment spoke to his hopes for his marriage, and hinted at an oncoming intense transference, it also nibbled at his weary concern that his personality was going to require a long, hard analysis for both of us. Further, he implied a hope that we would not abandon each other, which broached his depression. The humor revealed his *observing ego*, which took some distance from experience of himself, and suggested his capacity for reflective self-observation. It helped make the *unbearable bearable*, which, after all, is much of what the psychotherapeutic process is about.

The presence of humor, deriving as it does from the libidinous protective side of the parental superego and utilizing adaptive ego traits, suggests that a person may take away from psychotherapy precisely what it has to offer.

Communicative Pressure

Freud viewed psychoanalysis as a science based on his technique of free association. Unbiased observation of the freely flowing data would reveal hidden connections and meanings in the patient's words, emotions, and actions. Although we cannot expect the initially anxious and cautious patient to be this open, we can see whether the basic intent of the patient is to open up or clamp down on awareness. Does the person want to know what he or she is saying and want us to know it as well? As the pressure mounts to clarify past and present experience, more details, clarifications, and instances will be given in the hour. The extent to which we feel that the patient is attempting to merge our two minds and our understanding will be a measure of the communicative pressure. The pressure to communicate is based on many factors: anxiety over current distress, ability to communicate, the technique of the therapist in bringing forth this anxiety, the form of transference brought to the office, and the patient's conception of what is required in such a meeting. The sum total of these factors, however, will be the therapist's sense of how much this patient wants to bring out and reveal him- or herself, thus creating a world between patient and therapist that can be observed, thought about, and discussed further.

A number of years ago, I met Elvin Semrad, one of the

greatest exponents of the therapeutic arts, directly after he had interviewed a new patient. The usually taciturn and enigmatic man was beaming. The patient had been so wonderful, he said, full of details such as he said this, then she said that, then he did that, and she felt thus. For Semrad, the facts—the details—were close to the heart of real experience, and just exactly what he needed to know to go about what he felt was the real work of psychotherapy. It was Semrad's way of saying that free association is basically the only investigative tool we have, and the more inclined the patient is to take us into the special reality of his or her perceptions, the more likely it is that our comments will have impact and validity. In addition, communicative pressure is an indicator of basic trust, a willingness of the patient to fuse minds with us. As such, it indicates a potential for the therapeutic alliance, which rests, as discussed earlier, on a foundation of basic trust.

Warmth

Warmth is a very elusive concept, but it appears often in descriptions of patients whom therapists have found "attractive" and "engaging." Coldness in the physical world is defined as the absence of heat. When we meet a patient who is cold, lacks warmth, and is icily distant, we are responding to a lack of libidinous concern for us. We seem not to matter to the person. The fashionable term to describe this personality feature is *narcissistic*, a word often used pejoratively.

If this coldness is extreme and is connected with actions that hurt people, we begin to suspect psychopathy. This serious superego defect in patients is a stunning source of experimental failure for those hardy therapists who make the effort. Such patients may at times have charm, but not necessarily warmth. The con man is the common example of this personality type. The extreme lack of warmth they personify is very often associated with psychotherapeutic failure, spotlighting how much our analytic psychotherapy is based on the capacity for caring concern between two people.

The entire transference love that drives the motivation for treatment, sustaining the patient in the marked frustrations of the process, is another form of this character trait called "warmth." The two-body psychology of psychotherapy requires that both those bodies have a requisite degree of warmth.

Implicit in the quality of warmth is the presence of, or potential for, empathy. Reaching into the personality and experience of another is central to civilized behavior between people. It is a mental guidepost to behaviors that provide sustaining, gratifying relationships between people. Lack of these is often an important source of mental illness; attaining them is a major achievement, since doing so ameliorates much unhappiness. Thus, warmth suggests much about a person's potential for caring for the needs of others and the capacity to neutralize inner sadistic and destructive trends toward others.

When we encounter people who engage our feelings and give us a sense that they are responsive to our presence, we are attracted to them spontaneously. We feel we can work with them without necessarily articulating to ourselves that these people show personality traits that fit with the techniques of psychotherapy. Schizophrenics may display warmth; so may hysterical neurotics. The expression of warmth may vary, as may the leading defenses used to deal with it, but the impact on the therapist may be similar. A sense of warm involvement with a therapist can be communicated by the intensity of enveloping schizophrenic delusions as well as by voluble hysteria. Such an impact plays a leading role in the therapist's desire to know more about and grow closer to a patient.

Responsiveness and Dyadic Resonance

When patients seem to hear what they say in the hour and make new use of old stories, we are impressed with their capacity for insight. Similarly, when we offer a clarification or an early proto-interpretation and the patient works with it, we are impressed not only with insight, but with *insight in the interpersonal situation.* Psychotherapy depends on two peoples' working together. When patients have the capacity to use us to further their understanding, we are led to feel that this is a harbinger of good things to come. Unfortunately, this confidence is not always well placed, for what may appear early on to be insights may, in retrospect, turn out to be compliant, incorporative ingestions of the therapist's words. Patients' early affinity for insight, however, is significant often enough to warrant appreciation as a positive prognostic sign. This prognostic value exists even though the best of insights in early interviews is tentative, lacking the solidity and staying power that come only with long working-over of conflicts. Early on, we are concerned more with the *form* of insight, rather than the content. A serious attempt by the patient to use our observations, clarifications, and other interventions will, in the long run, provide a structure for constantly correcting, assessing, and reexamining our work together. Responsiveness is a rough estimate of the collaborative potential of the patient and is a strong substrate of the eventual working alliance.

Closely connected with responsiveness is the factor I call dyadic resonance. Psychotherapy depends on the interaction of two people. Does the patient, for example, seem to gain comfort, sustenance, or increased understanding from our relationship? Did the patient's anxiety decrease through the presence of the therapist, with a consequent increased capacity to bear depression and other affect? Does empathic mirroring of the patient's experience provide a usable tool for self-reflection? In short, does the patient give the impression that two heads are better than one?

Quite often, dyadic resonance is evidence of a good patient-therapist match. It is clear why we like certain patients. Their qualities may be those we know we are attracted to. Recall Semrad's pleasure in the example just cited. At other times, patients' qualities border on elements of ourselves that, at least initially, remain repressed. There may be similar conflicts, or experiences, in the lives of the therapeutic pair. In the absence of countertransference resistances, this resonance enhances accurate empathy.

Experienced therapists become increasingly acquainted with

the range of their therapeutic capabilities. When dyadic resonance becomes dyadic dissonance, it is wise to refer the patient to a therapist who will be more comfortable with that particular personality. A therapist, for example, whose narcissism is tender might have difficulty dealing with a patient whose narcissism is flamboyant and deeply embedded in important character traits.

On the whole, though, it is best to see a patient for a while before settling on a definitive impression of the therapeutic pairing. Early defensiveness, as mentioned above, often recedes as the patient finds interest and acceptance from an empathic therapist. Dyadic resonance may mount in amplitude as patient and therapist get to know one another.

Grains of Truth Magnified into Mythical Mountains

It is useful to recall that when Freud cautioned against analytic work with psychotics, he referred to these patients' conditions as the "narcissistic neuroses." His emphasis was on the narcissism of such individuals as a barrier to interest or investment (cathexis) in the therapist. No transference would form. The intensity of the interest in the self, to the exclusion of those outside one's boundaries, is the salient psychotherapeutic fact to focus on. A psychopathic con man is not psychotic. Yet, in terms of psychotherapeutic potential, it is exactly his narcissism that is the limiting feature in therapy. Our technique is an interpersonal one, although it has deep respect for the individual development of intrapsychic life. Therefore, in assessing potential for success with our technique, we must always be aware that we are limited in our effect if the patient refuses to allow us importance.

Apart from the issue of degree of narcissism, psychosis, as has been shown many times (Boyer 1967), is no contraindication to the therapeutic process. We may not cure a person who demonstrates deeply biological schizophrenia (a spectrum disorder), but we may nonetheless stem psychotic states through ameliorating the vulnerabilities of character.

Advanced age, with its supposed decrease in mental elasticity, was, until recent times, considered another mythical contraindication for analytic psychotherapy. Again, it cannot be denied that many people, as they age, rigidify and become encrusted with unbending habits and views. Others display a mental elasticity of people half their age. It is difficult, without the requisite therapeutic trial, to tell what age has done to a person. Many elderly persons themselves succumb to the cultural dogma that mandates, "You can't teach an old dog new tricks." They may approach the therapist with the forgone conclusion that they can't be helped. They need the experience of treatment to reveal their capacity for change and experimentation. Once again, it is best, regardless of age, for psychotherapeutic diagnosis to rely on intuitive guidelines, as outlined in this chapter. I have framed these in my own language, out of my own experience. Others may find a different language and different experience.

Conclusion

Clinical understanding is important to letting these factors coalesce into a therapeutic impression. For example, a 45-year-old man with a twenty-five-year history of severe alcoholism and poor response to prior treatments may show insight, motivation, flexibility, humor, communicative pressure, dyadic resonance, responsiveness, and warmth. Yet, (by history) assessment of his capacity to tolerate frustration is so outstandingly low that, for the process of analytic psychotherapy, odds are poor for a good outcome. A structured program along the lines of Alcoholics Anonymous might have a much better record and would be the treatment of choice.

On the other hand, a young man or woman who is a primitive self-mutilator and whose inability to tolerate frustration is obvious may reveal several of the other factors strongly present. In this case, the capacity to tolerate frustration may have to be provided by a long-term hospitalization in an inpatient setting until the patient seems capable of frustration tolerance on his or her own. In the ideal case, the inpatient milieu provides the missing psychological skill through the structure of the hospital until the regressed patient develops it or recaptures it.

My suggestion to work with all patients who demonstrate strong motivation may cause dismay to some therapists. What, they may ask, will happen to those passive or masochistic patients who will endure, without end, any open-ended or difficult situation? To some extent, if there is a history replete with sufficiently good therapeutic situations that turned out poorly, then one has reason to doubt the advisability of yet another therapy. Other modalities of treatment may then be considered. If the patient has not had such extensive therapeutic trials, then, no matter what the diagnosis, he or she deserves a try.

Perceptual set is an important element in framing the possibilities inherent in a person or situation. Traditional diagnoses may succeed in differentiating patients from each other in terms of signs and symptoms. The diagnostic approach is a task often quite different from the approach that seeks out possibilities for the process of psychotherapy. The therapist may find him- or herself confused when, culturally bound through training, he or she uses the diagnostic perceptual set for framing psychotherapeutic assessment.

"And so often, when you get to know a patient, they lose their diagnosis, you know" [Semrad 1980, p. 176].

7

Attachment: The Urge to Merge

Attachment, Understanding, Integration

Theology, science, philosophy, and art, through centuries of inquiry, have not produced agreement on the essentials of human nature. Small wonder, then, that discussions of the essentials of psychotherapy often end with irreconcilable polarizations. A balanced picture is not easy to obtain. Friedman (1978) attempted such a balance in his study of trends and fashions in psychoanalytic thinking from its inception to the present. He summarized the three outstanding, although shifting, preoccupations of analytic theory and therapy under the headings Attachment, Understanding, and Integration. If we augment these concepts, and place them in a dynamic relationship to one another, we emerge with a digest of analytic therapy.

Table 7-1 illustrates a large number of central concepts, almost all of which have been the subject of polemics and often bitter debate. Yet, in presenting a realistic picture of the clinical process, one would be hard pressed to eliminate many of these concepts. For each category, I have selected a representative sampling rather than a comprehensive listing. Many others could have been added or substituted, but they would have the disadvantage of lengthening the summary.

The overall process of psychoanalytic psychotherapy assumes certain developments based on Freud's technique of using the creativity of free association and the transferential backdrop of the therapist's neutrality. The analytic approach pays homage to the unconscious drives, defenses, and conflicts, as we see them in observable speech, affect, and behavior. These forces eventually focus on the therapist in a clinical transference. Therefore, a certain amount of neutrality on the part of the therapist will aid the patient in distinguishing fantasy from fact.

The arrows in the table pointing in two directions indicate that each process has an *ongoing* influence on the other. Patient and therapist both have a specific reality. The arrows indicate that as a group of two, they influence each other, as was indicated in my discussions of transference and countertransference. Attachment, understanding, and integration are in similar dynamic relationship. To varying degrees, they depend on and enhance each other. For example, a person experiencing attachment to a therapist is more likely to feel less anxiety. This reduction enables clearer thinking and understanding, which reinforce attachment, while integration enhances capacity for perspective, and thus understanding. The patient–therapist interaction, as well as special overall inherent factors dealt with in other sections of this book, are indicated here for clarity and completeness.

Attachment

Attachment is a special process, without which understanding cannot take place, and certainly neither integration nor enduring change.

> Dear Dr. Roth,
>
> After our meeting yesterday, it is clear that I need to say much more about my feelings toward you. I cannot let stand the impression I seemed to convey that I see you as cold, distant or unloving (and therefore unthreatening). This is far from true. I've never felt *more* loved or cared for, but with the important distinction that this love is contained in a strictly limiting reality. In turn, I love you – genuinely and deeply, and sometimes, no doubt, inappro-

Table 7-1
Factors Inherent in the Psychotherapeutic Process

Patient ←——————→ Therapist		
Attachment ←——→ *Understanding* ←——————→ *Integration*		
Diatrophic function	Clinical transference	Urge to complete psychobiological psychosocial maturation
Dedicated therapist	Insight observation clarification abreaction interpretation	
Real relationship		Working-through
Basic trust		
		Shift in psychic structure
Basic transference	Affective insight	
		Synthetic function of ego
Therapeutic alliance	Conflict-free ego	
		Eros
Transitional object	Working alliance	
		Cohesive self
Holding environment		
		Transference as integration
Symbiosis		
		Identification with therapeutic process
Narcissistic transference		
		Organizing function
Will to recovery		Triad of interaction internalization action
Time		

Special Overall Inherent Factors

Psychotherapeutic Diagnosis of the Patient

Personality of the Therapist

External Environment and Fate

priately. I recall a thousand times when I've desired your voice, your smile or your touch. Each week, I have difficulty leaving you because when I am with you, parts of me relax and I am "held" in your caring. Sometimes when I fall silent, I am merely marveling in that feeling. I have kept back my frequent fantasies out of embarrassment, but they are with me often . . . you have always maintained a formal distance, which I accept as necessary and appropriate . . . it is our relationship that has sustained and healed me, and on which I depend for continued growth.

This patient was in touch with the underpinnings of affection in her highly verbal and interpretively oriented treatment. Freud was equally straightforward about the issue of attachment:

If the patient is to fight his way through the normal conflict with the resistances which we have uncovered for him in the analysis, he is in need of a powerful stimulus which will influence the decision in the sense which we desire, leading to recovery. Otherwise it might happen that he would choose in favour of repeating the earlier outcome and would allow what had been brought up into consciousness to slip back again into repression. At this point what turns the scale in his struggle is not his intellectual insight — which is neither strong enough nor free enough for such an achievement — but simply and solely his relation to the doctor. Insofar as his transference bears a "plus" sign, it clothes the doctor with authority and is transformed into belief in his communications and explanations. In absence of such a transference, or if it is a negative one, the patient would never even give a hearing to the doctor and his argument [1917, p. 445].

What elements of the basic transference, and the structure of the treatment relationship, contribute to this sustaining attachment?
Freud stated:

It remains the first aim of the treatment to attach the patient to it, and to the person of the doctor. To ensure this, nothing need be done but to give him time. If one exhibits a serious interest, . . . clears away the resistances that crop up at the beginning and avoids making certain mistakes, he will of himself form such an attachment and link the doctor up to one of the imagos of the people by whom he was accustomed to be treated with affection [1913, p. 139].

In therapy these imagos will usually include those to whom one has entrusted one's physical, mental, and emotional well-being: not only the early parental figures and their substitutes, but also the succeeding series of doctors, educators, and friends.

The Early Mother–Child Relationship

Spitz (1956), drawing on long study of the impact of environment on early infancy, introduced the term diatrophic function (from the Greek meaning "nourishing through") to refer to the healing intention of the therapist, a willingness to maintain and support the patient. The diatrophic function is similar to the environment provided by the mother through the early years of life, in the face of a child's distress, anxiety, and confusion during daily and developmental crises. Gitelson (1962) elaborated this further: "In the way that the mother is the target for the child's drives and, in her capacity as auxilliary ego, guides their form and function, thus introducing the operation of the reality principle, so does the analyst draw the focus of the unconscious tendencies with which a patient enters analysis and, in his diatrophic function, provides the erupting instincts and revived developmental drive with direction and purpose" (p. 198). This is a workshop metaphor. The patient brings confused but potentially creative energies to the therapist. The therapist acts as a grid and provides an organizing target for painful, psychological incoherence.

Loewald (1960) added that the therapist, through interaction and interventions, conveys the view that he sees the suffering patient not only in the here and now, or in the analytic reconstructed past, but, most important, in terms of his *potential* for the future. This attitude suggests the analogy of the mother who sees the potential of her growing child. These elements imbue the patient with a sense of hope in the therapeutic process that joins the sense of suffering in maintaining motivation for treatment.

A brilliant, hardworking physician found himself indecisive about leaving an unhappy marriage for another woman. Obsessionally paralyzed in this position for two years, he developed disabling anxiety as he oscillated between these two women. As his work, always his bulwark against the pains of life, suffered, he experienced confused panic and sought psychiatric consultation. An encounter with the therapist seemed a new experience for him. Psychology and psychotherapy were areas of intellectual interest to which he had never given much credence. He was startled to find relief in unburdening himself of his dread and helplessness, and found the possibility of eventually understanding his dilemma a great balm. On his own, he had despaired of thinking himself out of his predicament. At first, panic eased only in the presence of the therapist, but soon the therapist was thought of as "my lifeline." This initial attachment increasingly held between sessions, and gave the patient mental breathing space to begin the longer process of understanding and integration.

Another angle of the diatrophic function is gleaned from Berman (1949), who emphasized the patient's sense of the therapist's dedication. This is conveyed through persistent attitudes of patience, kindly acceptance, and reliable pursuit of understanding through the repeated storms of the transference. Over time, patients are reassured by the therapist's stability, despite continued onslaughts of aggression and libido. A sense of safety and sanctuary envelops the relationship. It implies that the therapist does not mouth empty words when empathy suggests that understanding of the patient exists. Berman states, "The mature parent is the prototype of the analyst at work" (p. 163). This element of attachment is in part a reality of the therapeutic situation as well as of transference. We have considered this in more detail as the "real relationship" in Chapter 4.

Basic Trust

Part of the foundation of the "basic trust" (Erikson 1950) that the patient leans on in seeking help comes from the early mother–child relationship. As Greenacre explains:

> If two people are repeatedly alone together, some sort of emotional bond will develop between them. Even though they may be strangers engaged in relatively neutral occupations, not directed by one or the other for or against the other one, it will probably not be long before a predominantly friendly or predominantly unfriendly tone will develop between them. . . . The matrix of this . . . comes largely from the original mother–infant quasi-union of the first months of life. This I consider the basic transference; or one might call it the primary transference, or some part of primitive social instinct [1954, p. 671].

Greenacre suggests that if one person is troubled and feels dependent upon another, their ensuing relationship will enhance the former's tendency to try to reproduce the early infant's orientation toward the mother. This basic transference will impart a specific emotional tone to the patient's attachment. To the degree that the mother–child relationship was disturbed, special techniques will be required in treatment. With psychotics and borderline personalities, great activity on the part of the therapist will be devoted to interpreting anticipated failure of the patient's trust in the therapist.

Zetzel (1958) went farther, insisting that even with neurotics, it was necessary early in treatment to take steps to strengthen basic trust. To this end, she proposed that the therapist should promptly offer clarifications and interpretations and take an active role in "acknowledging a patient's basic needs and anxieties" (p. 188). Zetzel termed the bond created from this process of enhancing basic trust the *therapeutic alliance*. Without the therapeutic alliance, she cautioned, a regressive transference neurosis and interpretation will not be tolerated. In 1937, Edward Bibring had indicated similar views:

In my opinion, the analyst's attitude and the analytic atmosphere which he creates are fundamentally a reality correction which adjusts the patient's anxieties about loss of love and punishment, the origin of which lies in childhood. Even if these anxieties later undergo analytical resolution, I still believe that the patient's relationship to the analyst, from which a sense of security emanates, is not only a precondition of the procedure, but also effects an immediate (apart from an analytical) consolidation of his sense of security which he has not successfully acquired or consolidated in childhood. Such an immediate consolidation — which in itself, lies outside the field of analytic therapy — is, of course, only of permanent value if it goes along with the coordinated operation of analytic treatment [1937, p. 182].

Therapy as a Transitional Object

We are all familiar with Winnicott's concept (1953) of the "transitional object." This "object," which plays an important role in the child's development, is the element of life and fantasy that bridges the separation of the child from the mother. Reflecting the human capacity to symbolize, the transitional object shows the awareness of a "not me" part of reality. Such symbolization enables the child to bear the processes and anxieties of separation. The classic example is the blanket, memorialized in the United States through the "Peanuts" cartoon character Linus. Reflecting an insight similar to Winnicott's, Stone (1961) has conceptualized therapy as having two trends. One moves toward fusion, a bodily reunion with the mother and her soothing capacities and available gratifications. The second impels toward separation, individuation, and maturity. The therapist's words (symbols) mediate the separation process through interpretation. But the therapy as a whole can be viewed as a transitional object, a way station, a stepping-stone to further development.

Extending Winnicott's concept of the "holding environment," which was analogous to the mother's holding of the infant to enable development to proceed, Modell (1976) outlined a "cocoon transference": Narcissistic characters experienced the treatment relationship as a fortress that gave an illusion of safety and protection. Such patients felt protected from the internal dangers of libido and aggression as well as the external ones of reality. (This is similar to the descriptions of D. Burlingham and A. Freud [1942] of children during the bombing of London in World War II: They remained calm when with mothers who did not convey their anxiety, and displayed terror when they had been separated from their mothers.) Modell emphasized that full development of the "cocoon transference" allowed ego consolidation so that a stage could follow in which transference could be interpreted. Interpretation challenged the denial of internal and external dangers of libido and aggression, and was equivalent to revealing that the "cocoon transference" was a fantasy. Without this transition, therapy might be interminable.

Fusion

The element of fusion is inherent in all the formulations cited above; the therapist is unconsciously identified with an important figure or figures from the past, especially from the patient's earliest years. Searles (1965) elaborates on the importance of this fusion:

> Probably the greatest reason why we tend to rebel against our developing individual identity is because we feel it to have come between, and to be coming increasingly between, ourself, and the mother with whom we once shared a world-embracing oneness. I believe that the more successfully the infant and young child internalizes, as the foundation of his personal identity, a symbiotic relationship with a predominantly loving mother, the more accessible is his symbiotic level of existence . . . to the more structured aspects of his identity that develop . . . not as restraints upon him, but . . . as facilitators to release his energies and capacities in creative relatedness with the outer world [p. 42].

Man's identity enables him to perceive the world not merely by mirroring it, but, at a symbiotic level of relatedness, by literally sampling it through processes of introjection and projection [p. 67].

From the therapeutic viewpoint, in order to know oneself, one must first fuse in order to separate.

A psychiatrist consulted me about a case that was not going well. The patient, a woman in her twenties, was in a rage with him whenever he interpreted the transference. She persisted in experiencing him as her New York Jewish mother, with earthy humor, a humor often utilized to sustain the pains of unpleasant emotional circumstances. The psychiatrist, just as persistently, informed her that with this attitude toward him she avoided her unhappiness and sadness. This created great irritation in the patient, and she began to talk of breaking off the treatment.

I suggested to the therapist that since the treatment was only six months along, this woman needed time to make him familiar to herself before she could experience his strangeness. Submerged in the symbiotic weak points of her past were also her strengths. The psychiatrist was attempting to laud separation exclusively as the major factor in her acquiring understanding and in stimulating her growth and development.

Symbiosis brings one close to positive libidinous sources as well as to trouble spots, so one does not want to throw the baby out with the bathwater. Kohut (1977) has elaborated this point of view in terms of the narcissistic transferences, the merger, mirror, and twinship transferences. He delineates the roots of these fusion needs and fantasies as they occur in the course of normal growth and development. These transferences must all be lived through before being worked through. Kohut outlines how the therapist's impatience with narcissism forecloses the development of these transferences and severely limits a therapy's range of effectiveness.

Magical Wishes and Attachment

The complexity surrounding attachment and motivation for treatment was further expanded by Nunberg (1926), who outlined unconscious infantile wishes in "The Will to Recovery": "The wish to get well is essentially the antithesis of cure in the sense of an adaptation to reality, for the aim of the desire is to restore an infantile libido position in order to set up again the narcissistic untroubled ego-ideal." Nunberg's insight is everyday observation in clinical practice. For example, an obsessional man consciously wishes relief from hair-splitting intellectual brooding, compulsions, and his nit-picking, critical, and argumentative attitude toward others. Unconsciously, however, he wishes to maintain a notion of himself as a paragon of moral perfection second to none and expects treatment to justify this stance. The initial unconscious view drapes the therapist in the guise of an omnipotent magician-seer, a Merlin to an unformed Arthurian patient. Therapeutic guidance is expected to create our contemporary monarch, the "healthy" person, an individual subject to no discernible instinctual frustrations, the consummate master of external reality.

Outlining magical thinking, Nunberg states:

> The obsessive neurotic, for instance, considers the psychoanalytic rules as magic formulae which he has to comply with conscientiously to the letter. Even where this is not the case, psychoanalysis is sacred to most patients, and the analytic hour is an hour of devotion. Every patient has some kind of ceremonial with which he surrounds the analysis [1928, p. 110].

This wishful aspect of the relationship is maintained until the transference neurosis is established, at which point transference "becomes the bearer of the will to recovery, and substitutes for it, and is placed in the service of the real psychoanalytic task" (Nunberg 1928, p. 112). The "real task" referred to here is interpretation and resolution of the transference neurosis.

Success in brief psychotherapy, dramatic reduction in symptoms early in treatment, and "flights into health" are often due to this magical aspect of attachment before the transference neurosis emerges. When the transference neurosis crystallizes, it signals frustration of infantile wishes, and throws the patient into a characteristic and characterological impasse. This process can be observed across the whole diagnostic spectrum.

A young man, several months after he compensated from his psychosis, described the early images of me he had had while in catatonic stupor. He was convinced I carried the keys to a pink Cadillac limousine in my pocket and was waiting for him to master fully his murderous and sexual impulses. He often stood motionless, tiptoe on one foot, silent, lest the slightest activity should cause the world to explode. When he could prove to me that he was a totally good boy, I would reward him with the keys and untold sums of money. The son of a minister, this man, when compensated, led a life of unmitigated crime. He longed for forgiveness from his minister father, but this forgiveness was to be had in infantile terms with complete gratification. At a later point, when therapy seemed not to offer him justification for his angry and amoral life, he terminated treatment.

Time

The time frame that surrounds a relationship has a profound impact on the forms available for the development of that relationship. When I board an air-shuttle flight from Boston to New York City, I might do no more than smile at the person who sits down next to me. The flight takes a mere forty-five minutes. On the other hand, on a flight from Boston to San Francisco, which lasts five to six hours, it would be rather unusual not to strike up some rudimentary conversation and relationship with the person beside me. The opportunity for acceptance and formation of transference enhances attachment. Therefore, the initial attitude of the therapist and the manner in which therapy is presented to the patient will influence attachment. An open-ended, flexible approach that indicates that the therapy will go as far (or as close at hand) as the patient can or wants will provide a time frame which does not interfere with, and might possibly augment, attachment.

The Relationship of Attachment to Understanding and Integration

Throughout the forgoing discussion we have mentioned that attachment diminishes anxiety. Rational thinking, possible to the degree that the patient's anxiety is brought under control, can lead to the processes of understanding and integration. Painful comprehension, which of itself is central to furthering understanding, is also made more bearable by safe attachment. Affects bring a person closer to core concerns, conflicts, and memories. Incremental tolerance of affect allows for furthering of regression and the development of clinical transference, which becomes the guiding thread through the maze of psychological confusion. As we shall now find in our exploration of understanding and integration, the patient, as he or she finds clarity and resolution, also perceives increased rationale, both realistic and transferential, for maintaining what has become a productive attachment.

8

Understanding:
The Soft, Persistent Voice of Reason

Two Paths to Understanding

It was Bertrand Russell (quoted by Richfield [1954, p. 400]) who pointed out that "there are two fundamentally different ways in which we can know things . . . knowledge by *acquaintance* and knowledge by *description.*" Richfield goes on to say, "Knowledge about a subject may be independent of any acquaintance with that same subject" (p. 400). This dual road to knowledge is evident in the experience of transference. When description and acquaintance merge, the clinical effect is powerful.

An astute patient, fresh in the throes of newly developing transference feelings, exclaimed: "I can't believe how afraid I am of you; it's just like my father! It's totally irrational, and yet I feel that way. I'm terrified that you'll be angry with me, and it's the same feeling I have with Professor Ryan. All these *New York Times* things I've read about transference . . . it looks like I'm finally going to find out what they really are. I now see that I had only ghost terms for them, only words . . . like lace . . . a form, but not the entire substance."

This man has come to the truth described by Freud (1912a): "For when all is said and done, it is impossible to destroy anyone *in absentia* or *in effigie"* (p. 108). Or, as the old Chinese proverb put it: "I hear and I forget. I see and I remember. I do and I understand."

In therapy, acquaintance (affective insight) can lead to description, and description (verbal insight) can lead to acquaintance. The transference will introduce data for the mind to assimilate, which, once assimilated, will induce further transference development. The two processes go hand in hand. One without the other has marked disadvantages.

> The physician cannot as a rule spare his patient [the transference]. . . . He must get him to re-experience portions of his forgotten life, but must see to it, on the other hand, that the patient retains some degree of aloofness, which will enable him, in spite of everything, to recognize that what appears to be reality is in fact only a reflection of the past [Freud 1920a, p. 19].

The following comments of two patients illustrate two different forms of awareness of the transference: one descriptive, and the other experiential (by acquaintance). Each form, in its own way, furthers understanding.

> "I study you the way a physicist studies the atom. They bombard the atom with electrons and by virtue of deflection can determine the shape. You are a mirror, and I bounce things off you. If I can figure out my own distortions on that surface, what remains is you, and I can then sense who I am, and who you are . . . although a lot about you remains mysterious since you remain mostly constant, while I have lots of changing distortions."

> "I've been thinking a lot about what you said about my father . . . how I want to make up for some defect I think he saw in me . . . like my wanting to bring Julia here for you to see her, be dazzled by her beauty, knocked out . . . almost like saying 'Hey look, Dad! Look what I can get . . . I've done better than you!' It explains a lot for me . . . things which I've had only vague feelings about . . . just on the edge of my awareness, but never quite there. That's why I

always need special qualities in a woman . . . they make up
for my feeling defective, and I feel equal with other men."

For this latter man, the crystallization of his preconscious
awareness of fantasies of being defective in comparison to his father and how they caused competition with me, broadened and
deepened exploration of his relations with women as well as
men. Description and acquaintance augment each other. Affective involvement in the transference provides a realistic window
through which the patient visualizes past and present.

Earlier, we indicated how therapy is often broken off at some
early transference state, which is lived out rather than understood. Compensation may have occurred, but there is little or no
understanding of the transference cure, and further maturation
is foreclosed. An element of understanding that is bound in language – words – serves to frame and preserve a comprehension that often becomes buried under the emotional weight of
transference.

Words and the Psychotherapeutic Dialogue

Psychoanalytic understanding emphasizes insight through interpretation of the transference as the cardinal agent in therapeutic change. In his last years, Freud (1937a) stated: "We must
not forget that the analytic relationship is based on a love of truth
– that is, on a recognition of reality" (p. 248). In its ultimate
form, this reality is dosed out in words: verbal observation, clarification, and interpretation. Language plays the intermediary
role, the symbolic transitional object, between attachment and
the individuating, separating factors of integration.

Although the technical vehicle for communication of understanding is words, it is apparent to any serious practitioner of
psychotherapy that a great deal of communication goes beyond
accessible language. The varieties of psychotherapeutic dialogue may be roughly grouped into three forms, as Table 8-1 on
page 130 illustrates.

Words were of great importance to Freud in his formulation of
the "secondary process" and its binding capacity for energies of

Table 8-1
The Psychotherapeutic Dialogue

Words	Transitional Words	Beyond Words
Semiotic signs and signals	Dream words of waking state	Dream life
		Micro-kinesics
Observations	Psychosomatic verbalizations	body language
Clarifications	sighs	Unverbalizable somatic
	groans	affect
Interpretation (verbal	grunts	autonomic
myths)	vocal rhythms	tears
		sweating
Insight (descriptive)	Code words of therapist and patient	body odor
		flatulence
		musculoskeletal
	Words as objects	
	pain	Processes of integration
	pleasure	
	gifts	Transference
		Insight (experiential)

the ungraspable, unconscious "primary process." Secondary process is the realm of semiotic signs and signals, the language of consensually validated meanings, related to observable and clarifiable facts or thoughts. Words give form to the formless unconscious, and thereby possess a seductive potential, implying control as well as understanding. Or, as a patient put it, as he embarked on his psychotherapy:

> "I look forward to the use of words. I'm very good at it. As a matter of fact, that's how I make my living; I'm good at words. Words were special, you know, in ancient times, and even in modern cults. They were kept secret, for the person who knew the names of the gods had their power. By saying the words, one could call up the gods and demons and have them in his control. To know the word provided great power."

This is another way of conceptualizing primary-process demons and secondary-process names or words.

The therapeutic elegance of words to bind incoherent, emotional energy through verbal interpretation can be seen in the following example:

A woman came to see me a few years after her treatment had ended. She now reported a sudden and violent eruption of anxious dread, panic, and objectless depression. She felt this was secondary to her husband's hospitalization for a minor ailment, but the extent of her reaction seemed not to make sense. I reminded her of her mother's gruesome and lingering hospital death, her father's and her grandmother's. Her husband's hospital room was crowded with the dead, and therefore so was she. At the following session she remarked that my simple comment seemed to have thrown the whole situation into perspective. My phrase about "the hospital room crowded with the dead" recurred to her many times, stirred many memories, induced continued mourning, and had an enlightening effect. All her symptoms had remitted.

Naturally, her use of this interpretive effect of words was also based on several years of prior psychotherapy, but we must admire the shorthand value of the words to summarize, as a dream might, a storehouse of past experience. This is a combination of "descriptive" insight and "experiential" insight, which were gained through emotional living-through in her long treatment. My comment invoked the properly named emotional file (semiotic sign), which, when opened, induced the necessary experience of further mourning.

The process of mourning (which we shall cover in a later chapter) includes many elements of experience beyond words. Apart from the elements that can be described (who, what, where, when, how), there remain the unverbalizable elements of the body: feeling tones associated with the mourned person, tears, trembling, musculoskeletal reactions, and so on. These communicate, to the patient and to the therapist, much that never reaches the verbal descriptive level. In such states we are freed to comprehend, much like two animals meeting in the forest, through the language of the body (microkinesics) and the senses, without words.

Acceptance of Understanding

In offering words for therapeutic purposes, tact, timing, and the state of the transference are all important in assuring a receptive ear from the patient. The receptive state rarely occurs in a smooth fashion.

> For resistance is constantly altering its intensity during the course of a treatment. . . . We have therefore been able to convince ourselves that on countless occasions in the course of his analysis the same man will abandon his critical attitude and then take it up again. If we are on the point of bringing a specially distressing piece of unconscious material to his consciousness, he is extremely critical; he may have previously understood and accepted a great deal, but now it is just as though those acquisitions have been swept away; in his efforts for opposition at any price, he may offer a complete picture of someone who is an emotional imbecile. But if we succeed in helping him to overcome this new resistance, he recovers his insight and understanding. Thus, his critical faculty is not an independent function, to be respected as such; it is the tool of his emotional attitudes, and is directed by his resistance [Freud 1917, p. 293].

In approaching this "resistance" we appeal to the rational, observing ego of the patient in accordance with what the state of transference will allow. As a focus in therapy, the resistance becomes as important as the material that is resisted. In the resistances, we find the elements of conflict embedded in character. Thus, with the obstinate patients, we slowly begin to observe with them that, rather regularly, they tend to say "no" before they ever say "yes." This first line *observation* (E. Bibring 1954) is made without interpretation, without suggesting that we understand anything beyond what we observe. Indeed, we can go no farther until the patient consistently makes a similar observation. During this period of ferreting out the multiple expression of "no" before "yes," we have the opportunity to *clarify* our initial observations. They may be validated within the transactions of the office — obstinacy in setting appointment times — or they may be reflected in material from life outside the office (similar obstinacy with the patient's spouse, for example). Over time, when patient and therapist may have pieced together important past history and related it to current behavior, the time might be ripe to make an *interpretation*: "You tend to say 'no' first. Since your mother so often misled and misguided you, you no longer trust your own inclination to be trusting — this comes out in your interactions with me and with your wife."

Interpretation is a leap of psychological faith. We do not observe such material; it invokes the unseen, the unconscious. In this respect, it is purely hypothetical and now requires not only affirmation from the patient, but also redemonstration in other areas of life, both past and current. This is the working-through process. In general, observation and clarification by the therapist focus on an intellectual understanding close to experience, while interpretation is relatively distant from experience. Interpretation is nearest experience when it combines past history, present life, and an immediate corollary in the transference. For example: "You have the urge to run out of the office now to make me feel guilty so I'll care about you, just as you ran away from your mother, and as you walk out the house when you feel defeated with your wife."

At times, the therapist or the patient makes interpretations that pass over much unconscious material, but are still near to experience. This proximity facilitates the patient's acceptance of the interpretations. Such comments, although they speculate on unconscious material, are closer to observations because the patient is conscious of the material they describe.

> At the beginning of a therapy a young man dreamed that he had a triangle on his left knee. The triangle became a vagina as his right hand became a penis and began to penetrate the vagina. The patient laughed as he related this and said, "I feel like I'm fucking myself up by beginning this therapy!" This led to a discussion of his conscious anxieties concerning treatment.

> After several months of treatment, a woman had a frightening dream that as she sat on her bed, outside in the

street, a crane was ripping up the sidewalks and the foundation of her house. After I suggested that she felt that I
was undermining her defenses, without her being sure that
she had adequate psychological replacements yet, she discussed fears relating to her recent personality changes.
These fears were uppermost in her awareness and readily
available.

Words as Objects

The patient with the anthropological bent for words as names
for gods and demons warned me that this power could easily be
turned against himself. He noted that he has for words a use that
seems akin to self-hypnosis. His intellectualization and super-
logical systems often work to form massive rationales for
avoiding inner life. He suggested that I be forewarned that
words could be a two-edged sword in his psychotherapeutic dialogue. Here he was commenting on "transitional words": words
as objects, used for defensive or transferential purposes. In such
cases we cannot take words at their face value. They are often
meant for broader things:

> A very obsessional doctor came to see me with great sad-
> ness, fatigue, and world-weariness, seemingly unable to
> make emotional ends meet in his psychically frayed mar-
> riage and family life. He often began his sessions with a frail
> raising of his hand and requested me not to say a word, just
> to listen. Then, with great eloquence, detail, simile, meta-
> phor, and pointed anecdote, he would pour forth his tale of
> woe. At times he would smile wistfully and sympatheti-
> cally, as if to say: "I know, Dr. Roth, this is a lot I'm heaping
> on you. Please bear with me." And I always did. He would
> leave the office with a faint, tactful, and grateful smile and a
> world-weary shrug of his shoulders, vaguely murmuring
> "Thank you."

With this patient, although I note the words he uses and their
meaning, the task at hand does not concern verbal comprehen-

sion. Rather, it is to provide a safe and secure container for his overflowing, anxious helplessness and grief, a "holding environment," to share a burden he feels is close to breaking him when he holds it alone. The words are objects, parcels of pain, and he asks me to hold them with him as the essential meaning of this psychotherapeutic dialogue.

Dream Words and Family Code Words

A primary mechanism of dreams is the process of condensation, the focusing of multiple meanings on one symbol. When analyzed, the condensed symbol opens up in unexpected ways. Certain words take on this condensed form in psychotherapy, often inadvertently, but they become meaningful for the patient.

For example, I remarked to a patient that his family took a childhood illness of his in a rather "casual" way. This word *casual* reified over and over for him. Casual was the way he had to be toward a sister to show that he was cool about emotions, macho, and never flustered. "Casual" meant he sided with his mother against his father, who was anything but casual. To be less casual entailed a closeness with his father that he longed for but at the same time alienated him from his mother, earning him a loss in the oedipal competition for her favor. "Casual" meant one attitude toward his work and "noncasual" another, and the latter had meanings for the way his brothers handled work.

The word *casual* functioned as condensed symbols do in the primary processes of dream-work; it was like a nodal switchpoint in a railway yard from which the engine of the ego could roam and foray into many separate directions, yet interrelate them all. These code words accumulate and grow into a personal dictionary between patient and therapist. Any single interview will scarcely explain to the fly-on-the-wall observer the possible underpinnings of simple words to which dense meaning is being given by the therapeutic participants.

In an essay entitled "New Words," George Orwell commented on the use of words for the understanding of the "inner life." He described the shortcomings of words in illustrating and illuminating internal experience with the complexity and imme- diacy of experience of dreams. Great writers hedge this problem by evoking a feel for "inner life" through the multiple angles of literary technique, approaching the problem sideways as it were. Orwell proposed the creation of new words for inner life, but the idea seemed impractical since the vocabulary would of necessity have to be built upon mutual, similar experiences. He quoted Samuel Butler, who said, "The best art [i.e., the most perfect thought-transference] must be lived from one person to another" (p. 12). Orwell thought the family provided the best model for the creation of new words.

> All large families have two or three words peculiar to themselves – words which they have made up and which convey non-dictionary meanings. They say, Mr. Smith is a – – – kind of man, using some homemade words, and the others understand perfectly. What makes it possible for the family to invent these words is the basis of their common experience. Without common experience, of course, no words can mean anything. If you say to me, "What does bergamot smell like": I say, "Something like verbena," and so long as you know the smell of verbena you are some- where near understanding me. The method in inventing words therefore is the method of analogy based on unmis- takable common knowledge [1940, p. 9].

The communication process of long-term, intensive, psycho- therapy is very akin to Orwell's description of the creation of lan- guage within a family. Meaning is determined by common experience – intellectual, emotional, physical, and associated with symbolic images and time. It takes so long to obtain this commonality of language that at any given session, although we may observe some understanding gained or introduced, the keener process of steady accretion of meaning between patient and therapist is not overt. Understanding may hinge on a word, a phrase, a sound or emotion that has been replayed in many ways, many times, with ever-growing meaning. Two people are learning a language that is foreign to one of them or both of them, depending on the level of awareness.

Beyond Words

There are significant transference interactions in psychotherapy that are not immediately dealt out in the coinage of words or, for certain elements in the relationship, seem never to be put into direct verbal communication. Many elements of the pre-verbal, pre-oedipal transference are more theoretically conceptualized than interpretively verbalized in treatment. Others come closer to open expression, although mostly on a nonverbal level. Such moments give us a glimpse of the vast realms of experience that do not find expression in words. For example, Peter Blos (1984), commenting on fathers and sons, said:

> The residues of the pre-oedipal attachment experience of son to father lie, to a large extent, buried under a forceful repression once adolescence is passed. This infantile emotional experience, when roused into reanimation during analysis, remains usually inaccessible by sheer verbalization. It finds expression via affectomotor channels, such as uncontrollable weeping and sobbing, while the patient is tormented by overwhelming feelings of love and loss in relation to the dyadic father. One man in his late fifties exclaimed at such a moment, choked by tears: "Why did I love my father so much — after all, I had a mother" [p. 318].

Similarly, a patient of mine, a man in his late thirties, took his sons to a Boy Scout exhibition. As he described to me the scoutmasters and scouts, he suddenly and surprisingly found himself flooded with tears and sobbing. Ordinarily, he is a highly controlled, obsessional, and strictly rational man. He recalled his Boy Scout days with his own father; these were memories suppressed and repressed. A new idea occurred to him. Perhaps his father, a rigid and seemingly undemonstrative man who could never show him love, was able to show him some love through deeds. The patient said, "I felt in therapy I'd unearth all the bad things, the horror. I didn't realize there was love there also . . . it makes it more painful, but also more pleasurable at the same time, and I don't understand my feelings . . . but I can see that they are there."

With seriously disturbed patients whose difficulties go be-

yond neurotic conflict, Balint (1968) emphasizes that the regressive transference will move to a level in which words will not
describe the patient's experience. This is the level he calls the
"basic fault." He argues against "organizing" this material immediately, and suggests instead giving the patient sufficient opportunity to experience it. Then he attempts to frame a description and interpretation.

> The aim is that the patient should be able to find himself,
> to accept himself, and to get on with himself, knowing all
> the time that there is a scar in himself, his basic fault, which
> cannot be "analysed" out of existence; moreover, he must
> be allowed to discover *his* way to the world of objects — and
> not be shown the "right" way by some profound or correct
> interpretation. . . . Apart from being a "need recognizing"
> and perhaps even a "need satisfying" object, the analyst
> must be also a "need understanding" object, who in addi-
> tion must be able to communicate his understanding to his
> patient [pp. 180–181].

What is impressive in this paragraph is that Balint, whose forte
was bearing the depths of deepest regression, did not settle for a
pure corrective emotional experience with a patient. It was not
enough just to bear the transference and provide a nurturant setting of acceptance. It was also important, in order for the patient
to derive benefit from it, to provide verbal organization of the
experience.

Let us take, for example, the patient with massive vulnerability to loss and separation anxiety. After many years of treatment
it becomes apparent that this vulnerability has a rock-bottom
layer of nameless terror, which refuses to dissipate. After count-
less circumstances have been explored where such sensitivity
has led to irrational retreat or schizoid behavior, the patient and I
outline the area of vulnerability. I describe it as a "psychological
trick knee." Just as one might still perform many activities with
an unsure knee, there are certain activities to be chary of, to
move with care in, and some activities that must absolutely be
avoided. The understanding of the framework of possibilities,
plus comprehension of their source and stimulation, along with

a sense of security born out of our joint learning adventure, then allows the patient to chance life in many ways that were previously avoided. Without the verbal understanding, however, the patient would be ever vulnerable to an unnameable, unknowable, and worst of all, unpredictable terror. Verbal understanding is important even in the realm of the unverbalizable.

Cognitive Styles and Reality Sense

Hartmann (1964) provided conceptual tools to emphasize that nonconflictual areas of the ego are involved in insight. Our state of knowledge and ways of knowing are not entirely determined by the nature of our conflicts, defenses, and repression. Inborn intelligence and cognitive capacities are major determinants of our styles of knowing.

Intelligence is a complex set of mental traits, and people may vary in their possession of one trait or another. We note how certain patients are uncanny in their intuitive self-understanding, and grasp large emotional gestalts. Other patients may quietly and persistently collect data and hypotheses until they are convinced and overwhelmed with evidence that forces a final conclusion upon themselves. In working with dreams, certain patients are blank to the contents of a dream, but sharp in their awareness of the day residue that stimulated the dream. Others plumb the depths of dream material with striking ability. Among such patients, sparkling linguistic skills may aid in unlocking the metaphorical meaning of dream structure. The puns inherent in dreams are self-evident to them. Others are blind to the metaphors, but accurate in sniffing out the affectual underpinnings of a dream. Varying styles of intelligence will produce differing roads to insightful comprehension. The therapist must keep in mind differences in cognitive style. Individual routes to understanding must be allowed to take their course, and one does not seek for each patient to course the same road to Rome.

Cognitive ability, however, may be quite insufficient to provide a sense of reality in the face of unresolved conflict. Reality testing and the sense of reality are a problem not only for psy-

chotics and borderline personalities. When the important figures of early life acknowledge facts and achievements in one's
life, the stamp of reality is placed upon these actualities. Accepted and taken seriously by loved authorities, one's achievements feel real.

One bright young woman always knew that her high
school and college graduations had a gray, unreal, and incomplete feeling attached to them. During therapy she was
recurrently doubtful of the value of unusual academic and
professional achievements. She was surprised and confused when my comments indicated that I viewed her
achievements as remarkable. It became evident that she
was not able to recognize her academic brilliance until I had
pointed it out to her. This acknowledgment gave it a stamp
of approval and a sense that it was real, and realistically received by someone outside the realm of her personal fantasy. The enormous importance she placed on my
acknowledgment reawakened the unfulfilled acknowledgments never forthcoming from her mother. The mother,
while favoring an athletic brother and less intellectually
gifted sister, had consistently ignored the patient's superior achievements. Through her transference understanding, the patient began the mental struggle of intellectual
understanding of reality versus her affectual postpone-
ment of it. Unconsciously, she was still waiting for her
mother's excitement and acknowledgment of her achievements. Such insight does not cure her problem, but frames
the mental task for her. It describes the struggle that requires working-through.

Balancing Understanding with Unformed Experience

As we emphasize the rational comprehension of events in therapy, it is useful (and realistic) to remember that both patient and
therapist require the experience of the irrational (the unconscious) to be allowed to progress. To a large extent, we wish the

patient to suspend judgment, to allow irrational wishes, fantasies, and thoughts to emerge. There is an oscillation between this regressive movement and self-observation and judgment. Each patient will find to what degree this wavering is possible, and what balance between the two poles is most useful. The therapist, also, is not left merely to formulate. The therapist is "to surrender himself to his own unconscious mental activity, in a state of evenly hovering attention . . . and by these means to catch the drift of the patient's unconscious with his own unconscious" (Freud 1922, p. 239). Freud cautioned against excessive intellectual formulations in ongoing therapy:

> It is not a good thing to work on a case scientifically while treatment is still proceeding — to piece together its structure, to try to foretell its further progress, and to get a picture from time to time of the current state of affairs, as scientific interest would demand. Cases which are devoted from the first to scientific purposes and are treated accordingly suffer in their outcome; while the most successful cases are those in which one proceeds, as it were, without any purpose in view, allows oneself to be taken by surprise by any new turn in them, and always meets them with an open mind, free from any presuppositions [1912, p. 114].

Clearly, there are no cut-and-dried formulations for conduct in psychotherapy. Great variations will occur, depending upon many variables, including the nature and ability of the therapist and patient, as well as the clinical problem at hand. Ferenczi, one of the master therapists of the early years of this century, provided the most succinct summary possible of this process:

> One gradually becomes aware how immensely complicated the mental work demanded from the analyst is. He has to let the patient's free associations play upon him; simultaneously he lets his own fantasy get to work with the association material; from time to time he compares the new connections that arise with earlier results of the analysis; and not for one moment must he relax the vigilance and criticism made necessary by his own subjective trends.
>
> One might say that his mind swings continuously be-

tween empathy, self-observation, and making judgments. The latter emerge spontaneously from time to time as mental signals, which at first, of course, have to be assessed as such; only after the accumulation of further evidence is one entitled to make an interpretation [1928, p. 96].

Ferenczi's description of oscillation among the centers of therapeutic states of knowing — empathy, observation, and judgments leading to interpretation — reflects an integrative approach to the therapeutic process and, by this means, becomes a useful bridge to our next discussion: integration. Ongoing understanding becomes integration.

To summarize this chapter on understanding and its vicissitudes in meeting the challenges of the unconscious, I turn to the evocative art of the novelist Italo Calvino:

Only a certain prosaic solidity can give birth to creativity. Fantasy is like jam. You have to spread it on a solid slice of bread. If not, it remains a shapeless thing, like jam, out of which you can't make anything [Vidal 1985, pp. 3–10].

9

Integration and the Role of Mourning

Termination Begins with the First Interpretation

Therapy is like life. The initial emphasis is on attachment, developing a loving and dependable bond. Next, there comes an understanding of the pleasures and pains that are part of this bond. All this, however, points in the direction of ultimate loss of parent or the therapist. It is ironic that people seek treatment because of loss of love, fantasied or real, through a process that has loss as part of its inherent structure. Mastery of past pain occurs through mastery of present pain. This is the transference.

Human growth and development are always full of conflicts, especially with regard to sadness. The birth of a lovely child is loss of the special state of pregnancy. A woman in tune with herself will usually sense the sadness of parted symbiosis as the exclusiveness of the twosome is brought to conclusion. Inability to acknowledge, bear, and set this loss in place will contribute to postpartum states of depression. Conflicts about earlier states of dependency with an ambivalently held mother will, for example, make it harder to acknowledge the pleasures of pregnancy and will make a woman vulnerable to "postpartum blues." The unconscious longing for a loved relationship with one's mother, replayed in a loving relation with the unborn child, needs its due. One cannot proceed with the next stage of development without proper mourning of the last.

At every step of development, some degree of sadness requires acknowledgment, bearing, and being put into place. The
toddler often needs to run back to its mother for "emotional refueling." Going off to kindergarten, completion of schooling,
getting married, and forming one's own family all entail loss
of cherished places and people. It is commonplace to cry at
weddings and occasions of great happiness.

The best that therapy offers is culled from everyday life. The
constant underpinnings of transference-oriented therapy are
both minor and major elements of the normal process of grieving. Much of maladaptive defensiveness is geared toward
warding off sadness, often replacing this affect and its sequelae
with depression. Depression is a defense against the affect of
sadness.

As E. Bibring (1954) emphasized, simple abreaction is a one-
act therapy. It is rare that one outburst of grief dissolves the
encrustations of long-standing character attitudes and feelings.
The issues of grief may be embedded in several relationships
with several people, often at different periods of one's life. Integration of the impact of this series of griefs will consume a great
deal of time in therapy. The integrated outcome is often unknown to both therapist and patient. Consider the remarks of
the following patient after several years of therapy:

"When I first came to see you, years ago, I used to be tear-
ful and cry a lot, and have no idea what it was about. Some
of it seemed directly related to the loss of my wife, Maria,
but there was a deeper sadness than that. It's taken me
years to realize that it was you . . . having a man who was
bright, accomplished, and yet understanding, who was listening to me. It was so unlike my father, I couldn't bear it. I
had given up on that many years ago. I had become tough
and counterdependent. I didn't want to admit that I still
cared about him, still wanted him, or you, to be the father I
wanted . . . then I went through all those adoption feelings
with you . . . the sadness and bitterness about him all came
back. . . . I realize now I can be a lot of things I wanted to
be, through my experience with you, but sadness about
him still remains . . . no one has a period of life when they
are in nonconflict."

In succinct fashion, this statement informs us that understanding has focused on many elements of attachment, but
grieving and sadness were a constant thread. It represents integration, which, rather than a patch over a torn element of personality, is now part of the psyche's fabric.

Defenses against Grief

With neurotic patients, such as the man just mentioned, the
central mourning issues evolve slowly over time. The patient's
initial presentation to therapy may be the result of symptoms
and issues seemingly remote from issues of sadness and defenses against this affect. Phobias about elevators or crowds, or
indecision over a business career versus law, may seem remote
from mourning. With more disturbed patients, however, initial
clinical problems promptly announce mourning as a central issue, or rather rapidly herald its presence through fantasies and
dreams.

A young man dropped out of college in his first year. He
became remote and listless and ceased all former intellectual and athletic pursuits. Urged into therapy by his parents, he began to see me three times a week. Many sessions
were silent. He smoked, asked sarcastic questions, challenged my answers, and assumed a mystical, judgmental
distance. Yet he still came regularly.
In little bits and pieces, I developed the notion that he
saw me much as he saw his mother and father: I seemed
out of touch with his feelings, preoccupied with my narcissistic needs, and tied into corrupted bourgeois interests.
Gaining a therapeutic cure would be a feather in my psychiatric cap, just as his brilliant academic success would con-
firm his preoccupied parents in brilliant parenthood. In
small comments, now and then, I conveyed these ideas to
him. He remained mystical and skeptical, but still came
regularly.
Increasingly, after weekends or holidays, his sarcasm
sharpened, and anxious tension was more evident. Finally,

I made a gentle interpretation that he feared that I forgot him while we were separated. Even worse, like his father, perhaps he was afraid I would fail to return for our next appointment (the father was a diplomat, often away and canceling returns at the last moment). In the session following this interpretation, he reported a two-part dream: He is in the customs section of a New York airport. His father is there, but he can't tell if his father is saying hello or goodbye. Is he coming or leaving? He feels anxious, and then finds himself in a hospital room. He is watching himself in a hospital bed and, with terror, notices that he is growing smaller and smaller. He sees himself as he was in earlier and earlier stages of his life. Finally, he appears as an infant, and watches himself disappear into the wideness and whiteness of the hospital wall. No one is there to help him.

All the themes of seeking acceptance while fearing rejection are announced in this painful outpouring. The dream allowed us to state his fears in visual and metaphorical terms, to label them as his ideas, not just mine. He later revealed that this dream was a version of a recurrent childhood dream. All through a very long treatment of almost eight years, these themes maintained a steady presence. They grew in depth as they were attached to ever-increasing transference feelings, current life issues, and memories of the past.

The entire therapy was projected onto a background screen of longing for closeness while fearing abandonment. Whatever other conflict or defense was discussed, this implicit anxiety was always somewhere at hand. Although termination began with the first interpretation, it no doubt began from the moment when the patient first called me.

The listlessness and sense of emptiness that this patient suffered came from his depressive defense against mourning and sadness. Without the psychological presence in his personality of his loved persons, he vanishes into nothingness.

In the grieving process, as one allows the longing and love for lost objects to come to the fore, they are allowed into the personality. Mourning is a major source of identification. Or, as Freud epitomized in "Mourning and Melancholia," "The shadow of the object falls upon the ego" (1917, p. 249). As this young man was enabled to acknowledge all he wanted from me, it rekindled what he wanted from his mother and father (as well as other important figures of his life). Acknowledging, for example, his admiration of his father's political brilliance and sense of history allowed him to admire his own intellectual assets. Depression often discards the wheat with the chaff.

Defense against identification with a loved figure is a part of depression that enfeebles the personality. Out of fear of becoming a schizoid figure like his father, or a disorganized narcissist like his mother, the patient ground his personal development to a halt. It was better to be nothing than to be any embodiment of those terrible traits. The concentrated attention of the therapist reawakened buried longings for a good mother and father.

The process of continual mourning in therapy is what makes basic trust in oneself and the therapist so essential. Neurotic patients come with basic trust. Most disturbed patients need constant attention in maintaining basic trust at a requisite level.

A mildly paranoid woman found herself becoming isolative and suspicious after her mother's death. These were some of the mother's most dreaded traits. The patient was unaware of the similarity, while at the same time she showed few signs of mourning. When certain anniversary reactions were pointed out to her, she became increasingly distant, aloof, and suspicious. Rather than experience mourning, a direct reaction of loss, helplessness, and longing for the missing loved one, she maintained attachment through identification. This was safe; she need not acknowledge her loyalty. Over time, in small ways, I demonstrated to her that she cared greatly for her mother. For many reasons, her love remained suppressed.

The initial stages of mourning induce panic. There is the terror and reality of stark loss, helplessness in the face of the unchangeable. With vulnerable people, mourning induces a sense of terrifying aloneness. They fear subjection to the indifference of fantasied abandonment, and even the fate of death of the loved one, as they long to be close to those who are gone. In the face of these tensions, neurotic patients become more neurotic, and psychotic patients become more psychotic. "Better the devil we know than the one we know not."

Mourning brings one closer to the lost object, and this closeness induces a feeling of sameness. When this patient felt close to her mother, she feared she would possess all the horrible traits she had spent her life warding off. In such a process, she felt I was trying to drive her crazy, as her mother had tried. All my attempts to point out her love and similarity to her mother made her feel horrible. Constant reality testing was necessary to help her see who she was as opposed to who her mother was. *Similar* is not always *the same as.* During this period and over many years, the basic trust developed between us, supporting her attempt to sustain her feelings, which led toward a new consideration of old conflicts. As partial acceptances of her love were achieved without concomitant fears that this meant that she was her mother, her psychotic-like symptoms remitted.

This is not a process that is done once, at one time, or perhaps even completed within the time frame of therapy. Such painful and complicated mourning in a vulnerable ego remains an ongoing process. It may not always overwhelm the patient to the same degree, but it does erupt at key dates (anniversary reactions) or events that are emotionally combustible. At such times a person may show unexplainable irritability, distraction, or affects that defend against underlying sadness. When the significance of the anniversary is brought to the mourner's attention, these behaviors often dissolve into residual feelings of grief. Particularly in contemporary society, where religious ritual has been dropped, the hectic business of everyday life serves to mask unconscious time clocks. Memorial masses or lighting of candles (*yahrzeit*) are built-in forms of preventive medicine. Religious ritual provides structures to elicit and guide grief.

Loss in Everyday Psychotherapy

The mourning processes I have outlined are large-scale, but mourning is in the background of smaller, everyday therapeutic processes. Each time a fantasy or piece of characteristic behavior is examined and reduced to realistic considerations, a particular favored and loved way of doing or seeing things is lost. A young lawyer who was a public defender ended each session with a smiling, warm "take care" as he went through the door. When the meaning of this began to spell a cover-up for less benevolent feelings toward me, and deeper wishes for me to "take care" of him, it was no longer possible to use this parting salutation. It became too linked to separation anxiety, which induced anger at the end of the hour, and to older anger at neglectful parents. Part of his defender role was a defense against fears (and wishes) of being like his parents. Giving up the posture of the ideal defender entailed the loss of many lofty fantasies, as well as fear of losing his virtues. There is sadness and mourning in letting go of traits that one has carried for virtually a lifetime; they are old friends.

I once asked an ingenuous young woman who had a delusion that three hundred students from her school were following her, "Why do you think this is so?" Effortlessly, she replied: "When you are as lonely as I am, it's not so bad having all these people around!" When she compensated and lost these figures, she developed a massive depression. Often after acute psychotic reactions, when the symptoms have remitted, patients are left with depression. They become depressed over feelings that previously drove them crazy (Roth 1970). Indeed, a succinct way of formulating the recompensation process from psychosis is to say that the affects of sadness are now more tolerable. This formulation also dictates the technical process for this stage of treating the psychoses: initiating and completing the process of mourning. It is in this stage of psychotherapy that most therapies of the psychotic and disturbed patient founder. The work that enables mourning in such patients usually stretches out over years and remains incomplete with many patients. We shall return to this important topic in the chapter on stages of treatment.

Some Theoretical Aspects of Integration

Now we come to another of the endless series of psychological paradoxes. Through a process of terrible pain and grieving, one meets the highest of pleasures − the impulses of loving. The other side of the integrating features of mourning is Eros.

Semrad (1966) attributed much to the factor of "love" and "eros" in integrating personality through therapy. He felt that this was the basic factor in change and, although not understood, underlay shifts in personality. This, we must recall, was essentially Freud's view. Without transference love the patient would have insufficient motivation to endure the unhappiness of analytic investigation. This element of motivation for change has been emphasized through much of the preceding chapters. Semrad viewed hate and its vicissitudes as the central disintegrative destructive force to the ego.

Love neutralizes aggression and nullifies its disintegrative and regressive effects. In therapy, love becomes integrated and reworked through the transference love to the therapist. In clinical interviews carried out for teaching purposes, Semrad could awaken the lost loves, attained, frustrated, fantasied, however slight, in a seemingly "burned out" patient. The sudden blossoming of complex and poignant emotions, quite integrated and attached to narrative memory, moved the student onlookers. The patient invariably became, in the eyes of the observers, a comprehendible and absorbing person. The mobilizing passions of sleeping love seemed to be an integrative healer.

Without having seen such shifts in highly regressed patients, one would, for the most part, have been left with the impression that loving impulses, if any, were of a vague, distorted, and undefinable quality. Such patients often have their loving relationships reduced to terms such as *oral, anaclitic, primitive, a substitute for the breast,* and many other reductive simplifications. For Semrad, it was always otherwise: "Love is love, no matter how you slice it. A touch of love is like a touch of pregnancy" (1980, p. 33).

Nunberg, following the early psychoanalytic model, similarly focused on eros in delineating the "synthetic function of the ego." Eros gives the ego the capacity to mediate among the id, the superego, and external reality. The ego remains close to its origins, the id. Nunberg (1931) states: "Since the ego is derived from the id, it is probably from this very source (Eros) that it acquires its binding and productive power" (p. 122).

Silent Integration

Integrative factors are often "silent," representing processes that are more easily explained than understood. When integrative capacity is lost, its importance in everyday life is unmasked. For example, in patients who develop organic damage to the brain, the loss of recent memory and impairment in abstract thinking leads to confusion, terrifying anxiety, and poverty of thought and emotion. Similarly, the obsessional patient with excessive defenses of isolation and intellectualization disconnects thought from affect, so that integration of experience is interfered with. The patient feels anxious confusion over motives and ambivalences and often complains of an empty sense of boredom (Asch 1982). Synthesis is essential to healthy functioning.

Here is a historical progression of Freud's comments on integration:

> 1895: I have described my treatments as psychotherapeutic operations; and I have brought out their analogy with the opening up of a cavity filled with pus, the scraping out of a carious region, etc. An analogy of this kind finds its justification not so much in the removal of what is pathological as in the establishment of conditions that are more likely to lead the course of the process in the direction of recovery [Breuer and Freud, 1893–1895, p. 305].

> 1912: It must further be borne in mind that many people fall ill precisely from an attempt to sublimate their instincts

beyond the degree permitted by their organization and that in those who have a capacity for sublimation the process usually takes place of itself as soon as their inhibitions have been overcome by analysis [1912b, p. 119].

1919: As we analyze [the mind of the neurotic patient] and remove the resistances, it grows together; the great unity which we call his ego fits into itself all the instinctual impulses which before had been split off and held apart from it. . . . Psychosynthesis is thus achieved during analytic treatment without our intervention, automatically and inevitably [p. 161].

1933: [The intention of psychoanalysis is] to strengthen the ego, to make it more independent of the super-ego, to widen its field of perception and enlarge its organization so that it can appropriate fresh portions of the id. Where id was, there ego shall be [p. 80].

1937: The analytic situation consists in our allying ourselves with the ego of the person under treatment, in order to subdue portions of his id which are uncontrolled — that is to say, to include them in the synthesis of his ego [1937a, p. 235].

It is striking how little the general formulation of integration changes in all the forgoing quotations. In truth, although we have many techniques that begin a process of psychological change, the maturational and synthetic harmony that evolves is basically observed, rather then comprehended. Given this proviso, let us see how some have struggled to further our comprehension of this process.

Edward Bibring saw analytic technique as altering the balance among ego, id, and superego. As defenses shift and allow realistic expression of impulses, psychobiological maturation proceeds. The id develops throughout life, as, for example, through sublimations. The tears of childhood become the sadness of adult life. The toddler's rage at frustration becomes the forceful determination of the persistent adult. Lifelong inhibitions of basic impulses will stultify their growth into sophisticated adult emotional expression. Bibring (1937) viewed ego activities of integration and assimilation as perhaps the most important background forces for change: "We can assume their existence and need neither to evoke them nor to change them" (p. 187).

Of particular importance in this process is the modification of the superego, especially as outlined by Strachey (1934). To the degree that the superego remains based on an archaic infantile set of prohibitions, to that degree is the ego hampered in testing reality. Through excessive repression, libidinal wishes and aggressive and assertive impulses are denied access to awareness. Through the incorporation and identification of the benign attitude of the therapist, who functions as an auxiliary superego, the ego is modified and more of the id is allowed into consciousness. Energy the ego had expended in defense is freed up for other purposes.

Approached from the interpersonal and cultural point of view, as, for example, in the works of Erik Erikson (1950), integrative changes are seen in a psychosocial perspective. Developmental progressions that had been halted are noted to continue again. Isolation may open into intimacy, or stagnation turn to generativity. Renewed integration, when it develops, can be conceptualized from many angles and viewpoints.

Working-through

Working-through is the conceptual handle that is used most often to describe the hard psychological work that is necessary to maintain the understanding that the patient has obtained. Valenstein (1983) states that working-through is what goes on between insight and action. An exploration of the resistances to knowing and changing continues. In classical analytic theory, the reluctance to change was partially explained by the resistance of the id, and connotes a conflict-free quality. Once the libido has taken a position in relation to an object, especially in early life, the patient exhibits a sticky adhesiveness to this position. Generally one is reluctant to change one's interests and preferences. Psychical inertia acts as a drag against change. A person changes slowly, if at all.

Transference as an Integrator

Although transference derives from regressive trends, and is seemingly anti-integrative in its resistance to understanding the present reality, it too has an integrative function. Erikson (1950) has outlined developmentally the various forms of psychological disorganization prior to reintegration and the creation of a different identity. This disorganization can be seen in the identity crises and confusions of adolescence, which lead to firmer knowledge of a person's integral self. So too, psychotherapy can be seen as inducing regression as a precursor to integration of the split-off, repressed unconscious into a new, more acceptable, identity.

In this regard, the transference is seen as the *urge to mastery*, and, through language, a new synthesis of previously chaotic experience is achieved. Loewald (1960) emphasizes transference as the curative factor of treatment by virtue of its culling diverse elements of the past for an integrated treatment in the present. The therapist provides a framework for the multiple urges of transference, which seek a source of gratification. Transference provides opportunity for change in the unconscious.

The continual revelation of split-off parts of the unconscious results in such concepts as "cohesive narrative" (Sherwood 1969). The most useful goal of therapy is to provide the patient with a historically understandable, personal course of events: a coherence and stability to the patient's experience of self. In treatment, the therapist strives for comments that have "reconstruction" in mind. They comprise an assessment of the present in terms of the motivational building blocks of the past, which in turn provides an organizing framework around the patient's history. Such reconstructions of how we came to be who we are at the moment will reverberate up and down the developmental line and show itself in different ways at different stages of development. The terror of the preadolescent boy who fears being beaten up by his peers becomes the anxiety of the college student who fears the jeers and roughhousing of his college mates.

Kohut's concept (1977) of the "cohesive self" as a developmental goal provides a specific integrative process for therapy.

The therapist's empathic recognitions of the unrecognized and unempathized self will result in the patient's formation of a "cohesive self." The therapist's empathy provides the missing reality of self that the patient did not obtain in childhood. These pieces of new information are slowly put together into a new picture of the patient's self.

Gardner (1983) focuses on the identification of the patient with the therapist's "pursuit of truth." This identification does not take place entirely through the unconscious process of becoming like the therapist, but also — significantly — through *learning*. The therapist's techniques for searching out reality provide the patient with tools for investigation that ultimately become his or her own. As Fenichel (1937) observed, "When I recognize that what someone says is right, it does not necessarily mean that I have introjected [become like] him" (p. 24). Attunement to free association awakens a patient to his or her inherent capacity for self-observation, collecting data and drawing integrative conclusions. Gardner emphasizes the capacity of therapy to intensify the ability for "self-inquiry."

A Clinical Measure: The Role of Realistic Action

Toward the end of her career, Helen Tartakoff (1981), a highly respected classical analyst, shifted some of her traditional views. She had placed great emphasis on insight and understanding as being central to utilizing analytic psychotherapy. Increasingly, she felt that, in addition to insight, a special character in the relationship between therapist and patient provided an integrative structure for evaluating the effects of therapy in everyday life. None of the terms *transference, countertransference,* or *insight* fully captures the special *interaction-internalization-action* triad that is repeatedly pursued in therapy. This interactive triad results in new *solutions* to old problems and shows itself in some change in behavior, or *action*. Without this concluding experimentation — with action in life — the patient cannot measure or integrate insights derived from interpreting defenses and conflicts. Actual behavioral changes are the final measure of what has been understood in treatment. Returning from life's experience to a session, a patient works through impressions, feelings, and awarenesses that have arisen out of actual behavioral change. Action is integral to working-through.

Living-through as Working-through

If we concur with Tartakoff, then working-through is more aptly labeled "living-through." The understanding and insight the patient gains in therapy must be tried out in actual experience. In part, this experimentation occurs through the central focus of treatment, the transference. In fact, the transference is the fulcrum of, and conduit to, change. Sooner or later, however, no patient will be fully satisfied with transference alone, and some measure of success must be had outside of the office. There is usually some ongoing relationship between the living-through in the transference and the living-out in the rest of the patient's life.

A young woman had long been viewed as socially inferior to her brilliant and romantically successful mother and sisters. She was shy, tentative, and withdrawn, while they were outgoing and forthright. She had settled into a Cinderella-like role as caretaker of the various needs of her family. She dressed shabbily and affected an outward demeanor of naiveté. Since she was always reliable, the family and friends used her as confidante, caretaker, and even babysitter. Anna Freud, no doubt, would have summed up her defensive stance as "altruistic surrender."

Although she attempted the same stance in relation to me, her cleverness and psychological deftness poked through her humble demeanor. She had clear notions of the peculiarities of her mother and sisters, understood their foibles, and, more profoundly, fathomed their deep unhappiness. When I focused on this strength, she displayed anxiety and guilt: anxiety lest she be competitively challenged on her assessments and proved wrong, and guilt at feeling "superior" to her mother and sisters.

Over time she felt this mixture of anxiety and guilt toward me. She did not want me to feel that she was more than my humble and obedient patient, fearing both my anger and my destruction. These transference issues were observed, clarified, and interpreted in many ways over a few years. With me she became lighter in spirit, more daring in commentary, and generally confident. She felt sexually attracted to me, and told me so. With these new feelings about herself, in little steps, she tried on her new personality within her family. The smallest step involved complicated processes.

For example, she found a boyfriend, the first in many years. Would I be offended at her audacity? Would I lose interest in her if she became interested in someone else? She experienced the same anxiety in relation to her mother and sisters. New interests left less time to give to her family, listen to their problems, or do the busywork for which they seemed to need her. She feared loss of their loyalty and love, but also feared for their well-being without her emotional support. Bringing her boyfriend to dinner raised oedipal anxieties: would the mother be jealous, or would the sisters prove more attractive and brilliant, et cetera? At the same time, such activities and success would create new images for herself as a romantic woman, an intellectual woman, an independent woman, possibly even a mother herself. All this was brought back into the hours of therapy and worked-through in treatment (including the transference) while it was lived-through in her life.

Such changes in behavior provided not only intrapsychic conflict, but also actual conflicts with friends and family. She was changing a delicate equilibrium. At times this change induced regression and return to Cinderella status. Thus, a to-and-fro, trial-and-error pattern occurred, continuing the reworking of old behavior as it was brought back, as well as dealing with new conflicts as they arose.

This example is sketched in brevity. Even if I were to provide exacting detail, it would still only scratch the surface of the multiple ways that working-through occurs as integration proceeds.

Commonly, therapists expect that once understanding and insight occur, change follows as night follows day. Nothing is farther from the therapeutic truth. Change, if it occurs at all, occurs slowly. This is an important fact for a therapist to integrate.

Unless both therapist and patient have a deep appreciation for the lengthy process of working-through, unrealistic expectations of treatment may ensue. From this, only disillusionment can occur for both therapist and patient. It is often helpful to state this simple fact to patients. Accurate understanding has an impact; much of psychotherapy is the exploration of this impact. It is common to observe humiliation in people who find themselves engaged in undesirable behavior. They berate themselves since they "should know better." Appreciation for the complexity of altering personality is gained in detailed and repetitive working-through.

Integration Embedded in Attachment

Through attachment and trust, elements of the interactive therapeutic relationship are taken into patients' personalities. The elements may range from mentally hearing the therapist's supportive tone as they enter an anxious situation to totally unconscious identifications.

> An anxious professor got up to lecture before her colleagues, felt some terror, and could hear me saying, "They're people just like you . . . some might even have your very attitude at a lecture, eagerness to hear something fresh and new," and she calmed down.

Part of such a moment may include a vague feeling tone that is associated with the calming influence and self-esteem–inducing experience of the therapy hours. Often, even the feeling tone is preconscious. Only on reexamination of the situation can one find that the patient had the feeling tone of the safe and permissive therapist on the edge of awareness.

Other points on a spectrum running from incorporation to identification include unconscious utilization of the words, attitude, or other experiences with the therapist. The therapist may be surprised by such results, as parents are amazed to hear their words come back to them from children who, to all intents and purposes, had consciously rejected exactly the sentiments now being mouthed. It is important to stress that in the complex process of incorporation, the patient often introjects wishes that he or she has unconsciously projected onto the therapist. Such ego-ideal wishes are then experienced as part of the loved and admired therapist, and the patient feels greater freedom to act on wishes formerly tabooed by inhibitions.

A woman had parents who ignored her excellent intellect. Consequently, she was delighted that I was eager for her to complete training as a physician. She "knew" I wished this for her as intensely as she did for herself. In her mind, I was the wished-for good mother or father, rather than her actual parents, who never encouraged her.

For a long while I let the patient flourish in this nurturant sunshine. When I felt she was strong enough, this projection was taken up as a resistance to her seeing herself as adequate enough to make this judgment. She could accept achievement only to the degree that she felt I approved of it. These discussions developed into an analysis of her guilt, allegiance to her parents' view, and her identification with the aggressor.

Buried in this process is our ubiquitous mourning process. Taking her own individual stance implied independence, but also included loss and estrangement. Identification with the aggressor was a way of joining the enemy and avoiding the pain of "difference" and exclusion.

Such a tumultuous field of inquiry would not have been possible without her prior long period of feeling nourished in my presence. This attachment laid the foundation for painful and difficult understanding, which led to uncomfortable affects, including the major one of sadness. This underlying element of attachment is part of the integrative process. It is like the ground color the painter applies before the actual important images are superimposed on the canvas. The ground is not consciously noticed by the observer, but it quietly unifies the field.

The Blurred Field of Integration

I have dissected the integrative factors in this fashion to emphasize the multiple processes at work, both as they are revealed in
isolation and in collaboration with one another. As therapists,
we must be careful not to cling to one explanatory concept but to
have respect for processes that run before our eyes at great
speed and with great mystery. Although in this section I have
emphasized mourning and sadness and their roles in allowing
acceptance of current reality in contrast to the lost past, in previous chapters I emphasized attachment and bonding (the opposite of loss) and understanding. To a great extent, therapy sets
in motion an organic and self-directing process. We oversee this,
comment on it, influence some of its momentum, pull and lean
against its inertia this way or that, but for the most part, as
Freud said, the patient does what "he can or what he wants."
In Tolstoi's *War and Peace*, the Russian grand commander,
Kutuzov, is considering the question put to him of how he maneuvers hundreds of thousands of soldiers so masterfully.
Kutuzov in essence says, "It's rather simple. I look to see in what
direction the army is moving, and then I give the order to go in
that direction." In many respects, the attentive therapist does
the same.

10

Stages and Rhythms in Psychotherapy

All happy families resemble one another, each unhappy family is unhappy in its own way.

Leo Tolstoi, Anna Karenina

It is true that each psychotherapy has its own life. The unique personal quality of each patient, and our special response to this quality, provides a characteristic stamp to the work. At the same time, recurrent patterns shape similar experiences in all therapies. Awareness of these patterns stabilizes our position in relation to the patient and, in general ways, organizes our thinking, expectations, and responses. The very end of a treatment reveals qualities distinctly different from those of the very beginning. The bewildering murkiness of the midstages of treatment loses sight of both beginning and end. Once again, we shall find that the guiding thread in this confusion is the state of the transference. Its induction, development, and resolution provide useful reference points for the therapeutic journey.

Honeymoon Period

A number of factors converge to alleviate the acute pain and symptoms of psychological distress in the initial stage of therapy. Among them, the importance of expectant hopefulness is not to be minimized. The frustration of many wishes usually brings people to a therapist. There is the unconscious belief that these wishes will be granted by the therapist. Thus, symptoms produced by loss (real or fantasied) will remit to the degree that the person is hopefully expectant. To the degree that the patient remains pessimistic about help, the psychological pain and symptoms remain. On the whole, when the patient–therapist match is good, the patient experiences significant relief in the beginning of treatment.

A doctor had come from a home where his parents had maintained a loveless and unhappy relationship. He had spent his youth trying to make these people happy, a thankless and hopeless task. He buried himself in a career in medicine, where rescuing people seemed more possible. Taking a chance on love, he married. Like most marriages, his had its realistic difficulties. In addition, it had some extra ones, since his tolerance for conflict was low, and conflict spelled living out his parents' misery. Increasingly, he became withdrawn, lethargic, and pessimistic, and his alertness and efficiency dropped. In short, he became clinically depressed. He found his wife angry with his withdrawal and he longed for the kindness, empathy, and nonviolence he had dreamed of for his parents and then for himself.

During my first few weeks' work with this man, I was experienced as the wished-for mentor-parent. With little activity other than a naturally responsive interest, and questions and comments directed toward clarifications of his tale, most of his acute symptoms disappeared. My understanding of this case at this point was minimal. Nothing substantial had changed in external reality, and his character was the same.

Anticipating our discussion a bit, let me note that several months later when the negative transference developed, the depressive symptoms returned.

In contrast, a young computer engineer came to see me for heightened anxiety and increased impulsive angry outbursts at his new job. He came from a very intellectually competitive family, where the father and his three sons fought for the limelight. For several weeks I was as gentle as I could be in my manner and comments. This made no difference; he experienced me as similar in age, similar in level of achievement, and similarly competitive. Rather than reassurance and safety, he experienced humiliation in my presence. He felt I was quite competent, but he couldn't settle down in my presence. Notably, none of his presenting symptoms had remitted.

I referred this man to a much older colleague, quite grandfatherly, and semiretired. With this therapist the patient's anxiety dropped off rapidly and he relaxed into treatment.

The Negative Beginning

The beginning is a puzzling period of treatment. In the second case cited, for example, how was I to know that this initial negativity was not merely the patient's early defense against dependence, or homosexual anxiety? What if behind this irritating facade there was an earnest wish to be accepted despite his unpleasant demeanor? Certainly, this negative form of initial phase I had seen many times, especially in schizophrenic patients. Unfortunately, there is no ironclad meaning to early negativity and whether it indicates referring the patient to another therapist. In this instance, I relied on an unquantifiable factor — my clinical judgment. The patient seemed excessively insistent on his sense of humiliation, while at the same time acknowledging that I had seemed highly competent and had done him no true injustice. Furthermore, he continued having difficulties on his job. Perhaps most of all, he seemed relieved at the idea of stopping with me and being referred to an older therapist. He did not seem to feel rejected. Should this same pattern recur as he interacted with the next therapist, he seemed well enough motivated not to run away from it a second time. The combination of these factors — progressive humiliation, deteriorating work performance, good observing ego, and lack of rejection at a referral — dictated acceding to his request for a new therapist.

When the initial phase is not of the honeymoon variety, the clinical judgment of the therapist is markedly challenged. At all times we wish to convey to patients that the therapist is mostly neutral about their personalities and difficulties in life. That is to say, we have a tendency to accept patients for who and what they are. We are keenly aware that many fragile persons attempt to say "hello" primarily by saying "good-bye." This is the backward social stance of many schizoid and psychotic patients. We cannot be misled by the manifest behavior of such patients, who go through long periods of testing the therapist's power of endurance and survival. They do not wish primitive fantasies of death and destruction to actualize. They experience relief when the therapist continues treatment, unabashed by gross rejection.

But when the patient is not so severely disturbed, an initial negative phase is not always so easy to evaluate. It is probably best to err on the side of continuing, rather than stopping, therapy. When in the initial stages of treatment, however, the patient heatedly persists in suggesting you are intolerable, raising the issue of transfer to another therapist may be indicated. As in the case noted above, when the patient does not experience this recommendation as rejection, we are probably clinically correct to transfer the patient.

We are helped if the patient has a history of prior psychotherapy. The past experiences can be examined for similar or different responses to a therapist. If what is occurring with us has happened repeatedly in the past, we can demonstrate this fact to the patient. In that case, the patient is probably saved undue suffering if we continue treatment, rather than passing the therapeutic buck down the line. Delineation of past transferences to therapists is the single most useful source of data for evaluating the present transference.

Long Beginnings

As the chapter on transference indicates, for some patients the honeymoon period constitutes their whole psychotherapy. As soon as negativity threatens a safe and tenuous equilibrium, they will provide rationales for ending treatment. Often such patients are helped over a reality hurdle (change of job, birth of a child, et cetera) that overburdened their psychological balance. Once back on the track, they go their way. Just as often, these patients return to psychotherapy. In such instances, the therapist should view the therapy as having been interrupted rather than having been terminated. The beginning phase can stretch out over long periods of time, even years.

An artist in his twenties came to therapy seeking relief from severe sexual inhibition. Although handsome, socially skilled, and surrounded by many friends, he had managed to avoid sexual intimacy. As one might guess, the older he became, the more limiting this withdrawal made his friendships.

Ten months of psychotherapy ensued before he felt he was "finished." For the most part I had been warm, friendly, gentle, and nonconfrontational with this guilt-ridden and easily humiliated man. He had developed an admiring transference toward me and felt safe and protected in my office. He had some sexual relationships with women, surprisingly satisfying, but he was most captivated by a homosexual relationship. He had never had such an experience before. Although I suggested various areas of his life that might still have been only incompletely worked upon in treatment, he felt life beckoned more than therapy and he terminated (in my mind "interrupted"). He left an unpaid balance of about sixty-five dollars. I sent many bills, over a year or two, and then lost track of his address.

Almost nine years later he called for an appointment. He wished to "continue therapy." In the interim, he had been to at least two other therapists, spending several years with each. One was a woman, more a friend and social acquaintance than a therapist, and the other a stern and confrontational man. One was clearly his mother and the other a fair replica of his father. As for me, he stated that he always held fond memories of me, but was unclear as to why he hadn't returned to me, especially since he felt that the "batch" of therapy with me was useful. He returned with the same beginning-phase transference with which he had left. Our initial work, stretching over a year, consisted of helping him see how negative feelings about me had begun to surface when he left me the first time. Apparently, life had been kind enough to strengthen him to face less than happy thoughts about me and to continue analyzing the negative elements of the transference. And yes, he did pay those sixty-five owed dollars.

Beginning Treatment with the Severely Decompensated

When a patient has decompensated to a state where he or she is admitted to an inpatient service, the goal of the beginning phase of treatment is exceedingly clear. Such patients uniformly suffer from acute or chronic object loss, real or fantasied. They feel exceedingly vulnerable to rejection from others, and morbidly doubt their attractiveness as people. These findings are true across the spectrum of diagnoses. When we are able to penetrate the defensive veil of symptoms, and convey to such patients that we indeed have realistic concern, interest, and caring for their welfare, we will be taken into their world. Overwhelmingly, with inpatients, attachment is the primary goal (see Chapter 6).

The initial phase with inpatients and the multiple techniques that are recommended for treating them prove confusing to experienced clinicians as well as beginners. We observe many different styles and many different uses of personality in making contact with patients. Many seemingly disparate techniques seem to work. Many years ago, Dr. John Rosen developed the technique of "direct analysis." He played psychotic-like roles with patients. His becoming Lord and Master, God or Devil, was not unknown in his startling interviews with acutely psychotic patients. Just as startling was the technique of Elvin Semrad. Quite the reverse of Rosen, he was simple in comment, homespun, realistic, and he always took a back seat to the patient. Both therapists had remarkable success in reaching patients and compensating disorganized states of mind. Many other unusual and contrasting styles could be outlined.

What all these workers have in common is a depth of interest in their patients, an intense concern, and the wish to be involved. They keep knocking on the psychic door until they get an answer. They speak to the rejected elements of the patient, and finally make an attachment. Often this is on a psychotic basis, the only basis some patients have available. It does, however, allow the therapist into the patient's mind. Once this happens, provided the two continue working together, the possibility exists for the development of a clinical transference.

Decompensated patients are often emotionally wide open. They spill their psychic guts with intense, dreamlike revelations. During these periods there may be extraordinary discussion of psychodynamics, memories of the past and its relation to the present, and unusual forms of psychological insight. Without discouraging exploration and interpretation of fascinating psychotic presentations of psychodynamics, and without reducing its importance for the long-range goals of treatment, we must realize that the most important activity taking place early in treatment is that a dedicated therapist is listening. Attachment is fighting the regressive trend toward isolation and withdrawal. The patient's and the therapist's speech is a vehicle for attachment.

Another patient may attempt the same attachment through acting-out, which necessitates many hours of administrative activities for a therapist, or through uses of multiple psychopharmacologic agents. The bottom line is still the same: The patient is testing out the frail possibility that another person might be interested, is persistent, and will survive his or her distorted efforts at asking for help. If therapist and inpatient survive to the end of this psychological gauntlet, they will have earned a beginning to the treatment.

Transition to the Middle Phase

There are two factors that indicate that the beginning phase of treatment is over. One is the development of a clinical transfer-

ence. As outlined earlier, transference is the development toward the therapist of a persistent set of feelings, thoughts, and
attitudes that are relatively unchangeable. Simple reality testing
no longer modifies these feelings, and despite rational understanding of their irrationality, they persist. The second factor,
and perhaps the more important one, is the patient's realization
that the early fantasy that the therapist will magically provide
solutions to frustrations has not taken place. Dawning disappointment and frustration stimulate some return of early symptoms. Unpleasant feelings, stemming from the earliest days of
the patient's unhappiness, begin to surface and are directed toward the therapist. This is the advent of the negative transference. The honeymoon is over.

As variable as openings of treatment may be, infinitely legion
are the pathways that open up in the middle phase of treatment.
This is the period when attachment is deepened, understanding
attempted, and, most significant, the long process of working-
through (integration) takes place.

For the therapist, it is important not to surge ahead of the patient's capacity to apprehend and integrate the therapist's comments and interpretations. Sensitive attunement to the patient's
tolerance is essential for gauging the proper technical approach
to the transference and its leading resistances. One must be prepared to pull back and follow the patient's lead in handling the
anxiety created by shifting and changing lifelong attitudes and
defenses. We are the best therapists when we are lucky enough
to catch the patient's technical recommendations for good therapy, and have the good fortune and sense enough to follow
them.

> I once enjoyed a highly verbal beginning phase of treat-
> ment with a suicidal adolescent. Quite intelligent, charm-
> ing, and hungry for love, she responded with alert interest
> to my many clarifications and interpretations. I sensed that
> a portion of her remained secretive, but assumed that in
> time she would open up more.
>
> After about five months, the material began to dry up.
> She became increasingly silent, although outwardly polite
> and cordial. After several weeks of this tense interaction,

she finally blurted out that it was very difficult to be with me. She found my comments harsh, critical, and demanding. She did not know if she could tolerate this kind of scrutiny. The parental sources of this sharp negative transference were clear to me, but the patient found any comment of mine to this effect a form of useless commentary.

At a point when I felt at a loss to know how this state of affairs could be alleviated, the patient produced a small box, labelled "You can change life." With animated excitement, she exclaimed, "Dr. Roth, you must take a look at this!" She explained that it was a gift from her brother, only cost five dollars, and that it contained material and instructions for growing hybrid plants, creating different forms of life. The proper soil and nourishment were provided, and by creating the proper environment the plants would do the rest on their own.

Just as she was telling me how dead and hopeless things were, she was telling me that life and love are possible, something might grow if given a chance and the proper environment. Rather than make the slightest interpretation, I read the plant manual with her and discussed botany.

During the following session, she was quite communicative again and told me about an enormous pipeline that had been built in the Middle East over hostile and treacherous terrain. An engineer had staked his reputation on its success. He built this almost-thousand-mile pipeline, and when he finished and turned on the faucet, not a drop of water came out. He committed suicide. Two days later, the water came through. She emphasized how he had neglected to consider that despite his work and preparation, it would still take time for the water to come through the line, and he lacked the patience. I took these words to heart, and settled into a more languid pace of treatment.

In this case I had mistaken the extremely verbal initial phase of treatment for integrated understanding, when primarily what was occurring was the formation of a stable bond of trust and attachment. Fortunately, the patient was of a creative and communicative mind. Through displaced communication she caught my attention, when her withdrawal and anger failed to alter my techniques.

The case also demonstrates that during the initial phases of treatment (the beginning and the early middle phase), the transference must be allowed to flower without being analyzed to death. Unless the patient's feelings come to full fruition, there can be only intellectual experience of the transference. With this patient, the negative elements did not disappear with my reduction in activity; they remained, but were not excessively overwhelming. The slower pace allowed a more leisurely digestion of the process (and pain) of understanding.

The Triangle of Murder, Suicide, or Psychosis

One enormous barrier to entering the middle phase of treatment is the patient's terror of becoming murderous, suicidal, or psychotic. The deepening transference brings the patient to a psychological Bermuda Triangle, which offers only three intolerable options. Such terror occurs openly in those with egos vulnerable to the psychotic resolution of unbearable anxiety. It is also present, although more subtly, in borderline personalities, especially when "border" in these instances implies closeness to the psychotic border.

In our discussion of transference, I outlined the case of the young professor of medicine who was seriously suicidal and who improved remarkably in four months of intensive treatment. Although he saw me as a paragon of therapeutic virtue, he became paranoid and murderous toward another psychiatrist whose testimony might ruin him in divorce court. To avoid revealing our treatment in court, he felt forced to give me up, and ended his therapy abruptly. By this means he maintained his positive transference (and his compensation), and safely wished to murder an object he couldn't get his hands on. The basic ego vulnerabilities were not broached.

In the same section, I also referred to the young man who had multiple hypochondriacal symptoms and obsessions. When compensated, he felt that my office location was a source of virulent disease and psychosis. By keeping the psychosis located in me, he could walk off safely.

A third case in the transference discussion demonstrated how the barriers of murder, suicide, and psychosis are experienced, worked-through, and surmounted — the case of the patient who had become psychotic while a seminarian. The potential for murder, suicide, and psychosis arose as the transference recreated intolerable feelings toward his parents. The desire for, and terror of, a homosexual transference drove the patient into one or more feared states of the seemingly inescapable triangle. The patient was able to tolerate these fears, and he continued the middle phase of therapy.

Some patients break off treatment during the beginning phase, especially the honeymoon phase, before the transference induces these frightening states. They prefer a conservative, but safe, therapeutic outcome. Another group may become mired and regressively stuck for long periods at one angle of the triangle. Eventually the therapy is broken off in the early middle phase (which could last years), and compensation occurs at a distance from the feared object. Others, like the third patient just mentioned, are able to trust enough to experience this terror without complete crystallization of one of the three options. These patients, according to Zetzel (1958), have the requisite capacity to bear anxiety and depression or to develop it sufficiently during the therapeutic work. Such patients are able to move their therapeutic focus beyond the energy-draining terror of psychosis, murder, or suicide, and to consider elements of character structure that make them vulnerable to regression.

Three Technical Phases
of Therapy in Treating the Acutely Psychotic

The long-term treatment that begins with an acutely psychotic patient has an innovative course. First, the acute psychotic reaction must be attended to. Doing this requires hospitalizing the patient, possible psychopharmacology, milieu treatment, and perhaps work with the family. The therapist will need special techniques developed for penetrating the thick defensive webs of psychosis. These techniques, as mentioned earlier, vary with the style and personality of the therapist. The involved therapist carries out a great deal of activity during this stage.

When patients compensate, they typically enter a depressive phase (Roth 1969). Although patients may no longer be psychotic, they are mired in a deep and vegetative depression. Suicide becomes a special danger when psychotic defenses no longer drain off unbearable impulses. The therapist shifts from a technique that deals with the treatment of acute psychoses to one that more resembles that of severe, nonpsychotic depression.

The patient's processes of mourning are central in this phase of treatment. The therapist systematically pursues the losses that precipitated the psychosis. The patient's psychic pain is intense. Depression is the veil now used to screen off intolerable sadness. We constantly aid these patients to see that what formerly drove them crazy now makes them depressed. Not uncommonly, a patient will moan with desperation, "Let me be crazy again. Dear God, please! Anything is better than this." It is essential to point out to the patient that the depression is a sign of strength, increased tolerance to life's pains and challenges. And yet, we must go beyond the nothingness of depression to the pain of actual mourning.

Some patients, particularly people subject to recurrent bouts of increased psychosis, will show brief regressions from depression to psychosis. Mini-exercises in mourning may often recompensate the patient within the time span of an office visit. One lady, for example, would show up in my office with descriptions of black spots before her eyes, or reports of the black clouds that had followed her overhead right up to my office door. When we investigated the current status of her sense of object loss and were able to find the source, she would lose these psychotic trailers immediately. This source could be as simple as her husband's having left for a long business trip, or her mother-in-law's lording it over her and having cooked the Thanksgiving turkey. The ego that is prone to psychotic regression has an exquisite sensitivity to loss. And just as exquisite is its unerring ability to wall off such loss with a psychotic symptom.

The Danger of the Therapist's Narcissism

In this phase of treatment the attitude of the therapist toward mobilizing the patient is of central importance. If the patient is rushed, prodded, or pushed into getting on his or her feet, he or she is in great danger of regressive psychosis or suicide. Any therapeutic request or maneuver that seems more to answer a need of the therapist's narcissism than it does the specific need of the patient is doomed to failure. There will be great pressure on the therapist to mobilize the patient; it will come from the family, the hospital (if this stage occurs during an inpatient stay), and, ironically, from the patient, who will demand action from the therapist.

A keen therapeutic eye must always focus only on what the patient desires, never on suffocating conformity to the desires of others. Psychotic patients have usually spent their lives molding themselves to the wishes of others to maintain frictionless and safe relationships. As they compensate, the pathways to this old behavior are well laid out and seductive. One must keep close tabs on the recent expression of hidden conflicts of the acute psychosis, and not let patients waste their psychic effort. Patients must be reminded of what this episode is all about. The therapist, with timeless patience, must speak for the hidden portions of the patient: not always, but from time to time, as a reminder.

I cannot emphasize enough the enormous and limitless patience essential in this long phase of treatment. The patient often tries to cajole and nag the therapist into activity. Submitting is dangerous and usually results in the patient's regression. Semrad often referred to the stance of patients who in this phase were particularly neurasthenic as "studied ineptitude." This depressive phase may last from several months to about a year and a half.

Character Analysis and the Ego Prone to Psychosis

Should the two phases of acute psychosis and depression be sustained and worked-through, the therapist will be surprised at the new technical ground that is exposed. The last phase of treatment becomes the therapy of character and its defensive structure. The areas of character that are vulnerable to psychotic regression are studied: in particular, those that surround elements of separation anxiety, ego boundaries, differentiation of the self from objects, issues of basic trust, and sense of an independent self. In addition, usually many neurotic issues of competition of a romantic and professional nature will arise. These will funnel into the transference.

We must be especially careful not to deal with all issues as "pregenital" or "nurturing." Human beings, even those with a history of psychosis, are like symphony orchestras; the therapy is off balance if it follows a narrow focus. In this last phase, should we reflect back upon one's dealings with the patient during the acute psychotic phase and the early depression, one will feel almost as if a different person were in therapy. One's entire technique undergoes a degree of quantitative change that feels almost qualitative. The length and process of the treatment now follow lines of activity and development that resemble the treatment of neuroses more than those of psychoses. The patient's understanding, through transference interpretation, takes on increased importance.

If we follow this pattern of therapeutic stages, from acute psychosis to depression to treatment of neurotic character, an important discovery emerges. When the patient sees the same therapist during all three stages, both therapist and patient have a greater opportunity for continuity of work, and probably for success. Too often, a patient is treated during the acute psychosis by one therapist and then transferred to a second when compensation takes place. The first therapist was confronted by our active and vital patient who was caught in the wild throes of acute psychosis. Patients often demonstrate their woes in a compelling fashion during this period. The second therapist often meets a depressed, shut-off person, one who is going to remain so for a considerable period of time. This therapist does not have the advantage of the first one, who came to know the deeper and less defended side of the patient.

What all too frequently occurs next is that, with the shifting of the patient from the first therapist, neither the patient nor the second therapist can tolerate the other. The new therapist finds the patient inexplicable and often boring. In addition to the depressive phase of the illness, the patient is still suffering from rejection by the first therapist, and now he or she senses the distance of the new therapist. Neither person gains from such a shift.

At this point, patients frequently drop out of treatment entirely. We do not hear from them again until a new psychosis develops, and the whole sequence repeats itself.

It is important for the growth and development of both patient and therapist that they continue together throughout the stages of treatment. Only these two people can truly assess where the patient is coming from, and what goals are so desperately sought. The patient's initial attachment of the acute psychotic phase, usually won at a high psychological cost, is not easily transferred onto a new therapist.

The Middle Phase and Working-through

The vast bulk of transference interpretation and the long process of working-through, including living-through, comes during the middle phase of treatment. It is during this period that patients are most likely to experience despair, since they learn of the limitations of treatment as well as possibilities for unexpected change and exploration. How likely both may be is often indiscernible to patient and therapist alike. My own inclination is to give each patient all the time he or she requires and requests to work out this unknowable area of treatment. It is up to patients to discover which areas of their personalities have flexibility and which are immutable.

It is not unusual to have this period of treatment run into years. With patients who possess severe difficulties with separation, dependence, and basic trust, eight to ten years is not an unusual amount of time to be spent in this middle phase of treatment. When patients have reached a judgment about what is possible for themselves and what is not possible, and have found some degree of improved living through psychotherapy, they will begin to talk of termination.

Termination

With so much of the course of psychotherapy peppered with questions and doubts, it should come as no surprise that the question of termination is mired in its share of uncertainties. Even when we have evidence that therapy has achieved reasonable success, there is always a question of when to stop. We may have some bloom of assurance when we have witnessed the slow unfolding of a transference. We will have seen a period of induction, and will have felt satisfied that the transference varied and deepened as time proceeded. In particular, if we notice that when the patient expresses hostility it is expressed with great strength and persistence, we will feel reassured that we have encountered significant veins of troubling pain.

Unresolved negative transference accounts for a significant number of incomplete psychotherapies. Both patient and therapist have a disinclination to express and receive affects of hate. If the patient's expression of hatred as well as love has occurred in depth and for sustained periods of time, we will not feel very startled when he or she begins to discuss stray thoughts of finishing their work. During all such comments, I either remain interestedly silent or express some interest in the ideas. But I am not vigorous in my interest. I do not wish in the slightest to be seen as jumping at the first opportunity to put an end to this long and difficult therapeutic process. Indeed, at this stage, I am actually quite reticent, since I really don't know when the correct time for termination is. Certainly, I make no suggestion about actually terminating. I try to maintain an atmosphere of "Termination may well be what's best for you, but I don't know. As always, we shall depend on your thoughts and judgment, as you think about this over time."

Such floating preoccupations about termination will eventually (in several weeks or months) evolve into a more prolonged discussion by the patient about leaving.

"I think I have a recognition of how complex life is . . . or at least what I wished to accomplish versus what I have accomplished, or what I can do about it in therapy. I notice many ways in which I am much better and less miserable and tormented than I used to be. . . . I used to feel like a helpless, wounded animal. . . . I don't feel panic at difficulty now. I still have many goals, but I feel I can continue to work on them. . . . I will miss the lack of criticism here. It really frees me up to think. I have to try and do more of that on my own. Sometimes, in the past, I've wanted to leave you when you were too frustrating, wouldn't give me what I wanted. I often feel so much on my own, I get stuck on that. It's not so much *in* me as I want it to be, and I still have to work on that. . . . [The patient then reported a dream in which a figure with my characteristics made many mistakes.] I'm trying to see you as not perfect . . . it's a relief to think of you as human. You can have troubles just like me. I'm not such a freak, and we are more equal. . . . In a way, it's hard for me to admit that things are good for me; I feel the old guilt and depression. Also, admitting to you that I feel good reminds me that I could never admit that to my father. I was afraid he'd stop caring, if I was independent. That's what I've often felt with you . . . and I don't have to have my mother's miseries to show her that I love her, and won't abandon her. . . . I'm also pleased that I don't feel black rage toward you if I can't solve a problem here. What I feel is more like regret, or a sadness . . . it makes me feel that my decision to terminate isn't retaliatory . . . but, can I explore things on my own when I have challenges after I leave? [I said: There will always be challenges in life. It never ends.] Exactly! I thought for a long time that I was supposed to reach Nirvana here . . . everything would be fixed for all time. . . . That is impossible as long as someone is alive, and who would want it really? . . . I've been thinking of setting an exact date for termination. And I'd like you not to treat this as just something for further exploration!"

Since this therapy had gone on for nearly six years, and many elements of transference had developed slowly and been expressed intensely, I felt that the patient's judgment on this matter was therapeutically sound. We had indeed worked on many painful issues, and although, like the patient, I wished we could resolve more, the more realistic approach was to follow his move toward independence. He seemed during this period to show a flexibility in comparing irrational feelings toward me, their counterpart in his current life, and some idea of where they had originated in the past. Perception of me in a more realistic, nontransferential fashion, was also evident to some degree. Another feature of the terminal phase is the emergence of the therapist from the cocoon of transference into a more real figure. The patient has less immediate need of the transference object for gratification, and the transference loosens its grip upon the patient. A realistic view of the therapist (nontransference) is most evident to the patient at the very beginning of treatment (before clinical transference takes place), and toward termination, when the major transference elements have succumbed to some rational interpretation. In the case just cited, thoughts of terminating had floated into the patient's sessions for several months. Thus, these ideas did not seem like a manifest cover for some very recent hostility.

Once I have settled in my mind that termination is appropriate, setting a date is extremely important. Until a specific time is fixed, the wheels of the terminal mourning process do not click into gear. Many patients, after months of talking about termination, become gripped by a different reality when a date is settled. Although the analogy is farfetched, what comes to mind is the famous comment of Samuel Johnson: "When a man knows he is to be hanged in a fortnight, it concentrates his mind wonderfully." Time pressure brings out the issues of mourning. Loss is in the air, and the patient's response will be a combination of how greatly the original symptoms were brought about by object loss, how much this loss was resolved during treatment, the extent to which real-life replacements have been found, and the steadiness of the therapist in not losing sight of the importance of the patient's loss. How much time should be allotted to this process cannot be stated in precise terms, but at least one to two months for each year of therapy is usually in order.

Many patients will become anxious for fear they will have no opportunity to change their minds should they decide to. It is best to explore this anxiety and interpret it, but to stick to the termination date. It is usually the exception, rather than the rule, to have to extend the termination date, or to cancel it completely. The necessity to do so becomes evident if the patient has such marked deterioration outside the hour that it is clear he is in immediate, and continued, need of therapeutic attention. These cases arise, more often than not, when treatment hasn't been given a thorough and adequate trial. They are not usually cases where many years of earnest collaboration have taken place.

It is not unusual to have some recurrence of the original symptoms during the termination. This gives the therapeutic pair a final opportunity to run quickly through the relevant transference issues and to work-through in a manner that has taken place before. This whole process usually takes place on a smaller scale and during a shorter time period than it did in the original therapy. Not all patients follow this course.

A deepening and intense attention on the patient's part to the therapeutic work is seen rather consistently. Material that hadn't surfaced in the past may come to the fore. In the famous case of the Wolf Man, it was only when Freud, out of exasperation, set a termination date, that the Wolf Man suddenly picked up therapeutic speed. In the last year of the analysis much of the richest material was brought forth. In Chapter 12, we will note how dreams of this period will comment on work done, or not done, during the therapy. The dreams provide a rich source of sharp visual imagery depicting summations of the therapeutic work.

Some therapists describe very conscious attempts to shift and change their approach in the terminal phase. In tune with the patient's attempt to resolve transference feelings, they are freer with facts about their lives, are easier in technique, and in a sense loosen their therapeutic grip upon the patient. They wish the patient to finish the treatment with a clear sense of equality.

Other therapists are equally firm about maintaining their neutrality and professional stance during the whole of the termination phase. I must confess that I personally follow neither line in any strict or organized fashion. Once again, my behavior seems to accord with what each patient's needs and tendencies appear to draw out of me. With some people I am virtually the same to the very end. Something in their behavior leads me to feel that this consistency is most beneficial, and safest, for them. In addition, it preserves the possibility of my being their future therapist; I have not lost my special role. Perhaps this is what dictates my stance: a sense that I will be needed again. I certainly do assure all my patients that although we are terminating, they should feel free, should they so wish, to consult me later. Indeed, if the patient does not have this notion, I usually want to know why.

Even when we have spent many years with a patient, have engaged in a long terminal phase, and think all has happened that could happen, we actually never know. For example:

> Through close to six years of intensive treatment, a woman seemed to try to work at therapy with earnestness. She was as revealing as she could be, many anxieties and symptoms had remitted, but her termination decision was made primarily because she felt herself basically unchangeable. After so many years of work, considering that she was in no overt agony — indeed, had many blessings in life — I explored her reasons, but did not basically challenge them. The termination was not marked by any basic mourning nor deep feelings of loss.

> About two years later, this woman returned to me. During the interim she had separated from her husband and fallen deeply and passionately in love with a man who seemed quite appropriate. Entirely startling was her loss of phobias and certain inhibitions that we had tried to work on for years.

> She confessed to me that she felt that I was opposed to her divorcing her husband and, for that reason, subliminally, had always felt the therapy wasn't for her. I protested that I had made interpretations along those lines, but that she had always ignored these comments. The patient laughed, but could not recall I had said these things. I concluded that it was important, for reasons relating to her

overprotective parents, that she could leave her husband only if she did it entirely on her own. However, it now seemed possible to discuss these things. She seemed more open and available than before, and our therapeutic work resumed for about another year and a half.

This woman had never really terminated with me the first time. She quite unconsciously was taking a "break" from treatment. During this time she wished to be on her own (a reliving of adolescence), and could then return for a more adult collaboration. The next time we ceased treatment, her response to my loss reflected actual loss, and involved mourning.

This patient is still an example of incomplete termination. Even since the second termination, she consults me from time to time, and in this sense may never actually terminate. I remain an ongoing consultant whose presence seems to free up her noncritical thinking and allow her to make independent decisions. These visits take place a few times a year or over gaps of more than a year. With great efficiency, she capitalizes on our past work together. This is a useful pattern for a therapeutic pair. Much work goes into long-term psychotherapeutic work. Life is complex, often cruel in its twists of fate, and one is fortunate to have a reliable therapist to whom to air confused thoughts and painful feelings. At the same time, we therapists must be prepared for therapies that go well, for patients from whom we never – except for a few letters to "catch us up" – hear from again. It is hard to let go completely; we are naturally left wondering what happened after therapy.

Consistency and Variation

The clinical transference is like a flower, which has its beginning bud, a period of mature blossoming, and a time of sad loss of fragrance and petals. There is no end of variation to nature's offerings of different flowers, nor to the special qualities of an individual transference. I have outlined the stages above not to limit the unusual, individual possibilities of each therapy, but to

suggest an overall framework. Keeping an eye on the human relatedness that is both the source of our therapeutic inquiry and
the key to its success keeps us from being distracted by the shifting sands of clinical signs and symptoms.

11

Dreams

The Interpretation of Dreams . . . *contains, even according to my present-day judgement, the most valuable of all the discoveries it has been my good fortune to make. Insight such as this falls to one's lot but once in a lifetime.*
Sigmund Freud, The Interpretation of Dreams, 3rd. ed. (1931)

Dreams are very special. In one deftly drawn image they may offer commentary on past, present, and transferential life. Through dreams, the most nonliterary, unpoetic people produce mythic narratives, which are often so basic to human nature that they transcend the individual's concerns and reveal universal truths. Hazy and vague motives leap to life and are given form and hallucinatory substance. In looseness and freedom of expression, dream life illustrates what is expected of the patient within the daytime therapeutic hour: allowing the forbidden into awareness, and, to some degree, observing this process with a noninterfering eye. Unless there is countertransference from the therapist, a patient who never reports dreams is usually quietly resistant to the influence of the treatment or is massively repressed, and similarly immune. The uses of dreams within psychotherapy touch upon virtually all technical and theoretical issues of psychotherapy. A therapist who does not have a facility with this basic and daily unconscious communication center is severely hampered as an analytic psychotherapist.

Dream Imagery

A startling feature of dreams is their ability to translate ideas into visual images. A hidden thought, the latent content, is given concrete form in the manifest content of the dream.

A young man dreams of his father standing on the edge of a bathtub, naked, with an enormous and oversized penis. This feels like a totally new sight.

The dreamer states: "I now realize what a big schmuck my father is!"

A woman dreams she climbs up to the chimney of a house. She feels very high above the ground, and notices adolescents far below. They are from her past schooldays. She would like to get to them but finds she cannot get down.

The dreamer, adept at turning visual imagery into words, says: "When I was in high school, I became stuck up, felt I was above everyone else, and later, when I felt differently, I didn't know how to change, how to get out of my position."

The capacity to translate visual imagery varies from patient to patient and therapist to therapist. Some are naturally adept at such translation. Others may find different routes to the underlying meaning of a dream (we shall discuss these). However, keen attention to the pictures described by patients will aid therapists in comprehending the psychological drama staged by each patient. Freud likened the visual quality of dream-talk to Egyptian hieroglyphics, which dramatized language. As a patient recounts a dream, it is useful for the therapist to try to visualize the reported images in order to aid the therapist in placing him- or herself within the dreamscape. Naturally, trying to do this may lead to some questions. If a road is mentioned, how are we to know if the road we imagine is similar to the road the patient has in mind? At a later point, after the presentation of the dream, and during discussion of its interpretation, we can ask for further details of the images. In this process of visual clarification, the report of the dream experience broadens. To some extent, dreams will use the other senses to express the disguised latent thoughts, but visualization will predominate.

Between Freud's psychological genius and his propensity to think in visual terms there was a synergism that illuminated dream life for him. An examination of Freud's writing will reveal how often he resorts to visual imagery to express his thoughts. "Cathexis" is described as the movement of an army, with forward troops and others placed behind and holding the rear positions. When he gives the instructions for free association, he suggests that patients imagine themselves sitting by a window in a moving train. Next to them is a person who cannot see the window and is depending upon them to describe exactly what they see on the landscape. This visual metaphorical translation is a central feature of the expression and disguising nature of the dream-work.

The Hallucinatory Quality

Another important element of dream life is its hallucinatory quality, the experience of reality. This varies with the level and depth of dreaming regression. Some dreams are so real that we are startled to find ourselves awakening, amazed (at times relieved) that "it was just a dream." Other dreams maintain a watchful observing ego quality, and we can notice ourselves or the dream in ongoing action. Dream life is not turned completely on or off; it has various levels of waking ego available to it. In this aspect, it differs from the waking state. We often find ourselves unaware of our surroundings, such as when we drive a car and wonder how so much distance had gone by without our noticing.

The hallucinatory quality is important in distinguishing sleeping dreams from daydreaming. In daydreaming, although unconscious forces are unleashed, one still has significant conscious control of one's thoughts. More important, daydreams always remain at the psychological level of thought, rather than hallucinatory experience.

The hallucinatory quality of dreams combines with the regressive element to provide important clinical data. The dream takes one back to former states of existence, not just as thoughtful memories, but as powerful experiences. When dreams are combined with a return to former ways of thinking, we are aided greatly in reconstructing past influences on present life.

A woman dreamed that she was sitting at a round table with her mother and grandmother. Fluid was dripping on the table from above. The patient was frightened, puzzled, and made anxious by this fluid. She tried to engage her mother and grandmother in conversation about this, but they ignored her and behaved as if nothing were happening. They became irritable if she persisted. So, still frightened, she kept her fears to herself. She felt alone and helpless.

The dream represented the onset of menstruation, which began quite early in her life. Her mother ignored her and did not educate her, and the patient was frightened and withdrawn in reaction to this upsetting physiological event. The mother's tendency to ignore her in times of the patient's need had left her with great conflicts over dependency. These conflicts maintained her depressive tendencies and sense of aloneness.

In therapy, this dream allowed vivid recall of a time of life she had forgotten. Its affectual hallucinatory quality threw the patient back twenty-five years in time, to feel what she had felt then, and sense its influence in the present.

Condensation, Displacement, and Universal Symbols

The dream has a remarkable capacity for shorthand. Intense and complicated experiences of life are concentrated in symbolic expression. Condensation accounts for one's experiencing some dreams as taking place over long periods of time, when the actual dreaming time may have been short. Symbols, as they are used in dreams, are unconscious mechanisms that hide reference not only to past experience but also to painful affects. Unlocking the meaning of symbols unleashes both memory and frustrated longing as well. Patients show great resistance to complete interpretation of a condensed dream symbol. A patient will usually manage to unlock only those elements that the ego has been prepared to tolerate. However, it is not necessary to bludgeon the patient into accepting a complete interpretation; in fact, it is not usually possible to do so. At rare times, the events of therapy coincide to make possible the unlocking, in a single session, of enormous condensation within one dream.

A woman dreamed that she went to an apartment with an attractive man. Once inside, he turned to her and said, "Il faut parler francais."

In recounting the dream, the patient felt stunned by the implications of this phrase. The English translation was "It is necessary to speak French." The French language gave great pleasure to her. She had felt freed up during a stay in France. The visit liberated her from her dominating mother. Her emotional side came out in French. Indeed, she likened psychotherapy with me to speaking in French. I was teaching her a language for freedom.

"Il faut" means "It is necessary." This phrase related to all the obsessional "shoulds" of her nature, her fearful and rule-bound self. The "faut" also sounded like "faux" and recalled the false elegance of her family. "Il faut parler," when shortened, was "Il faut pa-," a "faux pas," a social mistake. The extreme social strictures of her family interfered with her enjoyment of life, particularly romantically. "Faux pas" reminded her of a verbal slip she had made in conversation with a friend, which had homosexual implications.

French returned her to her French-speaking aunt, her good-mother substitute, and to the rivalry with her own mother. Many memories came up in relation to this competition. From many men she wished gratifications designed to make up for maternal deprivations. The man in the dream was offering her what she had missed from her mother, and this was what she expected from me in therapy. The mother hated for the patient to speak French: it meant independence and choosing other models for life.

Condensation amalgamates multiple wishes. The man in the dream was attractive (he had features of several men she longed for), spoke French (like a favorite woman relative of the past, and like herself), and performed a function like me (encouraged her emotional freedom and sexuality). The fusion of past life, current life, and therapeutic life becomes palpable, vivid, and nontheoretical when the dream disguise is dissected. The extraordinary complexity of our feelings toward others is dramatized in a dream's condensation. Figure A looks like person B, talks like C, feels like D, and so on, all at the same time.

The latent dream thoughts are disguised not only by visualization, hallucination, and condensation, but also by displacement (with reversal) and the use of universal symbols.

A woman dreams of reading a book about German diplomacy of the eighteenth century. She feels sexually aroused as if it were a romantic novel.

Coming out of her history class, she had struck up a conversation with a young man who had attracted her. She was drawn to his ease, his polite and tactful manner (diplomatic). Her mind was filled with sexual fantasies about him. Certain conflicts over her sexual feelings caused a displacement from the young man to a disguised idea, represented in the dream by arousal from reading.

The universal symbols that appear in dreams are actually few in number and relate to consistent life experiences that are common to all people. These symbols relate to basic bodily sensations and perceptions, sexual feelings, and experiences of early childhood. Giants, for example, are usually a reference to our parents as we experienced them while we were still quite small. Similarly, kings and queens refer to fathers and mothers. Houses and their insides refer to bodily feelings. Long projectile images often have phallic meanings, while containers such as purses often refer to internal female organs. Dreams of flying, common in adolescent boys, refer to erections. Rhythmic activities often concern masturbation, and the climbing of stairs to sexual intercourse. Large bodies of water such as lakes or oceans often refer to early merging experiences, most frequently maternal.

These symbols do not explain dreams. They are merely reference points, guideposts to the themes and preoccupations of the dream. They are hints for patient and therapist. It still remains for patients to place such symbols into perspective with the rest of their associations, the day residue, and the current focus of psychotherapy.

Universal symbols, along with condensation, displacement, misleading hallucinatory experience, and visual translation of latent ideas, contribute to the disguised nature of dreams. The endless variations of these processes provide a dense and mysterious symbolic drama. In therapy, we open up bits and pieces of these processes – that is all. It is the exception, rather than the rule, to interpret amply the multiple meanings of a dream. In a sense, an entire completed treatment is such an interpretation.

The Special Role of Affect

The primary process of the dream-work (condensation, displacement, concrete metaphor) has an infinite capacity to deal with ideas. Rarely is the same idea dealt with in exactly the same manner in two dreams. Even in recurrent dreams there is some variation. Affect follows a different course.

Dreams are limited in their capacity to disguise affect. Affect may be present, absent, enhanced, diminished, or reversed (for example, hysterical disgust rather than sexual arousal). Apart from these maneuvers, the dream is helpless to disguise affect. This is important clinically: affect always refers to some real emotional experience! In the dark mystery of the dream, affect is the beacon that brings the light of reality into the world of fantasy.

A woman reported a long and richly complex dream involving two other women. One of these women slept in a bed with her and in the dream the patient found herself being masturbated by her. Although it felt good, she did not like this woman. Her mother and a man were also in the dream, which had a long narrative line.

Attempts to interpret this long dream did not get very far. Finally, I returned to the affect of "it felt good." The patient stirred into animated thoughtfulness. "It felt good" was clearly the feeling she got when she herself masturbated. This affect aroused additional feelings of frustration with women, originating with her mother and now felt in the transference. The guiding tidal wave of affect now flowed back over the dream story and images. With this affectual backdrop the patient could now relate the dream women to maternal and feminine conflicts as well as to the transference.

It often happens that a patient will report that he or she has dreamed, but draws a blank about any content. At times, inquiry as to the affect experienced will reveal that the patient remembers this aspect of the dream. Even if it isn't recalled, asking whether it was "a good feeling" or "a bad feeling" will draw forth an answer. We can then suggest further, "As you recall this feeling, what comes to mind?" For clinical purposes, it does not matter if the dream content is brought to light in this manner. What we are interested in is the most pressing element of the patient's preoccupations. The affect is the best representative of this state of mind.

Day Residue

As a historical document, the dream is not only a repository of the distant past but also an up-to-the-minute recorder of current events. In particular, it has a penchant for including events of the preceding twenty-four to forty-eight hours. We call this material the day residue. It is extremely important for several reasons. First, it allows us a glimpse of the most immediate and pressing concerns of the patient. In pragmatic terms, the past is important only insofar as it explains the present. After all, this is what the patient comes to treatment for: aid with daily living. The day residue focuses on central conflicts stimulated by events of the day. It is a clinical magnet that pulls our judgment toward choices for therapeutic attention.

A woman had a long complicated dream that took place at a party. She knew her husband was there but never could find him, and at times she decided he really wasn't there. She felt frustrated, and she was angry with the host for having such a large crowd of people. She kept her frustration to herself, since the host was a friend and she didn't want to hurt her.

The patient had actually been to a crowded party with her husband. She hadn't lost him physically, but she had felt his distance all night. This was the trouble with the whole marriage: he seemed to come and go psychologically. Her keeping feelings away from the host was displaced from keeping them from her husband. She liked her husband as a companion, as a friend, and she dreaded hurting his feelings by informing him that she doubted the marriage was viable.

Latching onto the day residue is important from a clinical point of view. We are always striving to be at the leading edge of the patient's awareness and experience. When we find ourselves near to these, our comments will be directed close to the immediate concern of the patient. We can be both comprehensible and empathic. Like a plant with hidden roots and a distant source of nourishment — its visible portion external to the earth — the patient's unconscious strivings are most evident in the day residue. The final common terminus of our past history is our life as we live it today. The dream uniquely teases out the myriad facts of everyday life and puts them into a central set of tightly knit themes that best express our current preoccupations.

Among those preoccupations that most interest the therapist is the transference. At a certain point in treatment, as described in our earlier discussion, a clinical transference crystallizes. When the therapist takes on such importance for the patient, very often the therapist and therapy hour itself become a central feature of the day residue. The patient often thinks of the therapist and the therapy. When a patient is seen regularly in intensive psychotherapy, after about a year almost all dreams contain some level of transference communication.

Dreams as Commentary on Psychotherapy

Even early on, the patient's dreams will express many feelings about the commencement of treatment of which the patient may have not been fully aware or may have been inhibited in expressing.

A man in the first month of treatment dreams that he has taken a train that he thought made all the local stops. He discovers it is an express, is frightened at its increasing speed, and fears he will miss his stop. He cannot find the conductor, who is busy with other passengers.

Here I gently suggested that the patient feared I would move too fast in therapy. I would take him into psychological places before he was ready for them, and he feared losing control of the pace. He was the oldest in his family and was indeed unable to get his mother's attention, which was taken up by other brothers and sisters.

A woman after her first week of therapy dreamed that she was very small and within a square of an ice cube tray. The water was cold and beginning to freeze. She was trying to climb up the side and she kept sliding down. She felt panicked and frightened.

This dream was helpful in getting quickly to this woman's fears of isolation and abandonment, and of my being cold and humiliating and freezing her into a rigid personality. Consciously, the patient had felt eager for treatment, and enthusiastic about commencing. The dream helped us be aware of her fear of the therapist's acting like her mother: cold, humiliating, and unreceptive to personality differences.

Early dreams often represent anxieties and wishes about treatment. The impact of beginning psychotherapy is enormous and stimulates many levels of impulse life. As important day residue, it is often strongly represented in early dreams. Some common images are *forms of travel* – long journeys on trains, planes, cars, buses, or boats – going from one place to another as representing an expectation of psychological change from one state to another; *forms of storage* – museums, attics, trunks, abandoned houses – all used to represent the past and what one has kept alive in some dusty corner of the mind; *sources of complete gratification* – amusement parks, movies, theatres, playgrounds, sports activities – suggesting places where many infantile (early) impulses are acceptable and satisfied; *the taboo* – entering strange rooms, buildings, and places, foreign countries, brothels, bathrooms – focusing on the inhibition against the hidden impulse that seeks gratification in treatment.

The dream has endless capacity to represent the patient's ideas about treatment, and the above is but a brief indication of some forms of dream representation seen at the beginning of treatment. Mentioning these may help alert the therapist to anxieties somewhat near to a patient's consciousness.

Opening the Therapeutic Door to the Unconscious

In these few examples, the reader will note that comments made relate to the manifest content of the dream: that is, the dream as it is reported by the patient. There has not been an excessive emphasis here on the latent thought, the hypothetical ideas and impulses that underlay the manifest images of the dream. Often in the beginning of treatment, what the patient will primarily see is how the dream represents treatment, for what is ahead is a conscious concern, and patients comment as much. If they do not, a simple suggestion that the dream might express some feelings about commencing treatment will usually allow the patient to begin to talk about the dream material. Generally, in the early stages of therapy it doesn't help to be excessively detailed in the study of a dream. Detailed dream study takes the therapist to deep material, which will, at the beginning of treatment, be understood intellectually rather than affectually, and most certainly will not be integrated.

It is important, however, to make some comment to the patient on these early dreams, which usually indicate a patient's willingness to unleash his unconscious to the therapist. The dream is a stark and concentrated dose of unconscious material. Even if we haven't the vaguest idea what the dream might mean, since we don't know the patient at all well, it is essential to say at least that much. We can briefly indicate that dreams are important material to discuss, that, say, this one remains mysterious for the moment, but that perhaps when we know more we can come back to it. Or we may indicate that the material will probably be reintroduced in some later dream. If we say nothing, however, the patient preconsciously or unconsciously feels that the therapist is not interested in dreams or irrational thinking. Early dreams that are communicated to the therapist serve to test the patient's receptivity to the unconscious.

When I make these recommendations to therapists, I am often asked, "Isn't this too much suggestion to the patient to produce dreams?" It is certainly suggestion, but I doubt whether it is too much. A great deal of psychotherapy is suggestion. Freud was the first to point this out and he reiterated it many times. He referred to the suggestion induced by the transference love; the patient feels that by enduring the discomforts of treatment, he or she will achieve the gratification of transference love. However, I am referring to even simpler forms of suggestion. We suggest that it is helpful if patients tell us what is on their minds, that they come to sessions regularly, tell us fantasies, daydreams, and feelings they may have about us. In the early stages of treatment, when we often talk about what the patient's role is, we can use part of this conversation to suggest simply that dreams are important and bringing them into treatment for discussion has proved helpful in other cases. Freud did this regularly.

In fact, although their extreme view neglected ego psychology and the analysis of defenses, the early psychoanalysts felt that psychoanalysis was primarily the analysis of dreams. In the early view, it was highly questionable whether a person could be successfully treated if he or she did not dream. In the therapeutic regression, one could examine forbidden and conflicted impulses as they became enlarged, emphasized, and visible. The deepest source of such evidence was the sustained nightly regression in dream life. Here primary process was king and ran rampant. The disguises in the dream, and the conscious response to the dream, revealed the adaptive and defensive ego side of personality. Through this back-and-forth focus, treatment could engage the whole personality.

There is much to be learned from the overemphasis on dream life in the first generation of psychoanalysts. For Freud, dream life was "bedrock." Whenever doubt and confusion assailed him, a correct dream interpretation restored his certainty. The early analysts used dreams the way a qualitative chemist uses color to indicate the unseen actions of molecular forces. If the dream did not corroborate, or if it refuted the therapist's clinical impressions, the therapist was on the wrong track. The uses of dreams were endless: diagnosis, prognosis, evaluating the effect of interpretations, revealing past history, gauging current conflicts through the day residue, tracking the development and stage of the transference, observing shifts in personality structure, and following the process of termination.

Diagnosis

Although it is usually impossible to diagnose a personality through one dream, a series of dreams over a period of time will often reveal consistent features.

About six months into treatment a woman complained that therapy wasn't helping her. She felt anxious and depressed and found me remote and inactive. It was hard to tell if she was regressing in too profound a manner or if this was the initial stage of an expected negative transference. Over several weeks she described dreams of the following nature: she is walking downtown in the city, the sidewalk collapses, and a large building crashes down on her; an atomic bomb hits the city, people are slaughtered and maimed, she is the only survivor; she is sitting in a car, it burns and begins to burn her, she sees her skin blacken and char, a woman outside is watching but does nothing to help her.

These dreams, accompanied by terrifying affect, showed a depth of anxiety and morbid fear which was not being provided through words in our sessions. I changed my technique to a more active, visible, and supportive one. This conversion helped the patient endure the pains evoked by the transference.

It is important to emphasize that, normally, one dream alone will be insufficient to make a holistic diagnosis of a mental state. Since we are all capable of remarkable regression in dreams, any single dream of a healthy person may be indistinguishable from that of a psychotic. This is especially true if that person is undergoing unusual stress such as the death of a loved one, a broken romance, moving to a new home, or any other normal life crisis.

For example, a young doctor told me that the night before his internship began, he dreamed he was in medical school again taking his national board exam. He did not understand the questions and he felt terrified that he was unprepared. He left the room to go to the library, lost his way, and felt totally alone and helpless. He awoke with much anxiety. This is a typical examination dream. In fact, in medical school he had been outstanding, always prepared, and had done well on examinations. This dream was intended to reassure the dreamer: Just as there was no reason to fear a poor outcome in medical school, so too you will do well in your internship. The isolation and aloneness (a state often found in dreams of psychotic patients) in this instance signalled the reverse – an ability to utilize one's surroundings and trust the environment.

Prognosis

An example of the prognostic value of dreams was given in the therapeutic history of Freud's famous patient, the Wolf Man. The Wolf Man's original childhood dream revealed an open window from which wolves in a tree looked in on the terror-stricken child. The landscape was wintry and bleak. When Freud developed cancer and could not see the Wolf Man again when reconsulted several years after termination, he referred him to Dr. Ruth Mack-Brunswick. During the treatment the Wolf Man became psychotically paranoid, and Dr. Mack-Brunswick feared for her life and Freud's; the Wolf Man was threatening to kill them both. At this point he had a new and clarified version of his old dream. The scene changed to a summer landscape, the frightening wolves were gone, and the branches of the trees intertwined in a soft, loving embrace. Correctly, Dr. Mack-Brunswick took this dream to mean that the patient had worked through central conflicts, and shortly this outcome would be seen more overtly. After a brief further period of disorganization, he began to recompensate. Prognostic features of a dream are often clearest when they reflect changes in recurrent dreams.

Assessing Therapeutic Change

Changes in recurrent dreams provide evidence for enduring and substantial changes in the structure of the personality.

A young man who was almost schizoid in his social relations began treatment, stating that his dreams were puzzling. There were no people in them, and their meaning eluded him, although many painful feelings appeared in the dreams. After the transference had been established, about a year later, he was surprised to find that there were people in his dreams. After a few more years he was stunned to realize he knew who these people were and could begin to talk about them. At this point his life had changed remarkably and his social involvements were restored to a level he had obtained earlier in life.

A woman described disturbing dreams in which there were no doors or walls in apartments where she was living. People seemed to roam freely without any discretion. She suffered from guilty symbiosis to a very disturbed mother. When she had moved to clearer differentiation from her mother, the dreams shifted. Doors appeared; there were clear walls and boundaries in the dwellings of her dreams.

In one very late dream, she had an apartment in one part of town, and her mother had one in another. She could not ever recall having previously had such a dream.

Belief in the Unconscious

Dreaming not only provides the therapist with corroboration from the patient's unconscious; it usually does the same for the patient. Despite education and cultural advancement, society retains its belief in the mystical validity of dreams. Many people take therapeutic progress more seriously when they find a change in their dreams. The dreams of very rigid, seemingly unimaginative obsessional people provide them with important data. One man complained to me that he was hopeless. He felt rigid and unemotional, but gradually became convinced that there was actually a viable, interesting person buried beneath all his stuffed-shirt obsessionality. With dreams as irrefutable evidence, I could then demonstrate how in waking life he fended off thoughts and feelings that erupted at night.

Assessing Termination

Dreams that occur around the period of termination are especially powerful. They often not only indicate successes in treatment, but also herald failures and dissatisfactions.

Toward the end of therapy a woman dreamed that she had a penis on the top of her head. It disturbed others, but she seemed not to notice it.

This woman was telling me that she still had a character disorder. Unusual aspects of her personality bothered others, but still didn't bother her. Several years later this patient returned to therapy to continue work on this problem.

A woman who was stopping therapy for "external" reasons (she had to move to join her lover) took a nap prior to her last session. She dreamed that she owed me money and that she missed her last session.

Indeed, she came late for the last session, and the check she wrote me bounced. An expensive lesson in dream interpretation!

After a joint decision is made to terminate and a date is set, the next dreams will indicate the patient's unconscious judgment about the decision.

> A man who usually dreamed of being pursued and victimized dreamed, after deciding to terminate, that he was a swashbuckling pirate. Freely commanding the high seas, he felt adventurous and master of his own fate.

> A woman had recurrent dreams throughout therapy of being unable to get into houses, castles, and homes. During the period of termination she gained entry, but could not find an exit. During the last weeks of treatment she began to find ways of not only getting in and exploring, but also of finding an exit.

The affects associated with such *resolution* dreams are of exultation, relief, and well-being.

If a treatment has been long, many dreams at termination will deal with themes of loss and abandonment, whether the treatment was successful or not. These become useful if the patient consciously denies loss, but will also facilitate grieving in the patient who is conscious of the impact of termination. These dreams rush past history to amalgamate past losses with the present one.

> A man dreamed of looking through a window and seeing his brother across the way in a large apartment. There were many empty rooms. The empty rooms symbolized all the dead members of his family. Now he was left with just one living brother, from whom he felt distant.

> Terminating was threatening to place me in the position of the distant brother, leaving him a lonely observer, outside of life (the apartment). This was how he felt after the multiple deaths in his family.

Such sadness of dream life thrusts patient and therapist into the childhood fears that are reawakened by impending loss.

The State of the Transference and Its Relation to the Past

The most relevant desires and conflicts of the past are eventually funneled into the person of the therapist. The past events and motives — greatly condensed — that are embedded in the transference are vividly demonstrated in the fantastical nature of the patient's dream life. The therapist and the patient go to the movies as it were, and get a chance to jointly view their mutual drama.

A woman who was often confused about her feelings toward me had the following two dreams: (1) She was exposing her vagina to an obstetrician-gynecologist. It was huge and overwhelming. (2) Her head nurse was working at a customs booth, making a chocolate cake. The patient stood by, watching.

There is a special structure in paired dreams. What is latent (the hidden thoughts) in the first is manifest in the second. And what is manifest in the first is latent in the second. The wish to be admired for sexual reasons in the first dream hides a different exhibitionist wish evidenced in the second. Behind the sexualization toward a father figure of the first dream is a hidden maternal figure, the cakemaker. The patient's associations (over many sessions) to these dreams were with her mother's multiple births. The patient was the oldest of ten children. Her childhood was spent on the sidelines. The mother's attention was devoted to each succeeding child. The patient spent many hours watching the mother change diapers (the chocolate cake) and powdering her brothers and sisters. She wanted the same attention and care from her mother, her "observant" attentions, but she had to be content to stand and watch. Later, she became a substitute mother, and never had a chance to be the cared-for child.

Exposing the vagina to me expressed the frustration of the little girl who watched her mother powdering, pampering, patting, and caring for the "bottoms" of her siblings. Chocolate cake was equated with the many bowel movements she observed her mother attending to with her siblings, who were like crowds of people at a customs booth.

The frustrations of the child of the past whose feelings still lingered in the present were evident in the transference. As well as sexual longings, there were wishes to be the apple of my eye and have me just watch her, admire her, and give her a chance to be the center of attention. The patient had been consciously embarrassed by her "childish" longings toward me. It was more comfortable to think of me purely sexually. The dream allowed these maternal needs to enter into the transference dialogue.

For the purpose of illustration, I have simplified the process of interpreting these two dreams. The condensations of the dreams were many, engaging us through many sessions as we returned to various images. A dream needn't be handled in a single session. Often dreams are referred to, through associations, in subsequent sessions, and further dreaming will make reference to the same themes. Putting dreams together with ongoing material gives credence to the persistence and coherence of unconscious drives and inhibitions. As in the paired dream just mentioned, it also gives substance to the conceptual notion that the past has influence on the present. As a road to the reconstruction of past events, dreams not only have heuristic value in stimulating hypotheses, but they provide conviction to the patient by superimposing past events on present images.

Many Roads to Rome

No one example can meet all the needs for exposition of techniques of dream interpretation. Each example, like clinical reality, uncurtains but a small window overlooking a variegated scene. At times we may make only the smallest comment on a dream, as in the beginning of treatment. Or in a complex paired dream, like the one just mentioned, perhaps only the most salient feature — the maternal transference — will be commented upon. In this case, we returned to the sexualized features of the patient's transference only later in treatment. The immediate clinical needs and receptivity of the patient dictate the level of dream interpretation.

Variations exist on the side of the therapist as well. Years of teaching the technique of dream interpretation have afforded me an appreciation for the diversity of therapeutic cognitive styles. Some therapists excel at translating the concrete visual image into its linguistic metaphor (they are often also good at verbal puns). Others are visually blind and respond to the affect of a dream, expressed or implied. Intellectual types may actually formulate a psychodynamic hypothesis that comes to a similar conclusion. Some are skilled at following the storyline of a dream; they reduce the dream to a narrative that encapsulates a conflict. For yet other therapists, a strange word, sound, or situation perks up their third ear, and this is explored. Relying on the stimulating effects of the day residue is yet another approach. This has the value of keeping the conscious conflicts in open attention. Many follow Freud's basic approach and allow the free associations to lead them to inevitable conclusions.

No one technique is superior to another if it is based on the therapist's leading cognitive ability and style and is honed by experience. Most people use a combination of these approaches, but each therapist characteristically employs some more than others. In learning the interpretation of dreams, it is useful to try to understand the dream from all these perspectives at various times. The attempt will broaden and enhance one's capacity to respond, even if one eventually settles into some favored style of listening.

Can There Be Rules for Interpreting Dreams?

Dream interpretation is a task as complicated and varied as psychotherapy. For an initial guiding orientation, however, we can offer the following flowchart as a paradigm, bearing in mind that facility with dreams over time and with experience will provide innumerable creative innovations and personal expressions of technique.

When a dream is first presented by the patient, silence on the part of the therapist is recommended. The dream is a virgin product of the unconscious. What direction the patient will take in conscious elaboration remains to be seen. We want to be guided by the lead of the patient's awareness and resistance, and do not wish to cue the patient in, nor to direct the material. So, first we listen. Does the patient take the dream somewhere, begin an interpretation, return to day residue, or move to the affect of the dream or to the affect invoked in telling the dream? The therapist's capacity to follow the patient is tested when a dream is recounted.

Suppose the patient tells the dream and then seems to ignore it and begins to talk of other things. Do not interrupt. Often fifteen or twenty sentences down the therapeutic road, the patient will realize that what is being said is related to the dream and will begin to connect the material. Some superficial resistance has been worked out by the patient in this manner.

On the other hand, ten or fifteen minutes may go by and the patient never returns to the dream in an open manner. It is important to point this out to the patient, thus speaking to the patient's preconscious awareness. We wish to appear receptive to unconscious material. In addition, we approach the patient's superficial resistance to discussing dream material. The various motives and feelings about this failure can then be taken up. It is important to focus on the resistance to the dream and to try to understand this resistance before focusing on the dream content itself. Once again, we emphasize not storming the patient's defenses, but moving with what the mental traffic will bear.

Despite all our efforts, patients may not take up the dream or they may suggest they have no notion whatever of what the dream might be about. If this reaction occurs early in therapy, we suggest that the patient think about some element of the dream we have singled out, a conflict suggested, an affect reported: in short, whatever our understanding has allowed us. If there was an elephant in the dream, we might suggest, "As you picture that elephant now, what comes to mind?" The same

treatment can be given to an affect or conflict or whatever symbol seems usable at the moment. It is important to provide some
initial education to the "naive" patient. This may be used by the
patient for resistance, but early in treatment it is better to err on
the side of the didactic. Do not expect the patient to be knowledgeable about techniques of dream interpretation by divine
inspiration.

In the worst-case scenario, the patient still draws an entire
blank on the dream. Undaunted, we note to the patient that
some part of his or her mind is quite active. The dream construes
affects and stories about which the patient's conscious self
seems to know nothing. Perhaps, we say, at some later point we
can return to this dream, or its images, when we have understood things further. The patient must have the clear idea that
the therapist is interested in dreams, even those that are totally
incomprehensible.

Since I have stressed the resistance side of dream interpretation, let us also remember that dreams can be used not just for
communication but also for resistance and obfuscation.

A young man in analytic psychotherapy with a psychoanalyst had been seen twice weekly for two years. Termination was necessitated by a prospective move to another
city. During the next-to-last session the psychoanalyst remarked to the patient that in their two years of work together he had not reported an entire dream. The patient
thought this interesting and notable. During the following
session, their last, he reported a long dream. It took a bit
more than forty-nine minutes to recount. There was barely
time left to shake hands and say good-bye. At that moment
the patient felt pleased that he could provide a dream for
his therapist.

When consulting his next therapist in a different city, the
patient made clear that the former therapist had enraged
him by criticizing his adequacy as a patient. The recounting
of the dream was not meant so much to communicate the
unconscious as it was to "dump shit" on the therapist. It
was not that the patient was a bad patient, but the therapist

was inadequate because he could not interpret dreams (especially long ones!).

When dreams are used in this fashion it is important to shift the focus from the unconscious meaning of the dream content to the use of the dream in the transference. This use may take many forms. Before a therapist's vacation, it is not uncommon for the patient to recount very long dreams, or a frenzied succession of dreams. This behavior is often an attempt to demonstrate how much the therapist is needed, and that therefore he should not go away. Or it may mean "Look how interesting I am; don't forget me!" The meanings may be many, but the point here is singular: In the transference relationship, focus on the use to which the dreams are put. If the patient feels that the therapist has a special interest in dreams, a profusion of dreams may be offered. This performance has to be related to the need to please, or to gain a favored position, or to whatever the meaning might be in terms of the individual patient's dynamics. On the other hand, I have found that some patients who spot my special interest in dreams will not report dreams. At times they are driven by paranoid fears, spite, envy, or a need to prove that I will be interested even if they report no dreams. Holding back becomes a test of acceptability. These resistances — the uses of the dream in the transference conflict — must be approached before interpreting the dream content.

Concluding Remarks

The psychology of the dream and the clinical technique for unraveling its secrets were the fountainhead of analytic discovery. The influences of the past upon the present (especially as revealed in the transference), as well as the vagaries and mental tricks of the unconscious primary processes are to be found in an understanding of dreams. For the alert clinician, dreams are a never-ending challenge to understanding mental life. In part, analytic technique attempts to turn the therapy hour itself into a quasi-dream state through the therapist's attempts at providing a controlled scene for regression. At times, a therapist can put a puzzling hour into perspective by wondering how one might think about this recent strange hour if it had been a reported dream. What was manifest, what was latent? Where were the condensations, displacements, and guiding affects? Such a turning of day into night will once again impress the therapist with the enlightening elements of the mysterious process of dreaming.

12

Gender and Personality of the Therapist: Are All Therapists Equal?

The transference has a powerful impact upon the therapist. As the patient assigns the therapist various roles, confusion may arise in the therapist's mind. Is my actual personality really too much like that of the patient's father to allow proper distance and perspective? If, in search of nurturing, a woman has always hypersexualized relationships with men, wouldn't a female therapist be best to begin with? Can a man help a woman who suffered great deprivation of female figures early in life? Is a female therapist appropriate for a man who lost his father during the crucial years of development? Should a male homosexual be in therapy with a man or a woman? Some perspective on these issues helps maintain our equilibrium, as the dreamlike vicissitudes of the transference assign us unusual gender and personality traits. Such dilemmas also arise in initial consultations, when the time comes to recommend a therapist.

The Influence of Gender

Usually, the gender of the therapist is not of prime importance in the evolution and development of the transference. There is, however, some question about what we mean by "the evolution and development of the transference," for there is no doubt that gender will greatly influence the experience of the patient

within a therapy. The expression of the transference – the objects to whom love and hate are directed – will clearly be
molded by the sexual reality of the therapeutic pair. The following clinical example will clarify what I mean.

A divorced mother of two, with no history of lesbianism,
had been in treatment with me for almost three years. The
deepening of the transference turned her attention to issues of late adolescence and to emotional abandonment by
her mother during that period. Powerful longings for close
relationships with nurturant women became evident in her
increasing fantasies and dreams about homosexual relationships with women. Although the years of therapy with
me had included experience of me as a steady, rocklike reliable figure, very available, supportive and nurturant, the
patient had not experienced sexual lesbian feelings toward
me.

For several months this woman was recurrently fascinated by the idea of giving up on men entirely, and turning
to lesbianism. She had long been frustrated and angry with
her current male lover. A few of her divorced friends had
become lesbian. Through dreams and fantasies we explored her desires toward the women she found attractive
in work and daily life. Through homosexual bonding, she
hoped to regain her mother and thus heal her sense of female defectiveness.

As the fantasy of female defectiveness was explored, interpreted, and eroded, the patient's homosexual urges
waned, and ultimately they disappeared. They also ceased
to be themes in dreams and fantasies. Her sexual life with
her lover improved, particularly as she perceived the maternal elements in his character and behavior. They were
analogized to the maternal warmth she experienced in the
transference to me.

Man as Woman, Woman as Man

It is not unusual for a male therapist to be the recipient of a female patient's early, maternal pre-oedipal transferences. All the

safe and nurturant elements of the psychotherapeutic setting re-call the safety and nurturance that existed in childhood. In most male therapists, there exist strong maternal identifications, which play a role in permitting the development of these feel-ings. When it comes to the woman's lesbian sexual feelings, however, reality plays a determining factor.

If female homosexuality is part of the important unresolved area of conflict, the regressive pull of the transference will even-tually draw this material into active expression. These transfer-ence drives are displaced away from the actual person of the therapist, if the aim of the drive is inhibited by the sex of the ana-lyst. The only times I have been experienced for any length of time as a female sexual figure (with breasts, clitoris, and vagina) have been with psychotic patients. Even among psychotic pa-tients, however, these were unusually disorganized. When such gender reversing phenomena occur in neurotics, it is usu-ally for a fleeting second or two.

Karme (1979), a female therapist, reported the working-through of homosexual issues with a male patient. Much as the woman just described did, Karme's patient manifested this element of the transference in dreams, fantasies, and experi-ences in outside life. Karme, herself, was not experienced directly as an object of homosexual desire. This did not prevent the expression of nor the working-through of the male homosex-ual themes. The sexual reality of the therapist flies in the face of this transference longing, but the impulse is not stifled.

It sometimes happens that a woman has a long psychother-apy or psychoanalysis with a male therapist, and these homo-sexual issues seem not to be part of the clinical experience. Or, if they were, they were dealt with purely in terms of the woman's longing for the nurturant mother of the first few years of life. This approach neglects a number of interests that certain women still have toward a mother: the desire to attain equality with the mother through sexual equality, knowing their bodies through sexual intimacy with a mother's body, rivalry with the father for the mother's attention, and desires to nurture and rescue the mother, perhaps including the wish to have a baby with her. When such issues are relevant to a woman's psychology and are forced into the mold of simplistic, nurturant longings for the early mother, they are not destroyed as psychic drives. They will manifest themselves when given the proper opportunity.

A woman spent several years in intensive therapy with a highly regarded male therapist. The pair covered many conflictual issues with some success. At times the patient raised what she felt were uncomfortable lesbian feelings, but these were interpreted as unfulfilled wishes for mothering. The patient ended this treatment feeling that, on the whole, it had been helpful, but vague feelings of dissatisfaction lingered.

After some time, deciding that life was still unsatisfactory, she entered therapy again. This time, the therapist was a woman. Within several months she experienced an intense, sexualized lesbian transference to this woman. The patient was stunned. She could not believe she harbored homosexual feelings of such intensity. For the first time in her life, with a new friend, she entered a homosexual relationship. She grew to feel comfortable with her femininity in this experience. All this material was explored actively with her female therapist. After a year or so her homosexual relationship waned. She began an intense relationship with a man, and then concluded her psychotherapy. Not long afterward, she married.

Attitudes of the Therapist

If the therapist is receptive to homosexual impulses and is willing to follow them wherever the patient's psyche determines they will go, these issues can be suitably broached regardless of gender pairing. In the cases just mentioned, the patients moved to heterosexuality. Such a result is probably most comfortable for most heterosexual therapists. Just as likely, however, is the possibility that the patient will move into a satisfactory homosexual position. The therapist must be able to appreciate and respect such a stance, especially when patients have used therapy to make a serious study of themselves. Having fathomed the unconscious as much as a person can, the therapist must have appreciative acceptance of a patient's conclusions. Certainly, often enough, the patient decides that neither sex is desirable for permanent living-together companionship.

Concerning cross-gender therapies and issues of homosexuality, if the therapist is alert to the burgeoning desires of the patient and is aware that they are stimulated by the transference, homosexuality may be reasonably explored and worked-through in displacement. This is true whether the patient decides on a life-style of heterosexuality or homosexuality. We can recall the extensive working-through of clinical issues that are possible with children and adolescents. Significant portions of the transference are dealt with in terms of displacement rather than direct transference interpretation.

When Gender Is Significant

Are there cases in which a therapist of one gender is definitely preferable to the other? I think there are. Early trauma will influence gender choice of a therapist. Some people come to therapy with intense, negative feelings about the opposite sex. At times these are overt; at other times they are irritating and nagging suspicions and doubts. If the patient's history is replete with sorry experiences with one sex, leaving great conscious enmity, assigning a therapist of that sex is asking the patient to enter a difficult endeavor with a marked handicap. This is particularly so if the early history was replete with open physical brutality or gross sexual abuse. Undoubtedly, such a background will be revived in the transference. If the recommendation is for a therapist of that same sex, one has to be sure that there was, in addition, deep love for this early figure.

A woman came to consultation because her professional advancement did not match her ability or potential. She fought often with her male supervisors and at times was fired. She had had two unsuccessful therapies with male therapists. These seemed to have ended in mutual argumentative fights, and she stormed out. Her father was sarcastic, sardonic, and contemptuous of her intellectual ability. At times he became enraged with her during adolescence and threw her out of the house. The mother was passive and helpless, but a kind and approachable woman.

I marveled at the patient's coming to me for consultation. She responded that she was strong-willed, and unwilling to let her father determine her life with men. Inquiry into her feelings during our few evaluation sessions revealed that she often felt that I secretly thought she was inferior. This feeling created irritation, which she was barely concealing. She interpreted this irrational feeling to herself with psychodynamic accuracy. Her interpretation did little good since her animosity mounted.

I suggested to this woman that her capacity to fight her difficulties was highly admirable. Particularly for that reason, I would hate to see her efforts wasted yet another time. It was the better part of valor to put the odds in her favor, and try therapy with a woman. Perhaps it was masochistic to storm with men against her feelings about men. I referred her to a woman and, from all I can tell, this therapy was able to develop.

In contrast, a woman described a very brutal early life with her father. He was physically and emotionally cruel. He accorded his wife the same treatment he gave the patient. The patient's hatred of this man was real and based on much reality, suffered not only by her but also by her sister and brother. Yet I noticed how smooth and comfortable her interview with me was. On this basis I began treatment with her. Later on, I learned that during the patient's early childhood, the father had been warmer, playful, and a source of deep delight. Only later in life, when she began to develop a mind of her own did his rougher side come to the fore. This change also coincided with the deterioration of the parents' marriage.

In this instance I relied on my intuition, which responded to an unspoken psychic reality rather than the overt facts.

Early Loss of a Parent

There is another class of historical facts that will influence the choice of a therapist's gender: early loss of a parent. When a person has lost a parent quite early in life, especially through death, the desire for intimate contact with a figure of that same sex is enormous. Treatment with a therapist who is of that gender arouses unresolved grief in a deep fashion. But perhaps this choice goes farther. There is a level of the long-term therapeutic relationship that is very real (see Chapter 4). The patient's years are spent, we hope, productively, in a joint venture with a valuable guide and mentor. This is a fact apart from the transference relationship. Although therapy can never replace such a tragic, early loss, it can at least provide a diluted and minimal facsimile. There is no reason not to take advantage of this possibility. As difficult as the therapeutic endeavor is, why not give it every possibility of usefulness?

> An 18-year-old college student came to see me because of a homosexual panic that developed abruptly while he was with his girlfriend. He was obsessed and terrified by ideas that he was homosexual.
>
> It seemed odd that sessions with me calmed him down. Traditionally, male homosexual panic yields most quickly to the presence of a woman.
>
> When the patient was 6 years old, his father died suddenly. His mother was attentive, loving, but domineering. He always missed the balancing presence of his father, but denied the loss in multiple ways. His recent involvement with a woman in an intense fashion evoked the longing for his father. Unresolved grief expressed itself in homosexual desires. A deep and intense relationship with a man had never been possible for him. He had kept a distance from similar circumstances. Consequently, he felt defective as a male. Throughout a long treatment, he often commented that just being with an older man (with me, in this case) was something he had always wanted. Even if the therapy didn't give him everything he wanted, nobody could take that from him.

Oedipal Issues Seen as Pre-oedipal

A cross-gender therapeutic pairing may inhibit recognition of the level of transference conflict being expressed. It does not feel very natural to a male therapist, for example, to experience himself as the oedipal mother, the mother of rivalry and competition.

A woman in her mid-twenties, with a significant degree of pre-oedipal issues of maternal deprivation, decided to make a bold and major shift in her profession. Immediately, she began to experience ominous anxiety, which washed over her endlessly for several weeks.

I interpreted her anxiety as abandonment fears. She feared to lose a number of carefully cultivated friends and colleagues. She also feared losing me should our treatment hours need rearranging with her new job. In short, I focused on separation anxiety, and yet her discomfort mounted.

One day she reported a tense, inhibited phone conversation with a woman who was in the profession that she was leaving. She had many fantasies of this friend's feelings of jealousy and competition toward her. She feared that this woman would consequently abandon her. When I commented that the tone in which she described her anxiety about the loss of this woman had the same tone as her separation anxiety about losing me with a change of hours, the comment clicked affectually. She was experiencing me as her jealous mother who turned cold and rejecting when the patient threatened to develop farther than she had. In many ways, the mother had blocked this patient's intellectual and creative advancement in life. The patient broke into tears, quite relieving in their effect, and said it all made sense. It was the first time in weeks that she could sense what was panicking her. The material broadened into maternal-competitive themes.

As a male I had difficulty sensing myself as an oedipal mother rival for this woman. It was more natural to feel myself as a nurturing mother who, the patient feared, could not tolerate separation and individuation. It took weeks for me to get this point, although it was explicit in the patient's discussion.

I do not believe this is pure idosyncrasy on my part. Oedipal rivalry with the mother, particularly professionally expressed, is alien to a male from the culture in which I was reared. Yet the important point is that gender did not prevent the development of these transference feelings. It remains for the therapist to be keen to these various possibilities.

Of additional note is the fact that the aforementioned patient arrived at this transference point as she improved in treatment. Improvement often revives oedipal guilt and anxiety. It is my impression that male therapists pick up oedipal competitive themes with their male patients more quickly, and with a greater surety, than they do with females. Males are less inclined to sense when women are making transference use of them as the rivalrous, oedipal mother. As has been noted earlier, male therapists are more inclined to see themselves as the pre-oedipal mother, nurturant and frighteningly dominant.

One possible explanation lies in the different histories of male and female development. In many ways the male experiences his pre-oedipal mother much as the female does. In the oedipal experience of the mother, however, the difference is significant. For the male in the oedipal situation, the mother is not the primary rival, whereas for the female, it is just the opposite. Female therapists are quite sharp in picking up oedipal-rivalrous transference feelings in their female patients. Male therapists tend to have a relative blind spot in this area.

An additional countertransference problem many male therapists have with female patients is insufficient attention and support to female aggression and self-assertion. There is a quiet tendency to ignore in female patients passive trends, both intellectual and sexual, that would be perceived as major therapeutic issues with their male patients. I have observed the counterpart in some female therapists: they have difficulty accepting passive trends in men. They wish them to be more assertive and forward and become anxious when a male patient wishes to be cared for and protected in the culturally traditional role of a woman.

Another dilemma among female therapists concerns the paternal transferences, particularly the competitive oedipal ones. It is more natural for a female therapist to see herself as the prohibitive mother, or the frightening phallic mother, than as the male, possessing a penis and competing with her male patient. There is often a time lag until the female therapist realizes that the male patient is talking about his father rather than his mother.

Members of each gender must be aware of the cultural biases that limit and inhibit their perceptions (see Mogul [1982] for an excellent summary review of these issues). With luck, a personal therapeutic experience for the therapist helps iron these out. To be more realistic, it is the clinical experience that helps disentangle them. Perplexities and failures (short-term or long-term) in clinical experience are the sharpest teachers of awareness of these issues.

Unconscious Choice of the Therapist's Gender

As in all things therapeutic, there is no end to variation and complication. In some instances abandonment by a parent early in life may not dictate therapy with a therapist of the same sex as the one lost. Especially in cases of severe maternal deprivation based on actual trauma, psychosis of the mother, maternal competition based on primitive envy, and other marked conflicts of the early mother–daughter relationship, the young girl will often turn to her father for maternal functions. The role of a male therapist then becomes central to the flowering of the female patient's sense of feminine pleasure, competence, and security. In such cases the way to the mother is through the *maternalized father transference.*

One woman came to me for treatment after several years of a terrible sadomasochistic relationship with a female therapist. This had fairly well reproduced her horrendous past with her mother. In her first session of treatment with me, she reported a dream of that morning: she was coming up my driveway, with her daughter, toward my waiting room and office.

Behind this dream-image child was the patient as a daughter, and then her mother in the same role with the patient's grandmother. At a minimum, the patient was saying, "I am bringing four generations of women to therapy."

In this woman's life, her father had deftly, and not so deftly, substituted for his psychically harassed wife's maternal functions. This historical nexus provided the dynamic thrust for recapturing female identifications through a maternalized paternal transference.

It is not uncommon for a man to have experienced humiliation at the hands of a cruel and jealous father. When the mother has provided the perception of her son as a strong male, and potential man, and instilled a sense of masculinity in her son, it is not uncommon for such a person to choose a woman unconsciously as a therapist. In this case, the way to the father is through the *paternalized mother transference* to a female therapist.

This is not to say that I am making specific recommendations about a therapist's gender for such historical circumstances. Often we understand these matters only long after the therapy has progressed. Rather, I am trying to suggest the complexity of unconscious influences that predetermine the choice of gender for one's therapist. When only one parent has been reasonably empathic toward a child, the parent who provided the acknowledging, affirming, empathic recognition of a person's talents and potential will be an important determinant in a patient's choice of therapist.

The Influence of Personality

In recent years there has been more open acknowledgment that particular personality characteristics enable certain therapists to work more effectively (and easily) with specific patient personalities. Although it takes a goodly number of years to discern these characteristics in oneself, because of the difficulty of factoring out lack of experience and the slow acquisition of skill, many therapists gradually, if not painfully, become aware that they do not do as well with some persons as with others.

It is with hesitation that I broach this topic. My major fear is that the reader's therapeutic maturation may be foreclosed short of adequate experience. In addition, I have stressed treating each new patient as a totally new experiment, which this discussion seems now to discount. The obvious answer is that as we grow with time and experience, we learn that we succeed with some patients more than we could have imagined, and perhaps not as well with others as we had once thought we could. In between these two categories there remain a vast number of possibilities. Over time, with further experience, we find that even the two extremes are subject to change. This leaves a great deal of space for coping with most clinical experiences in an open manner, without preformed opinion.

The realistic consensus of most therapeutic communities is that due consideration should be given to the personality (as well as skill) of a therapist to whom one is making a referral. In fact, some professional communities usually have a few persons reputedly skilled as "matchmakers." The matches of such people, if observed over time, may actually not be as highly successful as local myth would presume. This regard does not, however, belie the general view of knowledgeable professionals that the personal qualities of therapists are pondered when considering referral.

Transference and Reality

Freud (1937a), in reviewing Ferenczi's 1927 comments on the importance of the analyst's having mastered his weak personality points and having learned from his mistakes, goes on to comment: "This provides an important supplement to our theme. Among the factors which influence the prospects of analytic treatment and add to its difficulties in the same manner as the resistances, must be reckoned not only the nature of the patient's ego but the individuality of the analyst" [p. 247].

In 1936, Grete Bibring described a case she transferred to another analyst because the so-called transference distortions were not really distortions. Bibring decided that she was too much like the mother of the patient in reality, and there could be little "as if" in the transference. The patient could gain no observing distance on the transference experience.

Glover (1955) reported an earlier survey of the British Psychoanalytical Society. He asked the members: "How far do you think the personality of the analyst plays a part in the conduct of analysis?" More than half responded, "A considerable part." Glover noted that over years at scientific meetings, certain analysts repeatedly discussed clinical material from fixed angles of interest and could focus only on certain problems and issues.

Kramer (1979) detailed the unique experience of supervising two analysts on the same adult case. The first analyst was unreceptive to a theory of early development, especially concerning pre-oedipal influences, was uncomfortable with any disclosure of countertransference, and could not engage the patient in analysis. The treatment ended badly and prematurely. The patient, a woman, went for treatment to a second analyst (male, as was the first). Quite coincidentally, this second analyst called Kramer for consultation and supervision on this same case. The second analyst was a spontaneous and intuitive therapist, comfortable with irrational countertransference feelings and able to tolerate and understand his patient's immature and regressive needs. He managed to engage the patient and work successfully with her.

Berman (1949) surveyed several poor matches. His view was that these patients experienced the therapist's inability to warm up to them spontaneously, could not feel the dedication similar to that of a helpful parent, and broke off the treatment on one pretext or another. He also described patients whose innate psychological sensitivity and alertness to the moods and feelings of the therapist led them to confront the therapist. If the therapist could not acknowledge the correctness of these views, stormy periods of acting-out, inaccessible to therapeutic intervention, often followed.

Greenson (1967) admitted intense antipathy toward the reactionary political views of a patient, which inhibited him as a therapist. When these feelings were too intense and were not modified by other traits of the patient, he confessed as much, indicated that it was his peculiarity, and recommended treatment with someone else. I have seen therapists who were quite clear that they had angry feelings toward psychopathic criminals or drug-abusers with marked psychopathy. Quite out of hand, they dismiss any possibility of working with such patients. Other therapists find these individuals a challenge, have empathy for them, and possess the enthusiasm and energy necessary to work with these difficult issues.

Therapists' Affinities

A therapist's special qualities may draw him or her to a specific area of treatment. August Aichhorn's success with juvenile delinquents is legendary (1925). He fought fire with fire, and often was just as impulsive, mischievous, and perhaps even as psychopathic as his wards. Few others are so personally constituted to perform such tasks, let alone enjoy them.

In Boston, I heard one of our most highly regarded child analysts describe his joy at treating a child who had a capacity for psychological insight (Goldings 1978). He described his mounting pleasure as he became aware that the child was moving toward insight and awareness. Understanding was a highly vested value in his own orientation toward life. When this happened with a child, he felt a sharing of attention and an impulse to move physically closer to the child, which he concluded the child must notice and identify with; this may have helped increase his capacity for discovery. Certainly, if this response were not there, we might expect a different outcome in his interactions. This vignette must recall for us Tartakoff's summary triad of interaction-internalization-action in producing change in treatment: The personality of the therapist meshes with the process of treatment to produce change.

In situations of acute crisis, it is readily apparent to most clinicians that the patient requires a therapist who is comfortable with techniques that call for active reaching out. A distant, contemplative, and relatively intellectual approach is most comfortable for some therapists. They do not perform best in situations of emergency. For the same reason, many therapists shy away from work with children or adolescents. The quality of being a real object is too much of a disturbance and strain on their style of interaction.

Similarly, many therapists shy away from work with psychotics. The flagrant acting-out of fantasy, the demands, both rational and irrational, on the therapist, jar many well-mannered, -ordered, and -organized therapists. Many of us work best when our schedule is not disrupted and our hours not disjointed by sudden phone calls. Yet, there are those who enjoy the challenge of the psychotic's dream life that attempts to force its hand on everyday reality.

Work with psychotics often also demands close work with hospital staffs. The group psychology skills needed for doing this are often dissonant with some psychotherapists' personalities. Some primarily enjoy solitary exploration with one person, unimpeded by time or intervening group process, be it ward staff or family. The regularity of this endeavor may fit hand and glove with the needs of many patients. For example, obsessional patients are often comfortable with a therapist who makes no unexpected psychic moves. Such patients find great comfort in being able to view the passing therapeutic scene with control and predictability. They are most at ease with a therapist who is regular, predictable, and remote enough to seem noninvasive. For somewhat similar reasons, many paranoid patients are most comfortable with the inactivity of a contemplative and quiet therapist. An ebullient, energetic, hail-fellow-well-met therapist requires exhausting vigilance on their part. A number of examples of the effects of personality on treatment are sprinkled through Chapter 1, which discusses the personality of the therapist, and Chapter 4, which explores countertransference.

On the whole, we are not discussing specific countertransference problems here. Rather, we are saying that, given the wide range of personalities and problems native to humankind it is unreasonable to think that any one individual will be totally suited to treat every personality or problem. It is true that some gifted therapists have an amazing range of therapeutic effectiveness. It is not unknown to have one person show talent with children, adolescents, borderline personalities, psychotics, and even neurotics. But even these remarkable people are not uniformly effective with the total range of personalities that manifest a given disturbance.

As we conclude a topic that narrows the range of therapeutic adventure, I wish to reemphasize the importance of maintaining an open mind toward therapeutic "matches." Given a well-motivated patient and a good therapist, a therapeutic trial is often the best approach, if one cannot come to a conclusion about a "matching" issue. If the trial does not work, the people involved will know soon enough, and can take appropriate action. And if a seemingly unlikely match *does* work, all the better; it keeps us alert to our frailty in the face of so many unknowns, it decreases premature rigidification of opinion, and it furthers creativity.

Concluding Remarks

Although a well-trained and experienced therapist has a wide range of effectiveness, it does not encompass a full 360 degrees. Attention must be paid to the clinical realities we have noted, such as special influences of gender and personality on specific clinical problems. Given the proper therapeutic atmosphere, the transference will tend to develop according to the frustrated needs of the patient. There are certain circumstances, however, in which some of us will be more uniquely fitted than others to work with these transference manifestations. This is not a comment on the inadequacy of particular therapists, but rather a realistic reflection of the complexities of life and any one individual's ability to face them all.

13

Silence

Can Silence Be Golden Where Silver Speech Reigns?

Insight obtained through spoken interpretation is usually accorded a supreme role in the process of psychotherapy. Stone (1961) evocatively suggests that words form a psychosomatic bond between the young child and its mother and convey a capacity to tolerate separation. The mother's call of "I'm coming!" may provide enough presence to stem the child's crying. Indeed, as we have discussed, a valid verbal interpretation does initiate a mourning process to some degree. As fantasy is reduced, a slight separation is effected between patient and therapist. But, if words are paramount, what is the role and meaning of silence in the psychotherapeutic process?

One category of silence is the familiar one of resistance to conflicted transference feelings. Weisman (1955) deftly lumped these under one of two P's: protective or provocative. Paranoid patients, for example, may become silent in accusation against a therapist perceived as rejecting, unempathic, or devious. Further withdrawal will take on the quality of a protective barrier against pain and loss. Actually, paranoid patients are not entirely idiosyncratic in the use of silence in relation to the transference — they merely provide helpful magnification of a more general process. In most patients, once the transference has crystallized, silence and the blocking of speech indicate conflicted thoughts and feelings toward the therapist. Words are available, but the patient would rather not use them. In such instances, the therapist will find tactful comments to convert defensive silences into words.

Consider, however, the following tale of Rabbi Nachman of Bratzlav, our wonderful pre-Freudian, natural psychologist of the eighteenth and early nineteenth centuries:

> Nachmann has his survivors of a shipwreck pass the dark and stormy night in a remote castle tower, attempting to recall their earliest memories. He begins with the eldest among them, who remembers the first tree, another who remembers the first leaf, another the seed, a younger who recalls the fertile and receptive earth. Finally, they come to a small 4-year-old boy, who says, "Ich gedenk gornisht" — "I remember nothing!" And, the whole party agrees that this, indeed, is the earliest memory of them all.

Freud's basic model for the therapy hour was the dream. The dream is the integrator of current experience with past memory. This recovery of the past in the regressive dreamlike experience of psychotherapy reaches back beyond the verbal stage, leaving the therapist with the mystery of silences and nonverbal stages for which our verbally oriented therapy provides little explicit guidance. Moreoever, words are often useless for these aspects of treatment. Limentani (1977), in discussing preverbal states in treatment, quotes from T. S. Eliot's "Burnt Norton":

> Words strain,
> Crack and sometimes break, under the burden,
> Under the tension, slip, slide, perish,
> Decay with imprecision, will not stay in place,
> Will not stay still. . . .

The chronically silent patient, or silence in a usually loquacious patient, places a great strain on the organizational tendencies of the therapist. Silence is most often experienced as a "resistance," and the therapist's mind teems with schemes, both verbal and nonverbal, to reach past this state. The usefulness of silence often eludes our verbally dominated outlook.

Consider this following clinical example:

By chance I met a former patient several years after some successful work together. He had been hospitalized for almost a year and a half and then worked with me as an outpatient for another year and a half. I invited him to come by the office to chat and talk over his therapeutic experience.

In our meeting, I fully expected him to tell me how important and illuminating the last year and a half of our work had been, of his marked insights into his past life and continued conflicts, and of our fascinating and highly verbal analytic working-through of oedipal conflicts and pre-oedipal themes. Instead, he shocked me by commenting that the most important part of the therapy – perhaps the turning point of his life, he said – was the three-month period when he was confined to the ward in pajamas and socks after a psychotic suicide attempt that brought him near death.

During this three-month period he had been totally mute in our meetings. For over three months we met three times a week for fifty minutes of silence. What he enjoyed was my lighting up my cigar, sitting back, and puffing away for the whole time, asking nothing from him, seeming to be content to be with him, and waiting patiently.

Indeed, I did love these sessions and those cigars with their precious Havana leaf. I still allowed myself the unhealthy sin of cigar smoke in those times. And I loved the puffing of the smoke and the fused immersion in smoke and psychosis with this young patient, fully confident that, given requisite time, his biology would ultimately veer round toward some form of life that he deemed desirable. I was imbued with the romance of symbiotic fusion with psychotics.

Against my advice and will, the patient had been drugged, shocked, consulted, confined, and the family had even attempted to send him to a famous treatment center. Finally, when all the others had given up on him, the patient and I were left in peace.

In this atmosphere, more than any words could convey, he felt that I was the first person who wanted nothing from him except what he might want for himself, and I was totally willing to wait for it. His first pleasurable sense was his enjoyment of my énjoyment of that cigar, three times a week. (And we will of course bear Freud's comment in mind – "Sometimes, a cigar is just a cigar!")

The positive aspect of silence in a treatment is hard to *prescribe* for oneself, to *teach* to others, and it is hard to *communicate* its importance to patients who fear lack of verbiage in the hours. Encouraging experience of the nonverbal is the reciprocal of encouraging free association. In music we gain a sense of rhythm through the absence of sound. A similar process occurs in communication between two people. In teaching students a feeling for the correct dosage of verbal interpretations, I often use the metaphor of a pond. Toss one stone into it and rhythmic, harmonic waves emanate from the center of the site. A second stone may do more of the same with some overlap. But throw one stone too many, and the rhythmic organized waves become turbulent and chaotic. The pond needs to rest. The dosage of silence is harder to teach than the dosage of words: it is hard to learn and bear the uncertain consequences of silence in daily practice.

Let us note that in this quasi-practicing in the dark, theory acts as an important "holding environment" for the uncertain therapist. Anna Freud's "need satisfying object," Winnicott's "good-enough mother," or "facilitating environment," along with Khan's "protective shield," Mahler's "extrauterine matrix," or "symbiosis" and "refueling," or Balint's regressive "new beginning" (as summarized by Balint, 1979, p. 168), and more currently Kohut's merging "selfobject" transferences: All aid in providing an emotional stance for a therapist. Nevertheless, detailed, explicit, technical indications are missing in these formulations. They aid primarily in giving structure to a nurturant countertransference, an emotional ambience entirely necessary with disturbed patients. The therapist is left with a useful orientation but, in practice, very much on his or her own in generating spontaneous, intuitive, and meaningful action.

Personal History and Silence

Apart from the resistive nature of silence and the expression of preverbal states and communication, personal history provides endless variation to the meanings of silence.

"It seems strange . . . but your silence has been very important to me. I know at times I complain about it, but it has another side as well. Your silence gives me room to be myself. My mother was always chattering at me. From the moment I walked in a room she was at me. Yet she never knew me emotionally, for all her yacking at me. She just never knew who I was. I never got a chance to tell her. Here, I can experience myself, get to know myself, instead of listening to her . . . and to everyone else who has become her substitute. . . .

"When I take a nap, I am always fearful I will be intruded upon. She was always coming in on me. I need total silence in order to feel safe, to let go, and fall asleep."

In contrast, another woman needed a great deal of activity from her therapist. She had been raised by a hyperanxious and controlled mother, who utilized the most "scientific" childrearing methods of her time. They were quite mechanical and distant, and they emphasized minimal contact as a part of their efficiency for behavioral training. It was too silent.

This woman could not fall asleep unless she had company in the way of sound, which, in the form of radios, animals, voices, often seemed to come closer to noise. Silence kept her awake, since it invoked memories of her sterile and cold childhood experiences.

Speech as a Defense against Silence

Activity of a motor or verbal nature can be used as a defense against awareness of disturbing thoughts or feelings. In some of our subcultures, the frustrated housewife with no outlet for the rage maintains control by cleaning with a vengeance. Similarly, speech can serve as an activity defense against silence that gives room for submerged emotional life.

A patient had been running in high verbal gear during many of his therapy hours. During this valiant attempt at doing psychotherapy, he maintained an ongoing barrage of self-criticism, feeling his insight was inadequate. Finally, I suggested that he was extremely impatient with himself; there seemed little room for vagueness and doubt.

He replied, "My father was always coming down on me. I never had a chance to think. . . . You know, I began talking quickly as soon as you made your comment just now! It felt too good. I couldn't bear it, so I began to talk. . . . I should remain silent more, and let myself experience things. Those Japanese dudes are right . . . you've got to learn to silence your mind!"

Similarly, it is not unusual for therapists to use speech as an activity defense. The tensions that exist between patient and therapist are emotionally palpable during silences, especially after the crystallization of the clinical transference. Rather than bearing the uncertain consequences of prolonged silence, many therapists will break silence (transferential tension) with questions and comments that in effect serve as reassurances, whatever their content. Although this speech may be indicated in certain cases, mental states, or clinical emergencies, as a repeated pattern it places the patient in a passive position. It is misleading to suggest to the patient that the therapist can perform the therapy.

After several years of therapy, a female patient had settled into a pattern of silence for most of the hour. The therapist had increasingly attempted to empathize with the patient's walled-off silence and would make guesses as to what was on her mind, or what she might be feeling. When the therapist felt brave enough, she would venture to suggest what the patient was reacting to with silence.

These attempts at kindness were increasingly met with sneers, contempt, mystifying sparse answers, and often by continued silence. The patient would usually stare off in a direction that did not include the therapist, effectively negating her existence.

In consultation, I suggested to the therapist that she was trying too hard. Probably she was acting out some transference reversal. She was the patient as her childhood self, and the patient was behaving like her unavailable and unknowable mother. The therapist had to relax into the silence, allow herself to be vulnerable, unknowing, and begin to trust that the patient knew more than she, and consequently the therapist would have to allow the patient to lead the session. Basically, she knew only what she heard.

As the therapist gave the patient more room in her paranoid silence, she also encouraged the patient's active self. Rather than starting hours, or summing up hours, or guiding them along, she could acknowledge that the patient was in control, and she could only follow her, not lead her. Over time this woman came out of her provocative and protective lair and began to acknowledge her thoughts and feelings. As might be suspected, these were powerful feelings surrounding fears of trusting and caring for the therapist.

Silence at the Beginning of an Hour

The emotional tensions between patient and therapist are often evident in the first moments of a therapy hour. After the initial civilized courtesies at the door, as the participants sit down, there is a silence. At this moment a therapist has a choice: maintain silence or begin the hour. It is my contention that, barring unusual exceptions, therapists work against the aims of their intentions if they begin hours for a patient. What we are always striving for is to be at the edge of the patient's most immediate experience and awareness. When our patient walks through the door we have no real idea of what this might be. We want to behave as if excessive movement puts all of living nature into hiding, as it does at a woodland pond.

Particularly when the transference has formed, the patient is motivated (consciously or unconsciously) by the desire to please the therapist and be favored strongly. When the therapist begins the hours, there is instituted a subtle programming that the alert patient will follow. The patient's own interests and intentions are easily diverted by what is judged to be the therapist's needs and interests. Therefore, starting sessions by asking "How are things going?" or "Have you had any hallucinations this week?" or "Have you given any further thought to our last session?" will place the patient in the passive position, permitting both members of the therapeutic pair to totally ignore what is on the patient's mind. Often enough, once the therapy is under way, it is some set of disturbing feelings and thoughts about the therapist that is on the patient's mind. Silence will often allow such unspoken issues into the ambience with the crackling clarity of air just prior to an electrical storm.

The opening silence of an hour provides an opportunity to taste the concentrated tensions of the transference. If the therapist inhibits verbal action, the unique pains and pleasures stirred by the patient will well up into consciousness. It is a testing ground for countertransference.

The ubiquitous question in this discussion is this: How long can one allow this initial silence to continue? I have already indicated that in certain instances, it can be a rather long time, as long as the three months in the example cited earlier. But let us take a more common clinical course. Most patients, after a brief silence, will begin the hour with some material. Other patients will wait and ask the therapist what they might talk about, or plead poverty of thought and affect. If it is early in treatment, we explain to the patient how we try to follow patients' frames of mind, and that as much as possible, it helps the therapy if they loosen up and say whatever it is they experience. As much as possible, we encourage ignoring censoring thoughts. If the patient can't say what is on his or her mind, we can at least talk about the barrier to expression. If such resistance to expression occurs later in therapy, we are usually in possession of some modicum of understanding, which allows interpretation of the resistance or, as in some of the instances cited, living with and through the silence. Some patients, very interesting ones, maintain through all of their therapy more silence than speech.

I offer the following anecdote, not because I recommend the technique it reflects, but because of the unusual function of silence it demonstrates:

> I once knew an elderly, intelligent, and eccentric psychiatrist, now dead, who saw a young woman twice weekly for two years. Barely a word passed between them other than "hello" and "good-bye." One of the peculiarities of this man was that he often did not charge his patients, as was the case with this woman.
>
> He acknowledged that for two years, this woman would come into the office and sit on his lap for the entire fifty minutes. Then she would get up and leave. The physical relationship did not proceed any farther than this. Dr. X had no idea how the woman was doing in her life. I believe she had originally come for deep depression, but, truthfully, I cannot remember the details. One day the woman said she was better and wished to terminate, and she did.
>
> Not long afterward, Dr. X came across someone who knew the patient, and knew that Dr. X had seen her. Apparently the woman had done remarkably well during her treatment, and her life had improved significantly.

One can only imagine that this woman was either enacting something pleasurable from her past life or was fulfilling a childhood wish of great intensity. Unfortunately, I do not know any significant follow-up of this woman's subsequent life. One might easily imagine that if she had sought such fantasied perfection elsewhere in life, she might have come to grief. The period of treatment described, however, was one of immobility and silence. The patient remained at some nurturant level of symbiosis for a long and steady time. Since speech was never added to this equation, our understanding of it can be no more than our understanding of an uninterpreted dream. The manifest content is fascinating, but without the patient's associations, we are left with only our personal fantasies in place of the latent content.

Concluding Remarks

One realm in which silence is certainly golden is that of dreams. Silent visual images with only occasional speech is the usual format for our deepest state of regression, nightly dreaming. In this silent theater great symbolic dramas are enacted. Affects are experienced or cloaked in symbols, and speech is unnecessary. We should not be surprised, then, that silence figures quietly, but importantly, in the regressive experience of analytic psychotherapy. Silence will spring up as resistance to transference, but also as an enactment of wish and fantasy. It will often raise questions as to what must be lived through as well as worked-through. Despite the incoherent dreamlike nature of silence, it can be creatively utilized to recognize elements of transference and countertransference that are unbearable for both patient and therapist.

14

Psychotherapy and Psychopharmacology

One fact of contemporary psychiatry is the use of drugs for the treatment of emotional and mental disturbance. It would be unusual for a psychotherapist to deal with a person suffering from a major psychosis without resorting to medications at one time or another. Even nonpsychotic states of distress may require medications from time to time. Naturally, a large group of patients will neither need nor desire medications at any point. These latter clinical situations are not the focus of this discussion.

Today's psychotherapist is fortunate to have psychopharmacologic expertise available, should it be needed or desired. Although a therapist need have little detailed understanding of the biochemistry and physiology connected with psychotropic medications, it is important to possess a psychological sophistication about prescribing and taking medications. It is not a simple matter to suggest to a patient that he or she take a medication. Nor is it a simple matter if the medication is requested and a prescription is then offered.

A young man with cyclothymic swings of mood, not quite psychotic, but not far from it, was in therapy for about six months. Initially, during the "honeymoon" period, his moods evened out, and his work behavior became less aberrant. I had opted for an initial trial of psychotherapy without any medication.

When the negative transference began to emerge, he grew depressed. Soon his work performance was so poor that his job was in jeopardy. I suggested we try a course of antidepressants, described the symptoms he had, and the possible relief the medication might hold in store for him. He seemed agreeable, and began the antidepressants.

His mood improved, and he became more effective at work. However, he began to be quite late for his appointments and shortly developed a pattern of missing them entirely. I pursued the meaning of this pattern, and eventually he confessed his feelings. He took my prescribing of medication to mean I felt he was hopeless for the process of psychotherapy. He felt I had given up on him and had resorted to palliative measures. It was necessary to detail the use of medication in conjunction with psychotherapy, outlining how it could be an aid to psychotherapy rather than a substitute for it.

This exemplifies how prescribing a medication was equated with *abandonment*. The same meaning can be ascribed to ending medication.

A woman had been hospitalized with an intensely delusional and combative psychotic episode. Heavy doses of medication were used, not only to calm her panic but also to assure her physical safety as well as the safety of others. When she was discharged, she remained on high levels of medication.

After several months of well-compensated life, it was decided to taper the medications slowly to reach the lowest maintenance level possible. Within a few days she began to be delusional again. Investigation revealed that she felt that I thought she was cured and was going to lower the medications and then get rid of her.

These reactions are not unusual. Whenever considering initiating medication, or changing doses, it is imperative to discuss this plan with the patient. It is well to anticipate psychotic patients' thoughts of abandonment and to spell these fantasies out in early discussions. Even after the patient has assented, one must follow his or her experience with the medication over time. It may help to suggest that drugs are useful for symptoms that may get in the way of using psychotherapy. For example, disabling and terrifying anxiety makes it difficult to concentrate or to achieve quiet distance from oneself. Drugs may aid in symptom relief; they do not create enduring personality changes, which remain the hard work of collaborative psychotherapy.

The Bias of the Medical Model

A great cultural bias may influence all therapists, medical and nonmedical. This is the long history of the medical model and its associations with medications. The doctor prescribes and the patient receives in a passive manner. The doctor "knows" the effects of the medications and the patient doesn't. This stance is untenable and even deleterious in the psychotherapeutic setting.

The therapist must adopt an attitude whereby the patient becomes the prime source of information concerning the effects of the drug and, in particular, the psychological experience of taking the drug. The therapist must be active in gathering this material, or both therapist and patient will relax into the traditional medical model and not explore the effects and consequences of medication. Such exploration becomes especially important when the therapist has a psychopharmacologist administer medications, for there is a danger that many transference feelings may be siphoned off to this other "therapist" if the psychotherapist is dissociated from the patient's involvement with the medications.

Some Barriers to Accepting Medication

A psychotherapist who is steadfast and tactful in working with a patient's hard-won defenses may lose sight of psychotic reactions as serving the same psychological functions. A person will resort to psychotic defenses when more usual ways of coping fail. Consequently, when the ardent practitioner of mental health is eager to quell the ravages of psychosis, its functional aspect must be kept in mind. Psychosis is an obscuring night of safety. If this protective cloak is taken from the patient too rapidly, the patient may become anxious over what will replace it. It was only recently that his or her usual personality brought the patient to grief. In between psychosis and compensation, patients are like persons undergoing surgery. They feel their life and consciousness are in the hands of the surgeon; they require great and gentle reassurance that they will neither be abandoned nor left vulnerable in this strange state of altered consciousness.

It is not unusual to find paranoid patients, obsessional schizophrenics, and manic patients refusing medications. They *fear being influenced*. Their symptoms create what they feel is a safe titration between distance from and closeness to those around them. Too close, and they will engulf (or murder) or be engulfed; too far, and they will meet loss, depression, and possible suicide. They distrust medications and those who offer them. These patients are difficult in terms of management, and often require limit setting – either they take the medication or we cannot work with them. In extreme cases, one may need to resort to legal channels to assure the patient's safety. Throughout this route the therapist must constantly, despite great psychotic barriers, attempt to clarify the meaning of the medication. When the patient is better compensated, it is important to go back over this interpersonal struggle and reexplore its meaning. In long-term work with such people, a similar conflictual scenario is sure to recur. Persistent clarity by the therapist eventually helps to win the patient's cooperation.

During the course of compensation, painful feelings will be ascribed to taking medication. Depression that follows acute schizophrenic episodes will be blamed on the slowing effects of drugs. Manic patients, in particular, will often cease taking lithium when they move to depression. The underlying defense of manic moods as a protection against the exquisite sorrow of depression maintains a steady pressure to cease medication and take flight into manic moods. As medication proves a threat to magical solutions, it will be seen as an enemy. It is not uncommon for patients quietly to lower doses or stop taking medications altogether without fully informing the therapist. Active inquiry about the state of a patient's medication and the patient's attitude will do more good than harm in this phase of treatment. The patient plays out much negative transference, an expression of distrust of the therapist, through lack of adherence to the medication regimen. If a therapist treats medications as an exogenous issue, the whole element of distrust will be buried away in the patient's clandestine jugglings of medications.

Barriers from the Viewpoint of the Therapist

It is not only the patient who may see the institution of medications as a defeat; many therapists are imbued with the notion that any unusual activity on their part that is not considered to be observation, clarification, or interpretation is not psychotherapy. Removing from the patient's direct mental control any seeming modicum of autonomy is reducing the patient's chances of producing authentic and self-induced change. Such theoretical stances will not only inhibit the use of medication but, if medication is used, the therapist's disparagement may leak through to the patient. If the patient feels that psychopharmacology spells defeat for the therapist, he or she will have difficulty surmounting this aura of pessimism.

A converse problem occurs when a therapist is excessively imbued with the image of the efficacy of drugs. An overenthusiastic endorsement of medications may aid in getting over a patient's reluctance, but the high price for this eagerness is paid farther down the therapeutic road. A patient must not be led to expect that medications spell a cure. Otherwise, inevitable depression will follow. The patient will feel impervious not only to psychotherapy, but also to medications. Great hopelessness and abandonment of treatment, if not worse calamities, can then ensue. A conservative description, without a note of hopelessness, is useful when outlining the possible effects of medication. A balance must also be struck between describing possible side-effects and yet not arousing a nightmare of fantasied tics, tremors, and physical disabilities.

It is also possible for a therapist to feel doubt about the efficacy of drugs, and although using them, to feel improvement to be a "placebo effect." Even in cases where this impression may be valid, the effect is nothing to sneer at. Remember that the honeymoon period of psychotherapy, during which many symptoms may remit, is also a placebo effect. It is a direct result of transference fantasy, which must ultimately give way to analytic scrutiny and understanding. Nevertheless, both the "honeymoon" phenomenon of psychotherapy and the "placebo" effect of medications serve an enormous function. They allow persons to sustain the pain and frustration of engaging in a process that will challenge their personalities in an alarming manner. The placebo effects provide time to develop trust, transference, and working tools, in order to face the future unknown developments of treatment.

Using the Psychopharmacologic Consultant

Many therapists, including psychiatrists, use a psychopharmacologist when medications are necessary as adjuncts to treatment. While doing so assures a sound approach to the best medications, it presents certain problems. This therapist-pharmacologist split may cause the therapist to dissociate the element of medications from the psychotherapeutic process. Even though the consultant may be the source of prescriptions and may even follow the patient periodically, the therapist, in the patient's mind, is the ultimate authority. All of the issues we have been discussing come into play. If the consultant begins to cut down medications, the patient may react as if the therapist were preparing to wind down treatment. All the cautions noted still apply, and the therapist is well-advised to explore the patient's experience of the medications as if the medications were coming directly from the psychotherapist. By doing this, we also encourage keeping the transference in the therapist's office.

Attention must also be paid to possible splits in the patient's mind between the consultant and the psychotherapist.

A homosexual man entered therapy with a female psychologist. Prior to this he had seen a male psychopharmacologist at various intervals to obtain a minor tranquilizer for anxiety. The patient was insistent on continuing his relationship with the psychopharmacologist, although he had no current symptoms that required medication. The therapist felt no need to challenge this relationship.

Over time it became clear that as a homosexual, the patient was frightened to enter treatment with a woman. Having a man in the background reassured him and yet allowed him to explore his feelings about women. In this case, the medications were a spurious issue. More important was the use of the consultant as protection against intense dependency and sexual intimacy with a woman.

A depressed man had avoided introspection as a means of understanding and as a platform for launching change. He had seen a succession of psychopharmacologists, and received a succession of medications. Finally, he found a psychopharmacologist he trusted, and continued his drug regimen.

After a few years, it was apparent that his depression, while not overwhelming, still hamstrung his life. He kept losing the women he loved, and eventually he thought the cause might have something to do with his personality as well as his depressive tendencies.

He sought out a psychodynamically oriented psychiatrist and wanted to begin treatment. Although this new psychiatrist could administer medications, the patient requested that he be allowed to continue with his old psychopharmacologist. Recognizing this patient's ambivalence, and the long road he had traveled to get to this point, the psychiatrist agreed and began treatment with this inherent split.

This patient needed what he experienced as the non-intrusive role of medication to allow the more intrusive role of the psychotherapist.

Paradoxical Effects of Medication

A therapist told me of several years of intensive treatment with a severely inhibited man whose rage could not be evoked in treatment. Each time the patient reached this murderous material, he became symptomatic, so that his anger was reduced and he was distracted. During one such period he became transiently psychotic, and the therapist began medications.

While on this medication the patient began to talk openly of homicidal wishes, not only toward his wife and family, but also toward the therapist. The therapist realized that now that his patient was on medications, he himself felt safer. He realized that he was allowing himself to listen to material that, in retrospect, he felt he had cut off out of fear. The medication had calmed not only the patient, but also the therapist. This altered situation allowed working through material that had been avoided for years.

Psychotropic medication, in this instance, had an unusual additional target organ, the countertransference.

Concluding Remarks

This last clinical example highlights the synergism between the proper use of medications and the enhancement of the psychotherapeutic process. They are not inherently separate. When medications are used with the proper clinical indications, in the best interests of the patient, it is hard to see how, in the long run, they could be antithetic to the best interests of psychotherapy. Therapy should aim at dealing realistically with the problems of life. Danger does exist when mechanistic symptom change substitutes entirely for earnest live attempts at personality change.

For the psychotherapist, the watchword is "psychological so-phistication." Medications, apart from their physiological actions, never fail to have a psychological effect. It is the psychotherapist's job to be tuned in to these thoughts and feelings and to bring them onto the therapeutic table for open discussion. In this fashion, tablets become grist for the transferential mill, and accessible for psychological digestion.

15

Realities of Everyday Practice

It was quite early in my training when Dr. Jack Ewalt, the chief of our hospital, emphasized the stubborn resistances and blocked silences inherent in the treatment of disturbed patients. They were nothing to be anxious about, he reassured us. "Just be sure you have a comfortable chair!" This deft comment touched on the delicate interplay between the realistic, basic needs of the working psychotherapist and the requirements of therapy. The environment and work habits must be favorable to the personal needs of the therapist and yet fit the framework of treatment.

Along with the emotional deprivations that arise from holding a neutral stance toward patients, the therapist suffers a simpler deficiency from being indoors, confined to one room. I knew of one senior therapist who, one spring in her later years, decided to move her practice to her restful backyard porch. The backyard was large, private, quiet, and very beautiful. Within a month she had moved back indoors. Neither she nor her patients could concentrate; they were too distracted by the intensity of life around them. The inner world of the psyche seemed less alluring. Similarly, the environment of the office must be comfortable, but not distracting.

Arranging an Office

When furnishing and arranging an office, bear in mind that one must provide an indoor setting that will keep us sustained and satisfied and yet not unduly complicate the therapeutic task for our patient. Thus, while it is permissible to have pictures of our family members on our desk, painful reality will inhibit embarrassing transference fantasies if the pictures sit staring at the patient. Art, photography, books, and similar items, while reflecting our personal taste, have more universal connotations; although they may skew transference, they do not stunt or inhibit it.

In general, the more constant an environment remains, the more it fades into the background, so that the patient's inner imagination can come to the fore. Continual rearrangement or efurnishing of the office throws the patient back into environmental actuality and remagnifies his or her resistances to reality. The therapist grows, develops, and changes (although, one hopes, not radically and recurrently), and these accretions of life will be reflected in changes in the office, but a balance between change and constancy must be kept in mind.

A fetish can be made of having a soundproof office. I think the only true way to accomplish this is to have an office underground. The office must give at least adequate protection against sounds from the outside, particularly human voices. Background traffic noises become lost in the maze of the preconscious, but clear and audible human speech does not. After a number of years in a hospital-based office, I moved my practice to my home. I was amazed at the increased relaxation and decreased tension I felt when the sounds of passing voices, telephone bells, and announcements from the hospital paging system were eliminated.

One's specific practice may dictate other arrangements regarding noise and physical activity. A child therapist, for example, whose patients may scream or shout, jump or hop about the room, will have difficulty practicing in an office building above a sensitive neighbor. I knew of a child therapist whose technique was altered inappropriately on this account. She received repeated complaints from her landlord about the jumping and noise in her office (for example, the lights in the office below her flickered). She noticed herself leading her small-sized but active patients toward table games rather than physical expression of fantasy. These strategies were far from beneficial to either her technique or her patients. She found it necessary to find a new location, one that could absorb the activity of her practice without inhibiting it.

The physical arrangement of furniture may have clinical consequences. More than one therapist has been knocked aside (or suffered worse damage) during a paranoid patient's desperate dash to freedom. The therapist's chair should not stand between the door and the patient.

The actual distance between patient and therapist will be a matter of personal comfort. Some therapists need to be far enough away so that every physical sound and normal physiological motion they make is not under the patient's aural and visual scrutiny; others do not mind undergoing such intense observation. Furthermore, if the chair designated for patients has a degree of mobility, they can turn it a bit aside or come closer, as they feel comfortable.

The Clock

A small item of furniture, yet one that plays an immense role in psychotherapy, is the clock. The therapist, not the patient, is the guardian of time, at least for the duration of the therapeutic hour. Time is antiregressive and antidreamlike, and focusing on it will inhibit imaginative flights of transferential fantasy. Consequently, we do not want the clock facing the patient. Placing it somewhere behind the patient, yet directly in the line of the therapist's vision, allows one to keep track of time without distracting the patient. This arrangement also obviates quick furtive glances at one's watch or having a clock in an awkward corner. One should avoid insistent, ticking clocks. They are like Chinese water torture for anyone who treasures time with the therapist.

Tissues

Another item, small but of large symbolic value, is a box of tissues. Many patients have entered my office for the first time and immediately spotted the tissue box adjacent to the patient's chair. Frequently they will say, "I'm glad to see you are prepared. I'm going to need those!" Quite often, on the way out, a patient will take along a few tissues "for the road." They become a transitional object that transports the therapist a bit beyond the physical confines of the office. The absence of a box of tissues is usually unconsciously read by most patients as meaning that the therapist finds sadness and tears difficult to bear. Since mourning is inherent in analytic psychotherapy, a ready supply of tissues indicates that the office is a place to cry. People who fear dependence, or need sharp boundaries between themselves and the therapist, may be reluctant to use the therapist's tissues. Many transference conflicts may settle on the small, unassuming tissue box. Although there are few physical tools of the psychotherapist's trade, the box of tissues ranks as one.

The Waiting Room

A quiet, comfortable waiting room, with an adjoining bathroom, is helpful for the patient's entry into and smooth exit from the therapy hour. Many people come early to therapeutic hours just to sit in the waiting room. Some early piece of regression occurs here as the outside world is temporarily tucked away. Magazines that are readily available elsewhere are read only in this setting. Articles encountered here are often significant in terms of the patient's past life and current conflicts. The content of such articles may be used to start off the therapy hour and can be woven into several hours. The patient's preregressive state before the hour allows the reading material to have a heightened impact upon the patient. Such pieces are like the day residue of the dream: the latent, conflictual themes of an hour may crystallize around them.

If it can possibly be made so, the waiting room should be a place of quiet. Sounds from the office should not enter. A white-noise machine can be used in this area to keep the emotions of the consulting room from entering. Patients should not anticipate that they will have to inhibit their vocal intensity once they are inside the consulting room. New patients will find unpleasant connotations in plants that are brown and dying, magazines that are months out of date, and bare walls, even though older patients may have seen beyond such an apparent lack of hospitality.

After the hour, many patients head for the bathroom. Here, in one of our culture's sanctioned places of privacy, they may continue some process of the hour or begin to decompress before they leave.

The Location of the Office

Whether one's office is part of one's home or elsewhere is, to my mind, purely a matter of personal preference. I have practiced in both settings, and if I'd felt that either location had any significant advantage in psychotherapy, I would long since have reverted to that specific locus. As for practicing at home, I would only caution that a home office be consonant with one's family needs and that the family be attuned to the routine of a psychotherapeutic practice. Having one's family life abruptly and repeatedly intrude on one's practice is not conducive to the development of a neutral backdrop of constancy, which is necessary for the patient's unconscious fantasy to emerge. Not only does the patient become tense and on guard, too tuned to reality, but the therapist does too. Sometimes, however, the home sets the stage for unexpected learning:

> Quite late one evening, I was requested to see a man who was reportedly desperately suicidal. At that point my office was not separate from the rest of my home, and when I went to see this patient I took with me my dog, to avoid his barking and awakening my children.
>
> Once in the office, the dog found a quiet corner and settled into a half-dozing state. The patient told me his unhappy tale. As the hour drew late, I finally zeroed in on his suicidal feelings. He hunched over and began to speak quietly and intensely in the inimitable tones of one clearly set

on killing himself. Suddenly my dog lurched up his head, cocked his ears at the patient, and began to whimper. He arose and frantically clawed at the door, seeking exit. Obviously terrified, he had to be let out of my office. I feebly apologized to my patient, gently noting that old Faust was a psychiatrist's dog and had strong feelings about suicide.

Primitive murderous rage crosses many communicative barriers, in both man and dog. I have always remembered this episode as demonstrating the power of nonverbal communication of affect.

The major theoretical objection to home offices is that the setting interferes with the development of the transference. Practicing at home, if anything, has convinced me of the psychological power of unconscious transference. With the facts staring right at patients — my children coming and going from the side entrance of my home — I have variously been seen as: the father of twin girls, two boys, three boys, three boys and a girl, a girl and a boy, married a second time with two families, divorced and just using the office, or married to someone else and renting the office space while living elsewhere. It is well to remember that Freud discovered transference, and explored it for over forty years, in the confines of a home office.

Isolation becomes an issue when practicing in a home office. One must be sure to maintain teaching or research affiliations to allow frequent professional interchanges. They keep one's mind open to new developments as well as ensuring that one is still practicing a reasonable brand of "old" developments. Practicing in a group, or a hospital, does afford the therapist a source of daylong opportunity to interact with people on other than a transference basis. The larger social setting also offers more immediate support if one's roster of patients is exceedingly taxing in terms of suicide, exasperating acting-out, or disruptive forms of psychosis.

Money

In discussion of the initial interview, I indicated the complex motives that surround attitudes toward money. Money is as in-

tricate a topic as sex, and is dealt with in equally arcane and subterranean ways. It is important for the therapist to be direct and
self-understanding on both issues. One's financial arrangements should not be presented to a patient as if they were motivated by the patient's therapeutic needs. Charging for psychotherapy is strictly a business matter. While useful therapeutic
mileage may be made out of reactions to paying for treatment, or
from missed sessions, obtaining such reactions is not our purpose in charging for our services.

Many claim that patients will not be sufficiently motivated to
work in treatment unless they pay. I never found this claim valid
when I worked in clinics, in the days when third-party payment
was virtually nonexistent. Some of my patients paid perhaps
fifty cents a visit, and I wish I could ascribe success or failure to
so simple a matter as money. Unfortunately, the vast and unhappy vagaries of personal fates had more to do with therapeutic success than whether the patient paid a painful and motivating fee.

Freud altered his views on the motivating element of money
when the first studies of the Berlin Psychoanalytic Institute's
clinic were made (Eissler 1974). He observed that low-fee patients did well in treatment. A factor that was considered more
important than fee was the length of time over which the treatment was carried out; this time did seem longer for lower-fee patients than was usual. Additionally, these patients seemed more
often to be late and to miss appointments. It is quite possible that
anaclitic and extremely symbiotic patients will remain in treatment longer if they are paying low fees. I must say, however,
that in my own clinical experience I have found the major factors
in the length of treatment to be the nature of the transference, its
ability to be worked-through, and the state of the countertransference. Once again, I wish money were the essence of such prolonged treatments; it would make understanding so much
simpler.

Since significant portions of negative transference may become buried in patients' attitudes and behavior toward money,
the therapist provides guidance through clear ground rules regarding billing, expectation of payment, and a policy on missed
appointments. By noticing deviations from the ground rules,

one can sense that feelings are being buried in behavior involving financial issues. A therapist's policy about charging for missed appointments will vary according to personal financial needs, the financial practices of one's colleagues, and the press of one's caseload, as well as the needs of the individual patient. There must, however, be a standard policy. When arrangements are too open, great room is provided not only for the patient to act-out, but also for the therapist to do so. When a policy is clear, it is clearer to the therapist as well as the patient when something is awry. Guilt and discomfort over charging for a service so based on love and affection make many therapists brush financial matters under the rug of their superego. The patient's anger over paying will stem partially from similar developmental origins. When, very early in life, love and caring attention is furnished by one's mother, issues of payment are not part of one's experience. The unconscious transference expectation is that the therapist will play a role similar to the mother's, and the patient feels outrage at having to pay for such a relationship.

Some therapists state that they charge for missed appointments only if the patient is acting-out. This stance places the therapist in the role of omnipotent judge and seer. Acting-out is seen as pejorative, not normative for the awakening of the transference in the regressive pulls of treatment, and the patient is placed in a passive position. Such a judgment works against a collaborative effort. For many patients, paying for missed sessions allows the freedom to miss sessions without excessive guilt. They feel free to stay away as long as they feel it necessary, without a sense that they are causing the therapist financial harm. The idea may seem senseless when stated so boldly. Why would anyone bother to be in therapy unless he or she were serious and strongly enough motivated to show up? Well, the fact is that certain people can enter a relationship only in this backward manner. They say "hello" by saying "good-bye." Without this leeway, they might not be able to tolerate the heat of a close transference-oriented therapy.

In psychotherapy, money is like silence. Both have inherent power to heighten the therapist's awareness of feelings toward the patient. Unpleasant elements of countertransference become unavoidable, challenging the therapist's understanding and the conversion of this understanding into communicative technique. Practical clarity about monetary policies increases one's chances of taking due advantage of this unique source of transference.

Schedules and Caseloads

As a rule, psychotherapists work very long hours and specialize in overcommitment. Passion for work is a blessing, but great care must be taken against inadvertently squeezing personal living out of one's existence. It is easy to find oneself inflicting upon one's family and self the kind of neglect one spends the working day trying to repair in patients. A therapist should think realistically about limiting the workday and the total workload. All work and no play makes Jack and Jill not only dull therapists, but depressed ones as well.

The actual composition of a caseload has certain built-in limiting effects. Treating two, or at most three, actively suicidal outpatients will overwhelm most therapists. The strain of such cases is complex and intense, often requiring much telephone time. When we are in such a situation, we should not put ourselves in an untenable situation when offered another suicidal patient. It is not possible to handle more. The same holds true for impulsive, acting-out borderline personalities. Each such patient requires a long period of working-through until a stable relationship is established. During this period, taking on more patients with these disorders is too much to ask of oneself. Naturally, if borderline cases are being treated within a hospital milieu, one has greater energies, as well as additional human resources, to cope with these patients. Even within this setting, though, it is well to pay attention to the internal psychic thermostat that indicates one is being overwhelmed. A therapist is an entirely human therapeutic instrument and, as such, is heir to all the frailties of the human condition. Personal neglect and denial can only diminish one's therapeutic effectiveness.

The time of a session usually varies between forty-five and fifty minutes. I doubt that a shorter period is useful for analytic psychotherapy. There is always an inrun of minutes until the patient moves to deeper levels of concern within an interview. This usually takes fifteen to twenty minutes, although for certain patients, and at certain periods of treatment, the patient is off and running the moment he or she enters the office. Time cushions the patient's advance toward painful material. Too brief a session, thirty minutes for example, may suggest that one does not wish to have a lengthy discussion with the patient, nor an intense one. It is well to keep within the limits set for the "hour," and not to run under or over by excessive amounts. This vigilance is another built-in check for countertransference for the therapist as well as the patient. Most commonly, guilt over not providing relief and cure will cause a therapist to prolong one patient's hours regularly. Such mini-depressive behaviors on the part of a therapist are no more useful to the patient than growing up with a mother whose behavior is motivated by guilt. On the other hand, when a patient is in crisis, begins to shed tears for the first time in months or years, has suddenly opened up in a new way, or is in the middle of an intense story, one extends the time as needed. This is common empathic sense.

What about the time in between sessions? When I first began to practice, I allowed the standard ten minutes between patients. I soon found that my phone calls weren't so numerous that I needed an extra hour or two a day to handle them, nor were my notes so voluminous or regular that they absorbed the time. I found that I stood and waited, paced, and was actually eager to see my next patient, who was usually on the other side of the door in a similar state. I gave in to my natural inclination and did away with the ten-minute break between patients. I enjoy seeing patients, and when I am finished with one, I look forward to seeing the next. Others may be different and may feel revived by a break. From the practical point of view, since patient latenesses or missed appointments happen at random and are not infrequent, I find that I still have time to return most calls as needed and to jot down whatever notes seem necessary.

Smoking, Eating, Telephones

In the past several years our cultural attitudes toward smoking have changed. Fewer and fewer ashtrays will be seen in public waiting rooms, especially those of hospitals, and now there are none in the waiting rooms and offices of many psychotherapists. However, smoking will still be an issue for patients. It remains one of the most common forms of self-soothing and tension-absorption, despite its inherent potential for self-destruction. For some, of course, the self-destructive aspect is a strong element of the motivation to continue smoking. In any event, many patients will request permission to smoke, eat, or drink in the office.

I always recall the rejoinder of the late Dr. Elizabeth Zetzel to requests to smoke during the therapy hour. Dr. Zetzel, a chain smoker, puffed her way through sessions. In the midst of this cloud, when a patient asked if he or she could join in the activity, she refused permission. When the patient protested and noted her intense smoking, she explained: "What makes *you* anxious is good for the therapy. What makes *me* anxious is bad for the therapy!"

Many patients will give inhibition-loosening comfort and coziness as their apparently commonsense explanation for requests to smoke, eat, and drink during the hour. For me, at least, the answer is that I do not enjoy smoke and do not wish to have it linger with me for an entire day or week. As for eating or drinking, I find I am distracted by wondering when the negative transference will manifest itself through a spilled cup of black coffee on my office rug. Once burned, twice shy; I am a quick learner on this score and do not wish to provide any undue reason for irritation with a patient. I much prefer to take up countertransference material in other ways, no end of which exist outside of food and drink. Once again, some therapists may find this too finicky. It may be so, but what is important is to find one's own range of comfort within the confines of one's office and be practical, realistic, and consistent about maintaining it.

The issue of telephones is an important one, since it bears on the availability of the therapist. Therapists always have a dual responsibility: to be available to the patient sitting right in front of them, and to be potentially available for emergencies that might arise outside the confines of the office.

During the therapy hour, I almost never answer a ringing telephone. My answering service has instructions to tell the patient to call back and to continue indefinitely to ring in case of emergency. This persistent ringing is my signal that my outside availability may have to take precedence over the patient in my office, and I answer the phone. I feel that it is important for me to spell out to patients that I do not answer the phone during the therapy hour. It seems common practice for other therapists to lift up the phone, if only for brief comments, in the midst of psychotherapy. I feel that it is so hard for patients to unburden themselves of painful emotions and dreadful points of past life, that it asks too much of them to put themselves on hold while a therapist answers calls that almost always could wait. The patient is not an automatic device that can click on and off. Besides, masochism will allow many patients to deny their feelings about this practice.

Therapists can choose between personal answering services and answering machines. Both have advantages and disadvantages. The answering service provides a caller with a live body at the other end of the phone, one who could make suggestions as to how to find us if we aren't at the office, and who can make continued calls to locate us. On dark, cold, early winter mornings, helpful services will catch us at home before we come in to the office for the first patient, who has already cancelled the appointment. Answering machines, while they are mechanical and often freeze people's capacity to talk, do offer an opportunity for the patient to leave an actual message, complete with affect. In the treatment of dependent borderline patients, such a message can often be a tremendous boon. These people get great relief from calling in several times a day and leaving lengthy messages. They feel they can get through to the therapist. The quality of answering machines, like the therapists they serve, must possess great durability and the capacity to take multiple and lengthy messages. The economics of an answering machine are superior to those of an answering service. They will usually repay their costs by the end of the first year. Again, preference for one or the other will depend on one's personal style as well as the nature of one's caseload, and, not insignificantly, the quality of the local answering services.

Should one list one's home phone number in the public directory? Admittedly, if one deals with a large number of patients who express negative elements of the transference through strange and untimely phone calls, one would probably without a second thought choose an unlisted home phone number. All one needs is several phone calls of a life-threatening nature to one's spouse or children, and a personal therapeutic limit may be reached instanteously. If the caseload is not thus slanted in its demands on the therapist, however, it is probably useful to have a listed number. All many patients need for reassurance is the mere knowledge that the home number is available. They may never have to call. When the home number is not to be found, there may be recurrent calls to the office number in order to be sure that the therapist is reachable.

Concluding Remarks

There are many details of daily therapeutic life that could be included in this chapter. I have tried to cull out the few that seem to be of recurrent interest in clinical discussions. The major principle seems to be the one so aptly raised by Dr. Jack Ewalt: because the process of conducting psychotherapy is quite mentally demanding, one should be sure, within the context of these demands, to create a setting and administrative format that maximizes one's sense of comfort, security, and realistic achievement of satisfaction. This must be done with the framework and goals of therapy in mind, and with the realistic appreciation that there can be a sensible balance between personal and therapeutic needs. Masochistic self-sacrifices are no more desirable in a therapist than in a patient.

16

Selected Readings on Technique

There are certain readings to which one returns again and again. These works not only promote technical expertise but also add to our professional identities and philosophies. The inescapable fact is that no matter what has been discovered before, it is in the nature of our work to rediscover its validity once again for ourselves. We feel excitement in reading these works because they often highlight what we have discovered only that morning.

The listing that follows is not intended to be comprehensive, but merely a sampling, presented in a general chronological fashion. Interested therapists will no doubt augment this list, depending on their own interests and prediliction.

Sigmund Freud

"Recommendations to Physicians Practicing Psychoanalysis" (1912)
"On Beginning the Treatment" (1913)
"Remembering, Repeating, and Working Through" (1914)
"Observations on Transference Love" (1915)
"From the History of an Infantile Neurosis" (1918)
"Notes upon a Case of Obsessional Neurosis ('Rat Man'),"
    including "Addendum," and "Original Record of the Case"
    (1909)
"Analysis Terminable and Interminable" (1937)

"Constructions in Analysis" (1937)

"The Interpretation of Dreams" (1900)

"The Handling of Dream Interpretation in Psychoanalysis" (1911)

"Remarks on the Theory and Practice of Dream Interpretation" (1923)

These papers are striking for their clarity and direct advice. First-time readers are amazed at and enthusiastic about their clinical richness, relatively devoid of metapsychology. Re-readers are bemused and awed at their forgetfulness of Freud's capacity to speak to everyday clinical matters. The paper on transference love is written with exceptional literary giftedness; it reflects Freud's empathic awareness of the realistic elements of passionate transference. The two case histories provide a glimpse of a genius in the process of discovery and contain endless observations and speculations that will invoke admiration, agreement, or consternation on the part of the reader. In reading the "dream book," one may skip the first bibliographic chapter. Bear in mind that this historic book is basically an autobiography of Freud. Stimulated by the death of his father, it contains many of Freud's dreams. It is an exquisite example of an attempt at self-analysis. Enmeshed in this work are innumerable instances that further clinical understanding. Do not be put off by the metapsychology; the clinical portions stand on their own. The two papers on dreams are "how to" papers and have useful applications. The 1937 papers, written not long before Freud's death, contain some of his last thoughts on the methods and possibilities for analytic therapy and thought.

Sandor Ferenczi

"On the Technique of Psychoanalysis" (1919)

"The Problem of the Termination of the Analysis" (1927)

"The Elasticity of Psychoanalytic Technique" (1928)

"Child-Analysis in the Analysis of Adults" (1931)

"A Historical Critical Retrospect of Incorrect Methods in Psychoanalytic Technique" (with Otto Rank, 1923)

You may disagree with and be astounded by Ferenczi's leaps of imagination, but you will be impressed by the far-ranging and elastic therapeutic capacity and inventiveness of this pioneer of psychoanalysis. For many years, Ferenczi — the embodiment of the perfect therapist — was sent the most difficult of failed cases and was held in the highest esteem by Freud. His energy, clinical tact, empathy, and staying power are evident throughout his writing. Many of the themes about which he wrote still remain unresolved, especially the degree of activity useful for a therapist.

Ruth Mack-Brunswick

"A Supplement to Freud's 'History of an Infantile Neurosis' " (1928)

This is a tour-de-force of dream interpretation. In one article, dreams are used for diagnosis, prognosis, assessing defensive styles, interpretations, transference, reconstructions, gauging the future course of treatment, and deciding on termination. The fascination is heightened by revelation of the identity of the patient, the "Wolf-Man." Freud was stricken with cancer, was unable to see him for a recurrence of difficulty, and referred him to Mack-Brunswick.

Herman Nunberg

"The Will to Recovery" (1926)
"Problems of Therapy" (1928)

An original member of the Vienna circle, Nunberg is a master at fathoming a patient's irrational motives for seeking and sustaining therapy.

James Strachey

"The Nature of the Therapeutic Action of Psychoanalysis" (1934)

With appealing directness, Strachey outlines the "mutative" effect of living transference interpretations. The softening of the superego through identification with the benign analytic functions of the therapist is outlined. In this presentation, one sees many of the roots of today's object-relation therapies, which focus on the effects of symbiosis in the transference. Strachey is the major translator of the twenty-four volumes of the Standard Edition of Freud's works.

Ella Freeman Sharpe

"The Technique of Psychoanalysis: Seven Lectures" (1930)
Dream Analysis (1937)
"The Psychoanalyst" (1947)

A former professor of literature, Sharpe was one of the early British analysts. Whatever topic she touches is transformed into literary gold. She is superbly clinical, a model of tact and humanism, and constantly in tune with the unconscious roots of language.

Theodor Reik

Surprise and the Psychoanalyst (1937)
Listening with the Third Ear (1948)

At times one suspects Reik had more than three ears. He is the master of intuition and the leap into the unconscious. From Reik one gains confidence in intuition and the resonance of the therapist's unconscious with that of the patient's. These works are uncomplicated (nonmetapsychological) clinical forays into the use of "countertransference" long before it became a respectable subject.

Michael Balint

"The Final Goal of Psycho-Analytical Treatment" (1934)
"Changing Therapeutical Aims and Techniques in Psychoanalysis" (1949)

"New Beginning and the Paranoid and the Depressive Position" (1952)
The Basic Fault (1968)

Balint, a Hungarian, was the direct legatee of his analyst and teacher, Ferenczi. They shared the same warmth of personality and clinical fervor. With his emphasis on deep regression and courage in treating difficult patients, Balint integrated the child-analytic work of Melanie Klein into the treatment of adults. Many of Balint's clinical approaches find contemporary resonance in the empathic recognition central to Kohut's treatment philosophy.

Edward Glover

"Common Technical Practices: A Questionnaire Research" (1939)
The Technique of Psychoanalysis (1955)

The next time one feels that analytic technique is monolithic, a quick glance through the pages of Glover's 1938 questionnaire will dispel all such notions. The wide variety of practices among "classical" analysts, many of whom are now household bibliographic names, is extraordinary. Glover's very British practical sense is evident throughout his textbook, which is chock full of helpful everyday hints for the active practitioner, as well as theory for those who are theoretically inclined.

Frieda Fromm-Reichmann

Principles of Intensive Psychotherapy (1950)

Fromm-Reichmann was the kindly, wise therapist of "I Never Promised You a Rose Garden." Her text, nevertheless, is a rose garden! Even so, the bloom seems never to fade from her clinical and human wisdom. Fromm-Reichmann was a major pioneer in the psychotherapeutic treatment of disturbed and psychotic patients. Her work provides an analytic framework and rationale for intensive work with nonneurotic patients in a manner free of charismatic eccentricities. She offers a model consonant with the humble work of the everyday clinician.

Harry Stack Sullivan

The Psychiatric Interview (1954)

Probably the single greatest psychiatric talent of American origin and training was Harry Stack Sullivan. Many of his works are difficult to comprehend; tackling them, however, is deeply rewarding. Embedded in most of them is his extraordinary understanding of the development of defenses and their relation to anxiety in the interpersonal situation. Of all his works, *The Psychiatric Interview* is singularly straightforward. The reader will come away with a heightened sensitivity to the impact of one person upon another. One should not be put off by the underlying tone of irony, pessimism, and slight confrontation of the patient. With schizophrenics, he was a master therapist.

Donald W. Winnicott

"Hate in the Countertransference" (1947)
"Metapsychological and Clinical Aspects of Regression within the Psycho-Analytical Set-Up" (1954)
"Clinical Varieties of Transference" (1955)
"The Capacity to Be Alone" (1958)
"Counter-Transference" (1960)
"The Aims of Psycho-Analytical Treatment" (1962)

Reading Winnicott is an unusual experience. Even when one does not understand him, one still has the definite sense of having learned something. Steeped in a pediatric background, Winnicott brings concentrated attention to the infantile and regressed elements of treatment. Breasts, mothers, and babies are always in the literary air. Consequently, the reader's unconscious is stimulated in ways that escape consciousness. Many find this type of stimulation confusing, and unclear — almost mystical. Others come away from his work emotionally moved, pleasantly gratified, and fortified for work with regression in patients and countertransference.

Sidney Tarachow

An Introduction to Psychotherapy (1963)

Tarachow's early death deprived us of a first-rate teacher and clinician. His textbook, primarily consisting of conferences with therapists in training, raises an endless array of important clinical and theoretical questions. These conferences are not contrived; they are derived from a case or clinical question under discussion. Sensible, realistic answers are sought to difficult everyday clinical dilemmas. The case material has the advantage of being wide-ranging and not focused on one group of patients. Along with Fromm-Reichmann's, this is a text I always recommend to beginning therapists, and it is one to which I myself often return.

Harold F. Searles

"The Effort to Drive the Other Person Crazy — An Element in the Aetiology and Psychotherapy of Schizophrenia" (1949)
"The Source of Anxiety in Paranoid Schizophrenia" (1961)
"Phases of Patient–Therapist Interaction in the Psychotherapy of Chronic Schizophrenia" (1961)
"The Patient as Therapist to His Analyst" (1975)

Reading Searles's descriptions of therapy is like watching diffusion of the unconscious across a semipermeable membrane between patient and therapist. His capacity to organize primary-process experience and utilize it for understanding and technical intervention is breathtaking and inspiring. His maxims, derived from work with psychotics, are so well tuned into basic primary-process thinking that they partake of the universal and will influence the full range of one's work.

Phyllis Greenacre

"The Role of Transference: Practical Considerations in
  Relation to Psychoanalytic Therapy" (1954)
"Re-Evaluation of the Process of Working Through" (1956)
"Certain Technical Problems in the Transference Relation-
  ship" (1959)

Apart from her brilliance in theory and applied psychoanalysis, Greenacre is remarkable for her ability to state the plain
facts of clinical experience. Her commonsense approach to the
tensions of the consulting room recalls the straightforward
descriptions of the pioneer analysts.

Ralph R. Greenson

The Technique and Practice of Psychoanalysis (1967)
"The Exceptional Position of The Dream in Clinical Psychoanalytic Practice" (1970)

Greenson's textbook is clinically rich. One divines an image of
a hardworking practitioner, always striving to make reality meet
his theoretical conceptions. Such an endeavor may stretch the
reader's imagination at times, but the overall effect is a sweep-
ing look at technical concepts. His dream paper takes on all
"deviant" comers and, in so doing, makes not only his classical
views wonderfully clear, but unwittingly presents an opposing
side as well.

Otto F. Kernberg

"Prognostic Considerations Regarding Borderline Personality
  Organization" (1971)
"Technical Considerations in the Treatment of Borderline
  Personality Organization" (1976)

Reading Kernberg's exegesis of a clinical entity is like a foray
into the facets of a diamond. The multiple angles and brilliance

blind one but at a distance, the gem shines with enhanced complexity, and one feels more of a connoisseur for having studied it.

Brian Bird

"Notes on Transference: Universal Phenomenon and Hardest Part of Analysis" (1972)

Bird tackles the negative transference, the source of much therapeutic stalemate and failure. He does so, however, with a keen eye on the transference-countertransference factors that augment or reduce this frequently encountered impasse. His understanding helps serve as a sustaining model for those cases where the dead end may give way to working-through.

Arnold H. Modell

"The 'Holding Environment' and the Therapeutic Action of Psychoanalysis" (1976)

Winnicott comes to America. The holding environment becomes the clinical "cocoon transference," and Modell integrates object-relations and ego psychology. The thoughts in this short paper tend to remain with one for a long time.

Kurt R. Eissler

"On Some Theoretical and Technical Problems Regarding the Payment of Fees for Psychoanalytic Treatment" (1974)

Money! Do not let the obsessional title throw you off. This is one of the best papers ever written on money and its meaning in psychotherapy. It is replete with memorable anecdotes of therapists' struggles with this issue and does not lack for Eissler's own brand of recommendations.

Samuel D. Lipton

"The Advantages of Freud's Technique as Shown in His Analysis of the Rat Man" (1977)

Lipton amasses instances of Freud's encounters with patients that eschewed neutrality and a technical stance: providing meals, money, or books, and frequently offering his personal views and opinions. He delineates what Freud intended by technique versus the area of living together through a process shared by both therapist and patient. This is a provocative article.

Harry Guntrip

"My Experience of Analysis with Fairbairn and Winnicott" (1975)

This has to be one of the most extraordinary articles in all of the clinical literature. Three of the pillars of the British school of object-relations are revealed in clinical action. It is a realization of the old fantasy of wishing one were a fly on the wall.

John Klauber

"Some Little-described Elements of the Psychoanalytic Relationship and Their Therapeutic Implications" (1976)

What are the impact, strain, and effect of the therapist's living therapeutically with another person – the patient – in prolonged frustration? This excellent British clinician addresses this complex problem quite helpfully, in a remarkably brief paper.

Heinz Kohut

The Restoration of the Self (1977)
The Two Analyses of Mr. Z. (1979)

One need not be a self-psychologist to be enriched by Kohut's empathic wisdom. The techniques and attitude of Kohut are compatible with any system of therapy that emphasizes early development, keen listening, and attention to a fully developed transference. These particular works give the advantage of Kohut after he has shed his attempt to maintain an ill-fitting attachment to classical metapsychology.

Elvin V. Semrad

The Heart of a Therapist (1980)

The best of Semrad is not to be had in books. He himself used to refer beginning therapists to only one book, "the patient." His genius was purely clinical and could be appreciated only by observing him interviewing a patient. After one saw this, his maxims made sense. Yet if only part of his heart is imparted to the reader out of this collection of sayings and tales, that will be reward enough. One should try to picture most of these comments as coming from the chubby semblance of a Nebraskan Buddha.

17

Coming Full Circle

Healing . . . is not a science, but the intuitive art of wooing nature.
W. H. Auden, The Art of Healing

The therapist woos nature. Nature is not created by the therapist, but rather deeply respected, vaguely comprehended, and sensitively evoked. This is the transference. In this process, which has a beginning, a middle, and an end, the realistic therapist comes face-to-face with the form, tendencies, plasticity, and limits of human nature. Drawing upon so many pieces of personal experience, often at a split emotional second's notice, intuition is a mainstay of the working therapist. In this sense, therapy resembles the holistic amalgams of art. To the degree that it respects the raw data of experience, however, we must differ with Auden and recognize psychotherapy's scientific base. Facing facts with a patient, unflinchingly, tactfully, is very much a scientific process, though it be carried out in an artful manner. Nevertheless, Auden's phrase "wooing nature" captures essential elements of the therapist's role in the healing process.

Ariadne's Thread

A strange phenomenon occurs in our branch of the healing arts: The healer comes to depend on the patient for guidance and prescription. In the unknowable experience that awaits each new therapeutic venture, the transference is the guide through unpredictable mystery. The legend of Theseus and the labyrinth of Cnossus is an apt metaphor. Theseus was thrust into the labyrinth, a dark, nightmarish maze, the lair of the deadly Minotaur. Ariadne, who fell in love with Theseus, provided him with a ball of thread to guide him through the darkness. By this means, he slew the Minotaur and found his way back to freedom. Similarly, the therapist, in the awkward fumbling through unconscious and often dangerous processes, uses the transference to organize and guide a relevant approach for the patient. In the face of mind-boggling complexity, the therapist would otherwise be dazed and lost. Eventually, the patient, who tunes into him- or herself, uses the transference for the same sense of cohesive purpose. Through clinical examples, scattered throughout this book, I have tried to show how transference may occur during the beginning, middle, and end phases of treatment. If transference is given a full opportunity to flourish and then be resolved, what changes can we expect transference-oriented psychotherapy to bring about in our patients?

Change

We have discussed many factors that enter into the therapeutic process leading toward change. At one point I attempted to summarize these under the headings of attachment, understanding, and integration. These are complex and varied clinical entities. But what do they lead to?

Symptoms and Character

At the most evident level, the patient may often have a marked reduction of overt symptoms.

> An intelligent and well-organized woman came to her last session of a three-year psychotherapy, with a deft summary: "I want to summarize what I've achieved in

treatment. . . . My sexuality is at a level never achieved before. I now can have an orgasm, actually, several times a week, and to tell you the truth, I'd like more. I enjoy it and feel so released. . . . Divorce is no longer an issue. . . . I can tolerate my husband's anger, his depression, and how frustrating he can be. I think I understand him, not just myself, better. . . . It's wonderful to have a child. I feel I will make it as a mother. . . . And I'm not so burdened with guilt. I can argue with my husband and not feel so anxious afterward. . . . And, although I still have bitterness toward my mother, I feel I understand her better and can live with some of our similarities . . . although I am still almost devastated by her coldness and rejections."

In this deft summary, she virtually ignored me. When I pointed out this omission, we understood it as her still being afflicted by the same difficulty her mother suffered from: fear of dependence, a tendency to isolate affectionate and grateful affect, and the erection of icy, social distance. The patient felt this element in her personality was quite clear in her transference to me; it was dug deep into her character, and she suspected she'd spend the rest of her life struggling and coming to terms with it. While her astute intelligence discerned the obvious externals that had changed, the transference outlined for both of us the work left to be done.

Much of this woman's therapy had focused on images of herself as a female: nurturing wife, sexual wife, mother to a newborn child, daughter of a mother, and professional woman. She now felt a sufficient grip on these various areas of life, brought about by the understanding and change she'd achieved through therapy. With confidence, she felt that she could proceed on her own and master conflicts centered around her femininity as she wished and was able to.

This example provides three important expectations and possibilities for a reasonably concluded treatment. One is symptomatic change. The second is characterological change. Many of our clinical examples have referred to this process. Apart from its apparent importance in neurotic difficulties, I have repeatedly emphasized the importance of characterological change in egos vulnerable to psychosis. For those susceptible to psychotic regression, the strengthening of character in its ability to love and be loved, to depend and be dependable, to separate and allow separation, forms a bulwark against psychotic regression.

Developmental Thrust: Back on the Track

The third possible outcome is a return to one's developmental progress in life. This patient had been arrested in her young adult development as a woman. Although her block had its origins earlier in life, it now prevented her from further maturation. Therapy proceeds with such a case in a manner similar to the therapy of children and adolescents. When the patient is younger, it is more easily discernible that the child or adolescent is blocked in some essential developmental task, often surrounding separation from home and family. One can conceptualize older patients' difficulties and blocks in a similar fashion. The patient just described was brought to a phase of life to which many woman in their late twenties come: They are forced to confront the complex issues inherent to the multifaceted roles demanded of an adult woman. This is an ongoing confrontation, which continues throughout life. Conversations with women in their forties, fifties, sixties, and later years reveal how continuously they reevaluate themselves as women in relation to mother, grandmother, offspring, and the other significant people in their lives. The process is the same for men.

We can thus evaluate a treatment by the extent to which it gets someone "back on the track." A 36-year-old man, well-known for his laconic summaries of complex issues, added up the task of five and a half years of intensive therapy in ~~his~~ last session: "Forget Mom! Get married!" Rather effectively, ~~he had done~~ both.

Development and Human Nature

Taking up the developmental perspective returns us to the phrase "wooing nature." Useful psychotherapy restores a blocked individual's natural potential so that life may then proceed. Some people come to the therapist hoping to be given that which they do not have. Ironically, a therapist can "give" only what the patient already has. It is this element of nature that the therapist woos. A patient who feels unable to love may come to realize that he or she loves the therapist. This love is inherent in the patient; the therapist is merely an artful gardener, a cultivator, and like the patient, is also vulnerable to the wind, weather, and sun of fate in the therapeutic work. Even in the best of treatments, certain catastrophes may overwhelm recent gains. The death of a child or a spouse or a debilitating illness often reveal the frailty of apparent therapeutic successes. On the other hand, sometimes the Fates work in our direction, and good fortune supports the therapeutic work.

Being put back on the developmental track has no minor impact. When patients feel that life is open rather than closed, that they are expanding and maturing with a sense of continuity combined with change, life has a spontaneous appeal. It is another way of stating that hope is restored to one's outlook and expectations. Often hopelessness is present in the stagnation that brings people to therapists. The positive therapeutic result is variously conceptualized by different schools of treatment as self-actualization, development of a cohesive self, or other representations that emphasize the integrative, along with the progressively developmental, capacity of the personality.

It is hard to discuss this point of view without referring to Freud's sober and profound commentary on the possibilities for treatment: "Let us start from the assumption that what analysis achieves for neurotics is nothing other than what normal people bring about for themselves without its help" (1937a, p. 225). A few years of clinical experience will aid one in realizing this as no small achievement.

During the end phases of a very long treatment, a woman commented on Freud's remark: "One thing this process has done . . . it has translated tragedy to ordinary unhappiness. . . . I used to think such a notion was a travesty, but I no longer feel that. My whole life has changed, and, for the most part, for the better!"

Post-treatment: Terra Incognita

A large portion of the results of treatment will always remain unknown to the therapist. This obscurity is due only partially to the limited scope of our vision. Even more important, much change takes place *after* termination. Actual separation from the therapist allows the patient a more realistic completion of the mourning elements related to the transference. It augments the separate individuality of the former patients. For those patients who write, visit in subsequent years, or have need of further treatment, we have information about such developments.

I once treated a severely depressed and suicidal adolescent girl. Through two years of treatment she derided my comments, thoughts, manners, and recommendations. As a regular ritual, she would end each session by standing in the open doorway and stating loudly: "So what's it all mean? Nothing, nothing! All we do is talk, talk. What a waste!"

At our very last session, when she was about seventeen, true to form, she stood at the door and proclaimed: "So what did we accomplish? Nothing, nothing. All we did was talk, talk!"

About ten years later I received a call from a therapist in another city. She had just seen this patient, who was now a young woman of about 28. The patient had become depressed again. The therapist said that the patient told her how wonderful I had been at a time of crisis in her life, how excellent the therapy had been, and how it had sustained her until her current difficulties. The therapist was calling me to see how I had worked with the patient, thinking it would be wise to try to handle her similarly.

Affective Integration: Instinctualization of the Ego

Sometimes thoughtful therapists are dismayed when patients candidly acknowledge that insight is not their primary goal in psychotherapy; they just want to feel better. Actually, such comments are closer to the affectual wishes that bring people to seek the help of a therapist. As so often mentioned in this book, it is the loss of love, real or fantasied, that brings most people to grief. A hope of recapturing love is what motivates and helps a patient tolerate the discomfort of seeking aid from a stranger. Affectual longing guides the patient to the therapist, from whom "cure," a change in affectual experience, is expected.

It has been my observation that for most people, the most significant change in psychotherapy — the *product* of insight as contrasted with the *process* of insight· — is the suppression and repression of the moment-to-moment insights of treatment and their replacement by an altered, condensed, sustained affective state. This affective state is the crystallization of the personality changes achieved through the therapeutic process. It is reflected in an altered, basic characterological mood, dispositions to mood and affect, and new capacities to acknowledge, bear, and experience affective states.

The basic affect state communicates with remarkable rapidity a person's range of potential for work, play, and love. When we know a person well, one look will inform us whether he or she is available for work, play, or love. In brief, people usually comment on the results of their treatment as "I feel better" and, at times, "I still feel the same," or "It made me feel worse." As time elapses after termination, the details of the working-out and working-through — the clarified psychodynamics — recede from consciousness. A symbolic awareness is reflected in the affective state. An emotional aura surrounds the treatment experience and the psychotherapist. Certain images may remain. They are often quite incidental and seemingly trivial in light of many of the stormy emotions experienced in treatment. These picture memories are screen memories, on the order of dreams. If fully dissolved into meaning, they would open up to the repressed and forgotten experiences of the treatment. But there remains a central emotional feeling toward the experience and toward the therapist.

Symbolic awareness is reflected in the affective state. In a sense, it is like cruise control on a car: You set the car to run at one speed, and you don't worry about shifting, braking, or speed changes. You return to these details only when the traffic arouses conflict and anxiety. Before psychotherapy, the patient's emotional "cruise control" may have been set at obsessional vigilance, hyperstimulating anxiety, and a slight paranoid alertness. After therapy, we might see a person who has shifted the basic affective state to be careful in screening of detail, thoughtful in comment, and slightly studied when in motion, but far short of the former jarring screech of semiparanoid obsessionality. The patient might feel more comfortable, secure, and relaxed than before therapy, and others will also notice how much less angry the patient seems. We can also observe how others evaluate psychotherapy primarily by the affective states they observe. So and so "is friendlier; I can talk to him now. He's so much nicer!"

This is the use of the affective state as a *cognitive* and *communicative* system. The affective state alerts a person to his or her mental health. It is a constant ego-monitoring system that informs one that "all systems are go," that one can relax, respond, and act spontaneously without excessive calculation. The sense of pleasure and comfort in this state is derived from the fact that the id has suffused more of its instinctual energies — libidinous and aggressive — into the multiple outlets available to the ego, especially through sublimation. A successful treatment, to the degree that it is successful, will release the energies of the id, thereby expanding a person's life and opportunities for gratification and development in those areas where formerly they were blocked. The comment "where id was, ego shall be" suggests in this context that much of the ego still remains mostly a body ego, a development of the id, and successful treatment involves an *instinctualization of the ego,* which accounts for the pleasurable feeling tone of the post-therapeutic state.

I use the archaic metapsychological word id because it conjures up the desire for satisfaction through love of and being with others. Successful love must come to terms with the power of libido and the power of aggression. All close relationships invoke both, and difficulties with this simultaneous experience block growth and development. People have no end of trouble knowing what to do when they find they hate the person they love. Virtually all clinical transferences will confront this basic and disabling ambivalence.

Post-treatment Amnesia

The relative post-treatment amnesia for verbal insight and the salience of the affective state as a form of cognitive memory are among the reasons why insight is often played down as an important factor in change in psychotherapy. Emphasis is frequently placed upon the "corrective emotional experience," as worked out in the transference interactions. I do believe that the emotional experience with the therapist contributes, to a great degree, to the emotional growth of the patient. This is part of the "real" relationship. Perhaps the younger the patient, the more profound is this element of the therapeutic influence. However, understanding, both verbal and through emotional acquaintance, is a powerful factor. The voice of reason may be soft, but it has the capacity to be persistent.

The view outlined here is that insight is involved more in the process of change during the psychotherapy proper than in its undisturbed product, the therapeutic result. Children who have been in treatment, including latency-age children, usually have only the vaguest memories of many years of intensive treatment. Adolescents have somewhat greater recall, but it is not at all detailed, except for certain incidents or comments, which on inspection have the quality of condensed screen memories. Adults may recall more but, considering that a person may have been in psychoanalysis five times weekly for five years, the recall is amazingly scant. Most people, however, have little difficulty suggesting the affect they feel in relation to the experience and the therapist. This affectual, condensed mental symbol is the most evident residue.

The Fate of the Transference

The unconscious is indeed timeless. When post-treatment conflictual disturbances create unmanageable anxiety, we may find that a former patient has an active, conscious reawakening of the processes of the attachment-understanding-integration sequence. This has been seen dramatically in follow-up studies made years after *satisfactory* psychoanalyses (Balkoura 1974). Evaluating analysts, not the original treating analysts, observed a regressive revival of the transference neurosis. A woman, for example, while in the subway on the way to the evaluation meeting, experienced a resurgence of the anxious symptoms and thoughts that had long ago brought her to seek treatment. In the office meeting with the strange analyst, she found herself with the powerful transference feelings she had had with her original analyst. Over a few evaluation sessions, in a mini-version of her analysis, she went through the thoughts and experiences that had enabled her to resolve her difficulties years ago. Much of this new resolution was accomplished in between visits, reflecting a capacity for self-analysis.

This resurgence of feelings and conflicts, especially toward the therapist, reveals the *relative* dissolution of the clinical transference to the therapist. Some loss of unrealistic fantasy about the therapist occurs during the termination phase; he or she is seen somewhat more for the person he or she really is. A larger dissolution occurs after treatment, over a several-year period. A significant amount seems to remain untouched. Once an unconscious equation has been made between the therapist and the imagos of the past, "similar" becomes "the same" in the unconscious. A loved and lovable object, once hard won, is not easily discarded. It is important to bear this fact in mind during the process of termination. We must not be unnaturally relentless in expecting full dissolution of patients' feelings toward us. Similarly, in any future therapeutic consultation with a patient after therapy has ended, it is important for us to remember that powerful feelings still exist in the patient. Although therapists often wish to relate to former patients as old buddies, such an attitude may tread on sensitive ground, with painful results. Once again, it is best to ride with the tide of nature, and respect the unconscious persistence of transference. I should reemphasize, at this point, that many elements of the transference do come to be mastered by the patient and viewed perceptively through the lens of reality.

The Full Circle Come Round

What might it mean that the patient comes to encapsulate the memory of treatment predominantly in affects, feelings? For most practical clinical purposes, that is exactly the level of experience that brings a person to therapy in the first place. We are always uneasy with the person who enters our office and says "I have come to see you for understanding," or the mental health professional who says "I have come in order to understand the process, to help me with training." With such people, we always wonder what unconscious hurt has guided them in our direction. We want to know "what feels bad," "what is it that you don't like;" we are intuitively affectual in our clinical search. Most clinical complaints are affectually stated: "I am bored," "I am depressed, miserable," "I don't enjoy my marriage," "I hate my job," and so on. It is a change in this affectual state that a patient seeks in treatment, and treatment will be measured by the degree to which it alters the affectual state. Naturally, affect reflects a host of human factors, but it is through affect that people assess their relationship to these human factors.

It is also through affect that the therapist will often measure the ongoing process of therapy as well as its results. We may have observed, clarified, and interpreted with great accuracy, and the patient may have agreed. But if there is no affective response, we usually conclude that the patient has listened with two ears, but not with the third. There is a similar subtle process going on in the therapist with regard to affect. A patient whose nature has been more fully released, both libidinously and aggressively, has an effect upon the therapist; the therapist, despite his or her clinical training, which is slanted toward the conceptual, the formulated, will often feel differently toward the changed patient. Moreover, as the years go by, the therapist will forget the day-to-day, week-to-week, month-to-month, and year-to-year psychodynamic interactions. But a feeling toward the patient will usually endure and have a unique affective tinge, special to that patient. Should the patient return for consultation in a regressed state and have his or her specific emotional impact upon the therapist, it is startling how quickly past therapeutic memories will rise to the surface.

All this is to say how basically animal-like is the sum total of our therapeutic interactions. We use language, concepts, fantasies, dreams, and a host of observable and describable therapeutic events. Yet a very physical human state pervades our work, in process and product. Affect, which can be directly gratifying, or tension-releasing as in abreaction, cognitively useful in alerting us to our state of mind and existence, or uniquely social in its ability to communicate our state of mind to others, is the persistent current through all of treatment. This essentially physical phenomenon, a clear factor in all our lives, is also so tied to our past existence and so powerful in its influence that we have only a degree of influence over its expression. The force of nature is most evident in the evidence of affect. The artful therapist must respond to this with all due respect for the unchangeable as well as the influenceable. The therapist, in learning to live with and understand the nature of the patient, provides the same opportunity for the patient. And the converse is equally true.

References

Aichhorn, A. (1925). *Wayward Youth*. New York: Viking Press, 1945.

Asch, S. (1982). Review of *Psychoanalysis and the History of the Individual* by Hans Loewald. *Journal of the American Psychoanalytic Association* 30:265–275.

Auden, W. H. (1969). The art of healing. In *Epistle to a Godson and other Poems*, pp. 7–9. New York: Random House.

Balint, M. (1934). The final goal of psychoanalytic treatment. In *Primary Love and Psychoanalytic Technique*, pp. 178–188. London: Liveright, 1965.

—————— (1949). Changing therapeutical aims and techniques in psychoanalysis. In *Primary Love and Psychoanalytic Technique*, pp. 209–223. London: Liveright, 1965.

—————— (1952). New beginning and the paranoid and the depressive position. In *Primary Love and Psychoanalytic Technique*, pp. 230–249. London: Liveright, 1965.

—————— (1968). *The Basic Fault*. New York: Brunner/Mazel, 1979.

Balkoura, A. (1974). Panel report: On the fate of the transference neurosis after analysis. *Journal of the American Psychoanalytic Association* 22:895–903.

Barchilon, J. (1958). On countertransference cures. *Journal of the American Psychoanalytic Association* 6:222–236.

Berman, L. (1949). Countertransference and attitudes of the analyst in the therapeutic process. *Psychiatry* 12:159–166.

Bibring, E. (1937). On the theory of the results of psychoanalysis. *International Journal of Psycho-Analysis* 18:170–189.

—————— (1954). Psychoanalysis and the dynamic psychotherapies. *Journal of the American Psychoanalytic Association* 2:745–770.

Bibring, G. (1936). A contribution to the subject of transference resistance. *International Journal of Psycho-Analysis* 17:181–189.

Bird, B. (1972). Notes on transference: universal phenomenon and hardest part of analysis. *Journal of the American Psychoanalytic Association* 20:267–302.

Blos, P. (1984). Son and father. *Journal of the American Psychoanalytic Association* 32:301–324.

Boyer, B., and Giovacchini, P. (1967). *Psychoanalytic Treatment of Characterological and Schizophrenic Disorders.* New York: Science House.

Brenner, C. (1982). *The Mind in Conflict.* New York: International Universities Press.

Breuer, J., and Freud, S. (1893–1895). Studies on hysteria. *Standard Edition* 2:1–335.

Burlingham, D., and Freud, A. (1942). *Young Children in Wartime.* London: George Allen and Unwin.

Eissler, K. R. (1974). On some theoretical and technical problems regarding the payment of fees for psychoanalytic treatment. *International Review of Psychoanalysis* 1:73–102.

Eliot, T. S. (1943). Burnt Norton. In *Four Quartets.* New York: Harcourt, Brace.

Erikson, E. (1950). Eight stages of man. In *Childhood and Society*, pp. 219–234. New York: W. W. Norton.

Fenichel, O. (1937). Symposium on the theory of therapeutic results of psychoanalysis. In *The Collected Papers of Otto Fenichel*, Second Series, pp. 19–24. New York: W. W. Norton, 1954.

Ferenczi, S. (1919). On the technique of psychoanalysis. In *Further Contributions to the Theory and Technique of Psychoanalysis*, pp. 177–188. London: Hogarth Press, 1969.

_____ (1927). The problem of the termination of the analysis. In *Final Contributions to the Problems and Methods of Psychoanalysis*, pp. 77–86. London: Hogarth Press, 1955.

_____ (1928). The elasticity of psychoanalytic technique. In *Final Contributions to the Problems and Methods of Psychoanalysis*, pp. 87–101. London: Hogarth Press, 1955.

_____ (1931). Child-analysis in the analysis of adults. In *Final Contributions to the Problems and Methods of Psychoanalysis*, pp. 126–142. London: Hogarth Press, 1955.

Ferenczi, S., and Rank, O. (1923). A historical critical retrospect of incorrect methods in psychoanalytic technique. Chaps. 3 and 4 of *The Development of Psychoanalysis*. In *Sex in Psychoanalysis*. New York: Dover Publications, 1956.

Freud, S. (1900). The interpretation of dreams. *Standard Edition* 4:549–553.

―――― (1904). On psychotherapy. In *Collected Papers.* Vol. 1, pp. 249–263. Trans. Joan Riviere. New York: Basic Books, 1959.

―――― (1909). Notes upon a case of obsessional neurosis. *Standard Edition* 10:153–318.

―――― (1910a). The future prospects of psychoanalytic therapy. *Standard Edition* 11:141–151.

―――― (1910b). Wild psychoanalysis. *Standard Edition* 11:219–227.

―――― (1911). The handling of dream interpretation in psychoanalysis. *Standard Edition* 12:89–96.

―――― (1912a). The dynamics of transference. *Standard Edition* 12:99–108.

―――― (1912b). Recommendations to physicians practicing psychoanalysis. *Standard Edition* 12:109–120.

―――― (1913). On beginning the treatment. *Standard Edition* 12:121–144.

―――― (1914). Remembering, repeating, and working through. *Standard Edition* 12:145–156.

―――― (1915). Observations on transference love. *Standard Edition* 12:157–172.

―――― (1917a). Mourning and melancholia. *Standard Edition* 14:243–258.

―――― (1917b). Introductory lectures on psychoanalysis. *Standard Edition* 16:243–476.

―――― (1918). From the history of an infantile neurosis. *Standard Edition* 17:3–122.

―――― (1919). Lines of advance in psychoanalytic therapy. *Standard Edition* 17:157–168.

―――― (1920a). Beyond the pleasure principle. *Standard Edition* 18:7–64.

―――― (1920b). Group psychology and the analysis of the ego. *Standard Edition* 18:67–143.

―――― (1922). Two encyclopedia articles. *Standard Edition* 18:235–259.

―――― (1923). Remarks on the theory and practice of dream interpretation. *Standard Edition* 19:109–121.

―――― (1927). Humour. *Standard Edition* 21:159–166.

―――― (1933). New introductory lectures on psychoanalysis. *Standard Edition* 22:5–182.

―――― (1937a). Analysis terminable and interminable. *Standard Edition* 23:209–254.

―――― (1937b). Constructions in analysis. *Standard Edition* 23:255–270.

Friedman, L. (1978). Trends in the psychoanalytic theory of treatment. *Psychoanalytic Quarterly* 47:524–567.

Fromm-Reichmann, F. (1950). *Principles of Intensive Psychotherapy.* Chicago: University of Chicago Press.

Gardner, M. R. (1983). *Self-Inquiry.* Boston: Atlantic-Little, Brown.

Gitelson, M. (1962). The curative factors in psychoanalysis. *International Journal of Psycho-Analysis* 43:194–234.

Glover, E. (1939). Common technical practices: a questionnaire research. In *The Technique of Psychoanalysis*, pp. 261–350. New York: International Universities Press, 1955.

——— (1955). *The Technique of Psychoanalysis.* New York: International Universities Press.

Goldings, H. J. (1978). Unpublished discussion of paper by Hansi Kennedy, "On the role of insight in child analysis." Scientific meeting of the Psychoanalytic Institute of New England, East, November 4, 1978.

Greenacre, P. (1954). The role of transference: practical considerations in relation to psychoanalytic therapy. *Journal of the American Psychoanalytic Association* 2:671–684.

——— (1956). Re-evaluation of the process of working through. *International Journal of Psycho-Analysis* 37:439–444.

——— (1959). Certain technical problems in the transference relationship. *Journal of the American Psychoanalytic Association* 7:484–502.

Greenson, R. (1967). *The Technique and Practice of Psychoanalysis.* Vol. 1. New York: International Universities Press.

——— (1970). The exceptional position of the dream in psychoanalytic practice. *Psychoanalytic Quarterly* 39:519–549.

Guntrip, H. (1975). My experience of analysis with Fairbairn and Winnicott. *International Review of Psychoanalysis* 2:145–156.

Gutheil, T., and Havens, L. (1979). The therapeutic alliance: contemporary meanings and confusions. *International Review of Psychoanalysis* 6:467–482.

Hartmann, H. (1964). *Essays on Ego Psychology.* New York: International Universities Press.

Heimann, P. (1950). On countertransference. *International Journal of Psycho-Analysis* 31:81–84.

Hendrick, I. (1942). The discussion of the "instinct to master." *Psychoanalytic Quarterly* 11:33–58.

Jung, C. G. (1961). *Memories, Dreams, Reflections.* New York: Pantheon.

Karme, L. (1979). The analysis of a male patient by a female analyst: the problem of the negative Oedipal transference. *International Journal of Psycho-Analysis* 60::253–262.

Kernberg, O. F. (1971). Prognostic considerations regarding borderline personality organization. *Journal of the American Psychoanalytic Association* 19:595–635.

⸻ (1976). Technical considerations in the treatment of borderline personality organization. *Journal of the American Psychoanalytic Association* 24:795–830.

Kernberg, O. F., Burnstein, E., Appelbaum, A., et al. (1972). Summary and conclusions: the psychotherapy research project of the Menninger Foundation. *Bulletin of the Menninger Clinic* 36:1–275.

Klauber, J. (1976). Some little-described elements of the psychoanalytic relationship and their therapeutic implications. *International Review of Psychoanalysis* 3:283–290.

Kohut, H. (1977). *The Restoration of the Self.* New York: International Universities Press.

⸻ (1979). The two analyses of Mr. Z. *International Journal of Psycho-Analysis* 60:3–27.

Kramer, S. (1979). The technical significance and application of Mahler's separation-individuation theory. *Journal of the American Psychoanalytic Association* (Supplement) 27:241–262.

Limentani, A. (1977). Affects and the psychoanalytic situation. *International Journal of Psycho-Analysis* 58:171–182.

Lipton, S. (1977). The advantages of Freud's technique as shown in his analysis of the Rat Man. *International Journal of Psycho-Analysis* 58:255–273.

Little, M. (1951). Countertransference and the patient's responses to it. *International Journal of Psycho-Analysis* 32:32–40.

Loewald, H. (1960). On the therapeutic action of psychoanalysis. *International Journal of Psycho-Analysis* 41:1–18.

Mack-Brunswick, R. (1928). A supplement to Freud's history of an infantile neurosis. *International Journal of Psycho-Analysis* 9:439–470.

Matt, D. Unpublished translation from the Yiddish, compiled from several sources and oral tradition.

Menninger, K. A., and Holzman, P. S. (1973). *Theory of Psychoanalytic Technique,* 2nd ed. New York: Basic Books.

Modell, A. H. (1976). The "holding environment" and the therapeutic action of psychoanalysis. *Journal of the American Psychoanalytic Association* 24:285–308.

Mogul, K. (1982). Overview: the sex of the therapist. *American Journal of Psychiatry* 139:1–11.

Nunberg, H. (1926). The will to recovery. In *Practice and Theory of Psychoanalysis.* Vol. 1, pp. 75–88. New York: International Universities Press, 1948.

———— (1928). Problems of therapy. In *Practice and Theory of Psychoanalysis.* Vol. 1, pp. 105–119. New York: International Universities Press, 1948.

———— (1931). The synthetic function of the ego. In *Practice and Theory of Psychoanalysis.* Vol. 1, pp. 120–136. New York: International Universities Press, 1948.

Orwell, G. (1940). New words. In *My Country Right or Left: Collected Essays, Journalism and Letters.* Vol. 2. New York: Harcourt Brace Jovanovich, 1968.

Reich, W. (1933). *Character Analysis.* New York: Noonday Press, 1949.

Reider, N. (1957). Transference psychosis. *Journal of the Hillside Hospital* 6:131–149.

Reik, T. (1937). *Surprise and the Psychoanalyst.* New York: Dutton.

———— (1948). *Listening with the Third Ear.* New York: Farrar, Straus & Cudaby.

Richfield, J. (1954). An analysis of the concept of insight. *Psychoanalytic Quarterly* 23:390–408.

Roth, S. (1968). The schizophrenic wallet. *Psychiatric Opinion* 5:38–41.

———— (1970). The seemingly ubiquitous depression following acute schizophrenic episodes. *American Journal of Psychiatry* 127:51–58.

Sandler, J. (1976). Countertransference and role responsiveness. *International Review of Psychoanalysis* 3:43–47.

Sandler, J., Holder, A., and Dare, C. (1970). Basic psychoanalytic concepts. IV. Countertransference. *British Journal of Psychiatry* 117: 83–88.

Searles, H. F. (1949). The effort to drive the other person crazy – an element in the aetiology and psychotherapy of schizophrenia. In *Collected Papers on Schizophrenia and Related Subjects,* pp. 254–283. New York: International Universities Press, 1965.

———— (1961a). The source of anxiety in paranoid schizophrenia. In *Collected Papers on Schizophrenia and Related Subjects,* pp. 465–486. New York: International Universities Press, 1965.

———— (1961b). Phases of patient–therapist interaction in the psychotherapy of chronic schizophrenia. In *Collected Papers on Schizophrenia and Related Subjects,* pp. 521–559. New York: International Universities Press, 1965.

———— (1965). Identity development in Edith Jacobson's "The Self and the Object World." In *Countertransference and Related Subjects,* pp. 36–44. New York: International Universities Press, 1979.

———— (1975). The patient as therapist to his analyst. In *Countertransference and Related Subjects,* pp. 380–459. New York: International Universities Press, 1979.

Semrad, E. V. (1966). Long-term therapy of schizophrenia. In *Psycho-neuroses and Schizophrenia,* ed. G. L. Usdin, pp. 155–173. Philadelphia: J. B. Lippincott.

_____ (1980). *The Heart of a Therapist.* New York: Jason Aronson.

Sharpe, E. F. (1930). The technique of psychoanalysis: seven lectures. In *The Collected Papers of Psychoanalysis,* pp. 9–106. New York: Brunner/Mazel, 1978.

_____ (1937). *Dream Analysis.* London: Hogarth Press.

_____ (1947). The psychoanalyst. In *The Collected Papers on Psychoanalysis,* pp. 109–124. New York: Brunner/Mazel, 1978.

Sherwood, M. (1969). *The Logic of Explanation in Psychoanalysis.* New York: Academic Press.

Spitz, R. (1956). Transference: the analytic setting and its prototype. *International Journal of Psycho-Analysis* 37:380–385.

Stein, M. H. (1981). The unobjectionable part of the transference. *Journal of the American Psychoanalytic Association* 29:869–892.

Sterba, R. F. (1934). The fate of the ego in analytic therapy. *International Journal of Psycho-Analysis* 15:117–126.

Stone, L. (1961). *The Psychoanalytic Situation.* New York: International Universities Press.

Strachey, J. (1934). The nature of the therapeutic action of psychoanalysis. *International Journal of Psycho-Analysis* 15:127–159.

Sullivan, H. S. (1954). *The Psychiatric Interview.* New York: W. W. Norton.

_____ (1962). *Schizophrenia as a Human Process.* New York: W. W. Norton.

Tarachow, S. (1963). *An Introduction to Psychotherapy.* New York: International Universities Press.

Tartakoff, H. H. (1981). Panel report on insight: clinical conceptualization. *Journal of American Psychoanalysis* 29:668–671.

Valenstein, A. (1983). Working through and resistance to change: insight and the action system. *Journal of the American Psychoanalytic Association* (Supplement) 31:353–374.

Vidal, G. (1985). Remembering Italo Calvino. *The New York Review of Books.* Vol. 32, no. 18, pp. 3–10.

Weinshel, E. M. (1971). The transference neurosis: a survey of the literature. *Journal of the American Psychoanalytic Association* 19:67–88.

Weisman, A. (1955). Silence in psychotherapy. *Psychiatry* 78:241–260.

White, R. W. (1963). Ego and reality in psychoanalytic theory. *Psychological Issues,* Vol. 3. New York: International Universities Press.

Winnicott, D. W. (1947). Hate in the countertransference. In *Collected Papers,* pp. 194–203. London: Tavistock Publications, 1958.

_____ (1953). Transitional objects and transitional phenomena. *International Journal of Psycho-Analysis* 34:89–97.

_____ (1954). Metapsychological and clinical aspects of regression within the psycho-analytical set-up. In *Collected Papers*, pp. 278–294. London: Tavistock Publications, 1958.

_____ (1955). Clinical varieties of transference. In *Collected Papers*, pp. 295–299. London: Tavistock Publications, 1958.

_____ (1958). The capacity to be alone. In *The Maturational Processes and the Facilitating Environment*, pp. 29–36. New York: International Universities Press, 1965.

_____ (1960). Countertransference. In *The Maturational Processes and the Facilitating Environment*, pp. 158–165. New York: International Universities Press, 1965.

_____ (1962). The aims of psycho-analytical treatment. In *The Maturational Processes and the Facilitating Environment*, pp. 166–170. New York: International Universities Press, 1965.

Zetzel, E. R. (1949). Anxiety and the capacity to bear it. In *The Capacity for Emotional Growth*, ed. E. R. Zetzel, pp. 33–52. New York: International Universities Press, 1970.

_____ (1958). Therapeutic alliance in the analysis of hysteria. In *The Capacity for Emotional Growth*, ed. E. R. Zetzel, pp. 182–196. New York: International Universities Press, 1970.

_____ (1965). On the incapacity to bear depression. In *The Capacity for Emotional Growth*, ed. E. R. Zetzel, pp. 82–114. New York: International Universities Press, 1970.

_____ (1966). The doctor–patient relationship in psychiatry. In *The Capacity for Emotional Growth*, ed. E. R. Zetzel, pp. 139–155. New York: International Universities Press, 1970.

_____ (1971). A developmental approach to the borderline patient. *American Journal of Psychiatry* 127:867–871.

Index